T5-BBB-246

BRITISH ECONOMIC HISTORY ★ A
Garland
Series

Edited by
   PETER MATHIAS
   Oxford University
   and
   STUART BRUCHEY
   Columbia University

DOMESTIC SERVANTS AND HOUSEHOLDS IN ROCHDALE 1851–1871

Edward Higgs

Garland Publishing, Inc.
New York & London ★ 1986

Library of Congress Cataloging-in-Publication Data

Higgs, Edward, 1952–
   Domestic servants and households in Rochdale,
1851–1871.

   (British economic history)
   Revision of thesis (Ph.D.)—Oxford, 1979.
   Bibliography: p.
   1. Domestics—England—Rochdale (Greater Manchester)—
History—19th century.   2. Women domestics—England—
Rochdale (Greater Manchester)—History—19th century.
3. Domestics—England—Rochdale (Greater Manchester)—
Social conditions.   4. Rochdale (Greater Manchester)—
Social conditions.   I. Title.   II. Series.
HD8039.D52G7755   1986   305.5′6   84-46002
ISBN 0-8240-6682-0

All volumes in this series are printed on acid-free,
250-year-life paper.

Printed in the United States of America

DOMESTIC SERVANTS AND HOUSEHOLDS

IN ROCHDALE, 1851–1871

Edward Higgs

CONTENTS

CHAPTER 10. DOMESTIC SERVICE IN NINETEENTH-CENTURY
ROCHDALE: SOME IMPLICATIONS FOR
CONTEMPORARY HISTORICAL RESEARCH

PREFACE

The present work is a slightly amended version of a thesis submitted for the degree of Doctor of Philosophy at the University of Oxford in 1979. As such its does not correspond in every detail to the author's current views on the subject of domestic service in nineteenth-century England and Wales. Rather more emphasis probably needs to be given to the essential identity of the work and social role of female kin in the home and that of 'true' servants. The principal source used in this work, the manuscript census enumerators' returns, also need to be seen less as 'raw data' and more as a repository of the assumptions and perceptions of the men who took the census. Does the census hold a mirror up to the social and economic position of women in Victorian society, or does it reflect what male householders, enumerators and census officials thought these aught to be?

For the author's latest thoughts on these subjects see; Edward Higgs, 'Domestic servants and households in Victorian England', Social History, Vol. 8, no 2 (May 1983), 201-10; Edward Higgs, 'Domestic service and house-hold production', in Angela V. John (ed.), Unequal Opportunities. Women's Employment in England, 1800-1918, (Basil Blackwell, Oxford, 1986), 125-52; and Edward Higgs, 'Women, occupations and work in the nineteenth-century censuses', History Workshop Journal, Vol. 23 (Spring 1987).

ACKNOWLEDGEMENTS

I must acknowledge the help and advice of my supervisor, Professor Peter Mathias, and Dr Ross McKibbin, who both patiently read the drafts of this work and made numerous useful comments. Specific and invaluable guidance was also provided by Dr N. F. R. Crafts, Mr Brian Preston and Dr John Marshall.

I would also like to record my thanks for the services rendered to me by the staff at the Manchester Central Library, the Rochdale Public Library, the Lancashire Record Office and the University of Oxford Computing Laboratory. I must also acknowledge the help provided by the officers of the Census Room at the Public Record Office. Having worked as an assistant keeper of the public records for seven years I now realise the dedicated service they provide in difficult circumstances.

It gives me great pleasure to record my debt for all the scholarly encouragement and practical advice I received in discussions with my tutors at St John's College, with other senior members of the University of Oxford, and with friends and colleagues both in Oxford and elsewhere.

Finally, I must thank my parents without whom I and this thesis would never have been produced.

1. DOMESTIC SERVICE IN THE NINETEENTH CENTURY

I. The Domestic Servant in Nineteenth-Century Society

At any one time in late nineteenth-century England and
Wales over one million men and women were described as
domestic servants in the occupational returns of the contemporary censuses, making service the largest occupational
category after agricultural work.[1] Such people were to be
found in every part of the country, from the West End of
London to the industrial towns of Lancashire, forming one
of the recurring stereotypes of the Victorian world.

Similar occupational groups could be found throughout
Europe at this date. In France in 1866, for example,
domestic servants are said to have comprised 29 per cent of
the entire occupied female population, and nearly 45 per
cent of all working women in Paris in 1901.[2] Indeed
Laslett has gone so far as to claim that the presence of
living-in domestics was one of the factors which differenciated 'Western' society in the past from that of East
Europe or the Orient.[3]

Although the traditional servant class has all but disappeared in Europe it is still of great social importance
in modern developing countries. In Peru in 1961, for
example, there were 145,000 female domestics, representing
21.4 per cent of the economically active female
population.[4] In South America, Africa and Asia, domestic
service is still one of the most important paid activities
open to women and one of the most potent symbols of social
status. Even in modern Britain many of the functions of
the Victorian domestic are still carried out by the foreign
au pair or by the resurgent class of 'nannies'.

1

Many scholars have also argued that service had important social functions which add to its importance in the period. It has been claimed that for many women in nineteenth-century Britain, domestic service did not simply represent a source of cash, it was also their introduction to life in the city. In developing industrial economies, such as Britain in the nineteenth century, or South American countries today, domestic service could be seen as a 'bridging occupation' between the countryside and the city, providing female migrants with an introduction to the values and life-styles of industrial society, and providing a home and income whilst the traumatic transition was being made.[5]

The servant was also of paramount importance to his or her employer. Many scholars have seen the employment of domestics as of fundamental importance in defining middle-class status. For Karl Marx the household domestic represented the ultimate example of the use made by the capitalist classes of surplus value, showing that a whole section of society could live as 'unproductive labour' at the beck and call of the bourgeoise.[6] Mrs Beeton certainly believed that servants could be equated with income since she regarded a single maid-of-all-work as being sufficient for a family on an income of £200 per annum but expected a householder with an income of £1,000 to have six servants.[7] Indeed the larger the income the greater was supposed to be the percentage of it spent on this part of the 'paraphernalia of gentility'. According to one of the nineteenth-century household manuals quoted by J. A. Banks, a family earning £100 per annum might be expected to spend £4 on domestic help, or 4 per cent of its income. A family on £400 was expected to spend £24, or 6 per cent, and a family on £500 was held to spend £74 annually, no less than 15 per cent of its total income.[8]

An attempt to dismiss the work performed by servants as having no practical function is, however, unfair. Servants were not merely ornaments in the home, they fulfilled defined functional roles and produced necessary goods and services. The servant could provide his or her employer with three of the most sought after components of the 'good life' in Victorian society: privacy, cleanliness and free time.

In the nineteenth century the 'Englishman's castle' could only be secure if it was guarded, and this function was performed by the housemaid, or by the resident man servant. The very architecture of the middle-class Victorian house was affected by the need to create the 'no man's land' of the formal hallway where guests were received by the maid and vetted for undesirables. The act of paying calls and leaving one's card on the hall table exemplified the use of space in the Victorian home as a line of defence against the external world.

When not on guard many domestics were constantly employed in keeping the house clean. The Victorians may have been over-obsessed with soap but the harsh environment of the nineteenth-century city must have caused formidable domestic problems. In the words of F. M. Jones,

> The carriage-way was a ribbon of horse droppings converted by rain into a morass which passing wheels threw onto the pavement; hence the polished marble, granite, glazed brick base to buildings lining a highway; hence, too, the crossing sweeper. The block or macadam carriage-way slowly ground to dust; the manure dried up and powdered; grit and carbon poured from every chimney.[9]

Hence the symbolical importance of 'shine' in the Victorian home, with its polished brasses, gilt mirrors and glass.

Lastly, the domestic eased the burden of other women in the home. This did not usually mean allowing the rich to live an idle life since many lower middle-class families led lives hardly distinguishable from that of the 'aristocracy of labour'. The wife of a man earning £2 a week could afford a servant but would not be able to avoid household labour completely. Perhaps the servant would cook and wash whilst the mistress of the household looked after the children. The latter would have presented a very serious burden to many lower middle-class families who might have a shop to tend and whose geographical mobility might have limited access to the support of relatives.

II. The Historiography of Domestic Service

Until quite recently little work has been done on the social history of domestic service in this country in the nineteenth century, although several pioneering works have now been published.[10] Some of these works, although still of great interest, have tended to rely on anecdotal sources and national statistics which may distort the reality of social relationships in diverse communities.

Any attempt to write a national history of such a wide spread social phenomenon as domestic service is bound to obscure important regional differences. Recent work by geographers has shown that there were very great differences between the local servant populations depending on factors such as the availablity of alternative employment for women, the composition of the local elite who might employ servants, and the rate and nature of immigration

4

into a locality.[11] The use of national census statistics may be helpful when comparing servant populations in different countries but may obscure the regional contrasts which explain so much about the economic and social role of service within the national economy.

There are also problems in attempting to write the social history of domestic service from literary sources or even from family documents. The maid-of-all-work who was put out to service at 15 and left at the age of 21 to marry a labourer has left us comparatively few records and the same is true of the shopkeeper who employed her. The most voluminous records were to be found in the households of the rich and it is their servants who have, in general, left us their reminiscences. One recent study of the Victorian servant has drawn so heavily on this type of material that it has become biased towards a certain type of servant and servant employer. Of the 62 employers mentioned whose social standing could be indentified, 29 had titles, 14 belonged to the learned professions, 10 could be described as landed proprietors and four as farmers. Only three were retailers and only one was from the artisan class.[12]

The aim of the present work is to go beyond the general and anecdotal level of the present literature on this subject. It looks at several aspects of domestic service in one area. The servant population is examined to discover who entered the service, at what age, and from what background they came. The employers of servants are also examined to establish the identity of the 'typical' family which made use of their services. An attempt has also been made to quantify the factors affecting the employment of servants by individual households. The rural origins of servants are also shown to be linked to a conscious preference on the part of servant employers.

5

Having described the servant and servant employing populations, a section dealing with the turnover of servants and the channels of servant recruitment is used to give an insight into the dynamics of change within the apparently static statistical framework. The development of various forms of placement agencies and the importance of personal contacts in the servant market are also discussed.

The results of this analysis are finally used to gauge the validity of the popularly accepted servant stereotypes and the sources from which they are derived. The dynamics of change revealed by this study can in addition help us to understand some of the structural causes of the decline of the servant population in the late Victorian and Edwardian periods.

2. METHODOLOGICAL APPROACH

I. The Choice of Subject

As was noted in the introduction, much of the recent work published on domestic service in the nineteenth century has been anecdotal and literary in character. This is perhaps to be expected when attempting to analyse an industry which employed so many thousands of people in such small units across the whole country.

A study of such large numbers of individuals lends itself to the use of quantitative methods. Similarly, the distribution of servants in individual households suggests an analysis based on a source in which all such units appear. Such a source exists in the form of the returns made by householders in the course of the taking of the nineteenth-century decennial censuses. Every ten years the local registrars of births, marriages and deaths divided up their districts into enumeration districts and appointed an enumerator for each. This official handed each householder a schedule on which the latter was directed to give information on the name, relationship to household head, marital status, sex, age and occupation of each member of the household. These were collected by the enumerators and destroyed after being copied into books. The latter were fowarded to a Census Office in London where they formed the raw data for various tabulations published in the decennial census reports. When the research for this work was carried out in the mid-1970s the householders' returns for the censuses of 1841, 1851, 1861 and 1871 were available for public inspection at the Public Record Office.[1] Since the 1841 returns are not as detailed as those which

7

followed, the analysis was confined to the period 1851 to 1871.

The scholarly use of the census enumerators' books of this period is now a commonplace in the fields of historical and sociological research. This is advantageous since it has meant that many of the procedures and methods which have been used here have been tested in previous works and are well documented.[2] This work is perhaps unusual, however, in that it uses these methods to study a particular occupational grouping rather than the social structure of the community as a whole. Also, an attempt has been made to link the results of the numerical analysis of the local population with other local documentary sources. Thus statistics showing annual rates of turnover in the servant population have been linked to newspaper advertising and to the local institutions which were established to facilitate servant recruitment.

As a source of information on servants in this period these census schedules are unlikely to present serious problems of interpretation. The conditions under which the censuses were taken did not vary in the period nor does there appear to have been any changes in the contemporary definition of what constituted a servant. The censuses of 1851, 1861 and 1871 were all taken at the same time of the year,[3] and during periods of economic prosperity.[4] There do not appear to have been any alterations in the instructions for filling out the schedules which refer to domestic servants.[5] An examination of the printed works on the law of master and servant shows little, if any, innovation in the legal status of domestic servants which might have altered the classification of servants in the census schedules.[6] If the schedules contain any ambiguities as to the servant classification then this cannot be seen as a

8

result of differing conditions prevailing at the time of the different censuses. Changes in the census were probably not the cause of any changes detected in the observed servant population over time.

The choice of Rochdale for the study was dictated by the desire to analyse domestic service in a economic and social environment different from the locations hereto examined. An analysis of servants in an industrial setting provides a useful counter-balance to the picture of the service industry usually gained from an examination of London and country houses. It would be unwise to regard Rochdale as representative of British society as a whole but it is to be hoped that the district's social and occupational structures show certain 'modern' tendencies from which later national trends can be inferred.

II. Sampling Procedures

As was noted above, the information contained in the census enumerators' books were copies of the original census scheules completed by householders. They take the form of printed sheets with columns for the various types of information which the enumerators supplied from the original schedules by hand.

The unit of analysis used in the study of these returns was the 'household' or co-residing group. The household was defined as including the 'head' of the group, as designated in the schedule column headed 'Relationship to Head', and all persons enumerated after them until the next 'head' was recorded. Normally the enumerators themselves differentiated such households from each other by the use of a short line across the page in 1851 and a single slash in the name column in 1861 and 1871. There may well have been two or more such co-residing groups in one house, the latter being seperated from each other by a long line across the page of the schedule in 1851 and by a double slash thereafter. In the absence of the head, substitute heads such as wives or other kin were taken as marking the beginning of the group. The household in this sense can be seen as a purely administrative and bureaucratic artifact which did not always correspond to the reality of social relationships. Thus the families of two sisters might have lived on very close terms in the same house but were enumerated seperately. On the other hand two families may have lived in the same house, one paying rent to the other and leading a completely seperate social existence but only the first was enumerated, the second being regarded as a group of 'lodgers'. The definition of the co-residing group used here accords with the contemporary definition used by the census enumerators, as well as with other work on Victorian household structure.[7]

Having so defined the unit of analysis, each set of enumerators' books for each census of the enumeration district of Rochdale was examined in turn. The households in the schedules were grouped together by street or name of settlement. In these returns the streets were not enumerated in their entirety but were interspersed with households from other streets and areas. Each string of households with a common street or community name was counted as a single unit and distinguished from other subsequent strings in the same street or community by noting the numbers of the houses and names of any notable buildings, such as public houses, which might have been included amongst them. In this manner each set of census schedules was examined and each household placed in a particular string. If the first ten households in the

schedules were situated in Church Street, the next five in
Duke Street and the following ten in Church Street once
more, these 25 households were recorded as three seperate
strings, differenciated by street name and by the numbers
of the houses. A note was also made of which households
contained servants and in what numbers. Thus each household containing servants could be placed in a string of
households differentiated from all others in space. Taking
the three censuses of 1851, 1861 and 1871 together, some
56,000 households were recorded in this manner. It was
thus possible to calculate the number of households in the
Rochdale district in each census, to calculate the number
of households containing servants and how many they contained, as well as to place such households on a map of
the area with some accuracy.

The definition of a 'servant' used in this examination
was based upon occupational information and not upon an
individual's relationship to the head of the household.
This method was chosen so as to include in the analysis all
those persons who might have actually lived with kin but
who went out to do domestic work in other households.
Servant occupational categories included all variations of
the term 'servant' and 'maid' as well as butler, footman,
groom, coachman, gardener, governess, nurse and companion.

It became obvious in the course of examining the
original schedules that numerous 'servants' defined in this
manner did indeed live in the households of kin and were in
many cases the heads of households. When noting which
households contained servants a differenciation was made
between those households containing 'servants' in the more
usual sense and those households containing 'servants' who
were related to the head of the household by kinship.

After these preliminary examinations had been completed

11

and the total number of households containing servants had been calculated for each census, a random number table was used to generate a one in four sample of all households containing servants for each census. The same procedure was adopted to select a sample of 200 households from each census as a whole to act as a control on the results obtained from the servant-employing households. An additional sample was taken of individuals in institutions. Once chosen, the sample households, 2,641 in all, were copied manually from the schedules for further analysis.

It has been more usual in studies of Victorian household structure to take one sample from the entire population and then to study one sub-group from this sample in relation to the entire sample population.[8] This would not have been a practical proposition in the case of servant-employing households in Rochdale, since such households were comparatively rare. A one in ten sample of the whole household population in Rochdale in 1871 would have produced some 2,340 households of which only 183 would have contained servants. Compared with the method outlined above this would have doubled the number of households to be sampled whilst only producing some 20 per cent of the households with servants.

The households thus sampled were then divided into five groups for each census as follows:

1) The control sample of 200 randomly-selected households.

2) 'True servant households' - households containing persons in servant occupations whose relationship to the household head was 'servant'.

3) 'Wrongly enumerated servant households' - households containing persons in servant occupations whose relationship to the head of the household was one of

kinship and who were described as 'housekeepers' or 'working at home'.

4) 'Possible servant households' - households containing persons in servant occupations whose relationship to the household head was one of kinship and who may have been day-servants or may have worked in the households of their kin.

5) 'Out servant households' - households containing persons in servant occupations whose relationship to the household head was one of kinship or lodger but who were unlikely to have been working at home.

The criteria for placing a household in one of the last two categories was fairly impressionistic. In general, female servants living with kin were designated as 'possible servants' whilst male servants were categorised as 'out servants'. In many cases this accorded with common sense distinctions. Thus a seven year old girl designated as a 'nurse' in a household of young children would be placed in category 4, whilst the son of a labourer who was described as a 'coachman' would be placed in category 5.

Information on each individual in the control sample and on each servant in the other groups was then converted into a numerical series prior to computer analysis. This took the form of a numerical code for 47 defined variables (see Appendix A), 70 characters in length. The character in the first column was either '1' or '0', the former if a new household was being coded, the latter if the individual being enumerated was in the same household as the previous person. The next variable coded was the code number of the household; the third to the 29th variables recorded information about the household in which the individual lived, and the rest related to the individual or servant. The first coded variable was of great importance for the

13

strategy adopted for computer analysis. If there were three servants in a household then the numerical code showing the case number of the household and the data relating to the household were identical in each case. Only the coded information relating to the individuals would differ. Only the numerical code which referred to the first servant had a '1' in the first column, however, the other two having a '0'. This meant that when the computer was instructed to analyse the sample data it could be asked to choose only those cases with '1' in the first column. It was thus possible to record data referring to the household and the individual on the same line for the purposes of cross-tabulation but also to select only information relating to the household if an analysis of households alone was required.

This facility also enabled one to accommodate those cases in which a household contained persons with servant occupations whose relationship to the head of the household varied, one being kin, for example, and the other a servant. In such cases both individuals would have a '1' in the first column of their numerical coding and would be placed in differing sample groups for the purpose of computer analysis.

Once coded and placed in one of the five sample groups for each census, the information for each member of a family or each sevant was then punched on computer cards, some 5,200 in all, and entered on the ICL 1906A computer of the University of Oxford Computing Service. Since each card contained information on 47 variables this represented a database of some 244,000 individual pieces of information.

SPSS (Statistical Package for the Social Sciences), a well-developed computer package, was used to analyse the data. This provided a wide range of techniques for data management and statistical computation, was well documented and easy to use.

III. **The Statistical Framework**

The results of this statistical analysis are given in the text in the form of tables or of summary statistics showing what proportion of two or more populations had a particular characteristic in common. Such statistics are often compared with similar information drawn from later samples. The percentage of servants born in Rochdale in 1851, for example, might be compared with the same figure in 1871 in order to see the changes in the origins of servants over time. In such cases it is necessary to remember that one is comparing statistical results gained from samples of populations, which are therefore subject to statistical sampling error. It is necessary to discover if the difference between the two figures reflects actual differences in the underlying populations or is caused by the chance selection of untypical individuals and households in the sample.

Standard statistical procedures exist which enable one to measure the likelihood that such differences are caused by sampling error. This can be done by calculating the difference between the two percentages involved and then comparing this to the likely magnitude of the statistical error derived from standard statistical techniques.

Confidence testing allows one to calculate , at a given level of statistical significance, that the true sample error will be only of a certain magnitude. A statement that the difference between two percentages was significant at the 95 per cent level indicates that there was only a 5 per cent chance that the difference between the two figures could be caused by sampling error. Whether or not such a difference is significant depends on such factors as the size of the difference, the number of cases and the level of certainty required. The larger the number of observations the greater the likelihood that the sample proportions represent the true population proportions. Similarly, the greater the difference between the two percentages the greater the probability that the sampling error will be smaller than the difference. Finally, the tests for statistical confidence can be performed for differing levels of probability, 95, 90, 80 per cent, and so on. This implies that one can be certain that the sampling error is smaller than the difference between population percentages with differing levels of conviction. At the 95 per cent significance level there is only a one in 20 chance that the sampling error will be greater than the difference between the two proportions. If the sampling error appears too great at the 95 per cent level, a less rigorous test at say 80 per cent, can be used. This will allow one to say that one can be 80 per cent certain that the sampling error is smaller than the difference between the two percentages.

It is normal to use the 95 per cent probability level as the test for statistical significance. It is not always possible to reach this level due to the small number of observations in some cases. It has sometimes been necessary in the present study to accept statistical significance at a lower level, 80 per cent constituting the lowest level accepted. All differences between percentages quoted in the text are significant at the 95 per cent level unless otherwise stated.

IV. Other Sources

Although this machine-readable data formed the basis of the subsequent numerical analysis of the servant population of Rochdale, a secondary analysis of the original household returns was undertaken in an attempt to relate service to the geographical distribution of the district's population. Six inch Ordnance Survey maps of the Rochdale district published in 1851 and 1892 were used to construct plans of the entire enumeration district of Rochdale in 1851 and 1871. The entire area was divided into 100 yard grid squares, some 16,000 in all, and the settlements recorded in the censuses of 1851 and 1871 were drawn in. Using the classification system outlined in Appendix A (Note 28), all settlements were classified as belonging to certain settlement types. The census returns of 1851 and 1871 were then used to record the number of households in each grid square, as well as the number of servants and servant-employing households. It was thus possible to calculate the number of households in differing types of settlement and any changes in settlement patterns over the period 1851 to 1871. It was also possible to produce a numerical coding showing the type of settlement and the status of the area in which each servant lived in 1851. This information was included in the machine-readable database.

Sources such as local newspapers, workhouse records, local account books and correspondence from the period were used to add substance to the numerical analysis. An appeal was also made through the correspondence page of the Rochdale Observer for any information or personal reminiscences from people who had been in service, or remembered others who had been, in the Rochdale area.

17

3. ROCHDALE IN THE NINETEENTH CENTURY

I. The Economic and Social Development of Rochdale

The district of Rochdale is situated in the valley of the
River Roch which runs southward from the Pennines towards
Manchester and the Mersey estuary. The modern metropolitan
borough lies in the comparatively level area that was once
the bed of Lake Littleborough, a lake formed between the
Pennines andthe south-eastward flowing ice sheet of the
last Ice Age. This lake was fed by rivers and streams
descending from the high moorlands, creating valleys
through the Pennines along which trade routes and human
settlements have penetrated into Yorkshire. Rochdale
itself was not in fact a single township but a conglomerate
of three adjacent settlements (Castleton, Spotland and
Hundersford) grouped around a fording point on the River
Roch which gave access to these Pennine routes to
Yorkshire. These routes were extensively used from the
Roman period onwards and by the 11th century there was
already a castle and toll bridge guarding the ford. All
subsequent communication systems followed this general
pattern. Thus the road between Halifax and Rochdale, over
the Blackstone Edge, became a turnpike in 1734. The canal
and railway followed in their turn.[1]

It would be a mistake however to confuse the Registrar
General's District of Rochdale with the metropolitan
borough of that name. The former was a far larger area
which stretched from Heywood in the south to Bacup and
Todmorden in the north. The parliamentary borough and the
adjacent built-up area covered approximately 2 square miles
in 1851, whilst the district covered a much larger area of

perhaps 50 square miles.[2]

Within this area there were a large number of settlements ranging in size and function from the 'urban' centre of Rochdale proper down to isolated 'rural' farmhouses. In all, only some 43 per cent of all the households in the district were to be found in the urban centre of Rochdale in 1851, whilst the rest lived in other settlements, some of which, like Littleborough and Smallbridge, were small towns in their own right. At the same date over one third of all households were situated in settlements which contained under 100 households. (See Appendix A, Note 28 for settlement classification) There was thus a wide diversity of settlement types within the area under study and it would thus be incorrect to equate statistics derived from a sample of households in this district with a single 'urban' type. Such a typology cannot easily be superimposed upon a district which included small industrial villages, isolated farmhouses and country mansions, as well as parts of at least three 'urban' areas, in Heywood and Bacup, as well as Rochdale itself. (See Table 1)

In the nineteenth century the Rochdale district was undergoing an extremely rapid population expansion. In the period from 1801 to 1871 the average decennial increase in population was no less than 22.5 per cent , a rate which decreased considerably in the decades between 1871 and 1901, when it was only 6.4 per cent per decade. (Table 2) This growth was the result of a rapid industrial development which encouraged a large influx of migrants. Thus in a sample of 200 households from Rochdale in 1851, 35.3 per cent of the household heads had been born outside the Rochdale district, and by 1871 this percentage had increased to 41 per cent. This migration appears to have been over short distances, as Redford suggested, since in 1851 nearly 60 per cent of all migrant heads had been born

19

within 20 miles of Rochdale.[3] This figure, however, had dropped to 46 per cent in 1871, but this was due to an influx of Irish migrants into the area.

Rochdale's industrial expansion was based upon its obvious natural resources. The district's importance as a route centre led to its early connections with the textile industry as the wool produced by the sheep of the Abbey of Whalley, which grazed on the moorlands, was transported via Rochdale to the sea.[4] By the fifteenth century the area had a market dealing in woollen cloth and in the sixteenth century the area developed a flourishing woollen textile industry, based on local wool, water and good communications. Court cases of the 1570's also give evidence of local mines of coal and other minerals, which led to the production of iron in bloomeries.[5] Despite these economic advantages the introduction of steam power into the woollen industry of the district only appears to have occurred in 1831. However, by 1790 the manufacture of cotton textiles had been introduced and the first cotton power loom was established in 1820. By 1772 there were already three Rochdale 'engine makers' noted in the Manchester trades directory and the textile industry appears to have spawned a considerable local engineering trade. Rochdale's great industrial expansion came late but because of this its rate of growth in the early nineteenth century was prodigious. By 1866 the Chief Constable's general returns show that the borough alone contained 47 cotton mills, 19 woollen mills, nine dye-works, two hat factories, 26 machine works, four saw mills, three corn mills and 21 foundries.[6]

It was thus only in the mid-nineteenth century that Rochdale began to accumulate the institutions and paraphernalia of bourgeois civic life. The 1832 Reform Act created the borough of Rochdale and in 1856 the town received its charter of incorporation. The Rochdale Merchants' and Tradesmen's Association was formed in 1864 and was followed two years later by the Chamber of Commerce. The 1860's and 1870's were the peak of the town's civic history with the establishment of the Borough Police Force in 1857; the acquisition of the local waterworks by the corporation in 1866; and the construction of such public buildings as the Town Hall, Post Office and Public Baths and Library, in the years 1868 to 1875.[7] Linked to this assertion of maturity by the town and its ruling elite was the rapid expansion (and often equally rapid contraction) of various newspaper ventures in the 1850's and 1860's. No fewer than eight local newspapers were founded in the twenty years after 1850, although only two survived into the present century and only one, the Rochdale Observer, is still printed today. This journalistic effervescence represented not only the activity of the town's commercial classes as a whole but also the party conflicts which divided them, since the newspapers appear to have been established, almost invariably, as the organs of particular sections of Rochdale's political society.[8]

II. Rochdale in the mid-Nineteenth Century

In the period 1851 to 1871, the years with which this work deals, Rochdale was still undergoing a rapid population growth. In 1851 the total population of the Rochdale Enumeration District was 72,515 but this total had risen to 109,858 in 1871.[9] (Table 2) As can be seen from Table 1, this population growth was concentrated in the urban areas of Rochdale and Bacup, and in large nucleated settlements within the district. In 1851 the urban area of Rochdale itself contained nearly 6,000 households, but this figure had doubled by 1871. During the same period the number of households found in large nucleated settlements had increased from 2,179 to 5,836. This does not indicate a movement of population within the area but rather a gradual increase in the size of existing settlements, as small communities grew and merged with each other. Thus it is no surprise to find that small nucleated settlements and all dispersed communities were actually losing households in these decades. Some of the large expanding settlements, mostly situated in the valleys to the north of Rochdale itself, were becoming towns in their own right. In 1871 the single settlement that had been formed out of the merging of Shawforth and Facit contained 850 households, whilst the settlement comprising Littleborough, Caldermoor and Featherstall contained 700 households. Since the mean size of households in Rochdale at this date was 4.7 persons, both these 'conglomerations' may have contained over 3,000 people.

This meant in effect that the population of the Rochdale district was living increasingly in an industrial environment. As can be seen from Table 3, agricultural workers in 1851 were heavily concentrated in small settlements and isolated dwellings, whilst workers in industries such as textiles and engineering were concentrated in the large nucleated settlements which were becoming an increasingly important part of the whole settlement pattern of the district. As the same time the urban area of Rochdale, although also containing industrial workers, was the district where persons providing personal services and retailing were concentrated. Thus even in nineteenth-century Lancashire we can still detect a shift from 'rural' to 'urban' living in this period.

22

The urban nature of life in the district was a function of its economic developoment. As can be gauged from Table 4, Rochdale was an area with a high degree of industrial employment. Such employment was concentrated in the textile industry, resulting in a high occupied rate for women in the area. Thus 51 per cent of all women in the Rochdale district, aged over 20 years, had stated occupations in 1861, whilst the comparable figure for England and Wales at the same date was only 41 per cent.[10] Every other category was under-represented except in the case of those employed in commerce and retailing. We may note in the case of males an absence of workers in the professions, in domestic service and, above all, in agriculture. The same pattern is to be found in the employment of females, although the deficiency in the class of persons providing dress is also significant.

The employment structure in Rochdale was more diversified than in other Lancashire textile towns because of the presence of a substantial woollen industry. Thus, in 1861, of the males aged over 19 and employed in textiles, nearly 40 per cent were employed in the production of woollens. In the case of females the figure was just over 25 per cent. This can be compared with Oldham in 1861, where the woollen industry employed under one per cent of the occupied population over the age of 19. In Preston in 1861 the manufacture of woollen textiles employed only five women in the same age group.[11]

The comparatively small number of persons employed in agriculture underlines the urban and industrial character of the region. Even those farms which did exist were hardly more than smallholdings. Thus of the 17 farmers appearing in the control samples who gave the acreage of their farms, only one man farmed more than 40 acres and the majority had less than 20. Possessing an average of only 17.2 acres, it is not surprising that at least three of the 'farmers' had other jobs as well. This agriculture could have been little more than a family enterprise and could not have generated much demand for agricultural labourers of either sex.

The scale of industrial enterprises in the district was much larger. Although a thorough examination has not been made of the size of all companies and industrial plants in the area, some idea of the concentration of labour can be established from an examination of the numbers of hands which capitalists claimed to employ in their census returns. The results of an examination of employers' returns (pooled from the household samples of the censuses of 1851, 1861 and 1871) are given in Table 5. Some capitalists failed to give the numbers of hands they employed, so these averages are based only on cases where manufacturers actually recorded the relevant information.

It can be seen from these figures that there were some very large employers in the district, especially in the case of cotton textile production and the manufacture of machinery. The averages in fact conceal a good deal of variation. In the case of cotton manufacturers there must have been a considerable difference between the standing of a man who employed 30 hands in 1871, and John Bright who employed 980 in 1861.

Rochdale was area dominated by large-scale capitalists but who were nevertheless outnumbered by a population of small semi-independent producers, and an even larger group of wage labourers. The great manufacturers appear to have been isolated in society because of their considerable wealth and by the absence of a professional class which might have acted as a bridge between them and the extensive group of retailers in the town.

This was reflected in the politics of mid-nineteenth century Rochdale. Formally the capitalists accounted for only 9 per cent of the electorate in 1857. They were easily outnumbered by the craftsmen with 23 per cent, the drink interest with 14 per cent and the retailers with no less than 26.5 per cent of the electoral votes. However, according to J. H. Vincent, who has studied the politics of the area, 'Standing out above all these details there emerges a general picture of the domination of Rochdale politics by a narrow class of Nonconformist businessmen, itself dominated by half a dozen great firms and families'.[12] Thus the Brights, Ashworths and 'Flannel Lords' controlled the local Liberal Party as effectively as the local Conservative Party was controlled by the local squire, the Royd's banking house and the Rev. Molesworth, the Vicar of the parish.[13] This political dominance of the town was reflected in the very names of the streets which were built in the period, amongst which appeared 'Reform Street', 'Free Trade Street' and 'Kossuth Street', as well as the inevitable roads named after Cobden and Bright.

In studying the history of domestic service in this area, one must be aware of the social and economic structure of the locality. Rochdale was dominated by a relatively small class of large manufacturers and the town lacked a large profesional class such as might be found in the market towns of southern England. This meant, in effect, that the petite-bourgeoisie of small retailers and innkeepers had an unusual position of pre-eminence in the social hierarchy. At the same time, large-scale industrial production of textiles meant that there was plenty of employment for young, unmarried women, who elsewhere would almost inevitably have gone into domestic service.

4. THE SOCIAL POSITION OF THE 'SERVANT' IN THE MID-NINETEENTH CENTURY CENSUS

I. 'Servants' in the Census: Sources of Inaccuracy

An examination of the census schedules for Rochdale in the mid-nineteenth century soon reveals that many people in servant occupations were not living in households as servants in the social sense. According to F. R. Blatt writing in 1929, 'The term "domestic" servant has the same meaning as household servant, the true criteria seems to be the personal proximity of the servant to the master by sleeping in his house and the personal character of the services rendered.'[1] In the enumerators' books, however, many 'servants', 'housekeepers', 'nurses' and so on, were actually related by kinship to the heads of the households in which they lived. In 1851 for example, James Schofield, an innkeeper of Balderstone near Rochdale, had a family of eight children, one of whom was described as a 'nurse'. By 1861 Schofield appears to have died because his family reappears in the census with his wife, Alice, as the widowed head of the household. By now all the family is at work but Mrs Schofield remains at home and is described as a 'housekeeper'.

Men and women so enumerated may have been day-servants and examples of such persons can be found amongst the schedules. In Sheffield Tillot has discovered two girls described as 'in service - sleeps at home'. However, as Tillot adds, many, if not most, of such persons were in fact helping at home, 'that they are part of the vast domestic labour force the census officials described as

26

"well understood". [2]

This problem of misspecification was inevitable, given the manner in which the census was taken in the mid-nineteenth century. The enumerators in charge of collecting the data were supposed to be literate but an examination of some of the scripts from Rochdale, especially from the country areas in 1851, shows that the standard was often not very high.[3] The enumerator was to leave a schedule with each household head, who was to fill it in, according to the instructions, on the census night. The instructions were vague as to how a 'servant' was to be defined. In 1851 no instructions actually mention servants and in 1871 the only aid appears to be Instruction 20 which reads, 'Domestic Servants should be described according to the nature of their service, adding in all cases "Domestic Servant"-Examples: "Coachman-Domestic Servant"; "Gardener-Domestic Servant".'[4] The latter instruction was certainly not followed in the vast majority of schedules in Rochdale in 1871. Even assuming that the householder could read, it does not appear that the census instructions gave him any clear definition of what constituted domestic service.

After the schedules had been filled in it was the job of the enumerator to collect them and copy them into his book, which formed the basis of all subsequent tabulations. It was perhaps inevitable that enumerators should have standardised the returns whilst copying them mechanically into their records. In some cases this process of standardization was carried to great lengths, especially in the manner in which many housewives were recorded as 'housekeepers'. Two examples can be cited from the 1861 census of Rochdale. In the first enumeration district in the Castleton area, for example, out of 235 households some 49 contained wives described as 'housekeepers'. Similarly, in the tenth enumeration district of Wardleworth, no fewer

27

than 141 households, out of a total of 249, contained wives enumerated in the same manner.[5]

Unfortunately we do not have any of the correspondence between the enumeration districts and the Registrar General's Office for this period. We cannot therefore follow in detail any of the day-to-day difficulties encountered in taking the census. All that seems to remain are the outward letters for the period 1889 to 1894 to local census officials, local authorities and individuals. These relate to pre-census organization, fees to officials and matters arising from the returns and publication of the results of the 1891 census. These reveal, however, that even at this date the local enumerators were not sure of the position of girls helping in the home. For example, on the 25th March 1891 the Registrar General wrote to inform the Reverend Latter of Gutwell Rectory, Wisbech, 'that in the case of sons and daughters living at home with their parents and having no property of their own the columns for Occupation or Profession may be left blank...'.[6] Paradoxically this was the very census in which the servant category and that for 'home helps' were compounded in the final tabulations. Other queries at the time suggest uncertainty as to the position of daughters helping in the households of farmers[7], and to the correct enumeration of a mistress/housekeeper.[8] It is to be assumed that similar problems had been encountered in previous years, although we cannot be sure what decisions were made about them at the time.

Once the enumerators had filled in their copies of the census schedules, they were sent to the district registrar's office where they were checked. They were then passed on to London where they were checked once more. It is at this stage that we would assume that many of the

28

wrongly enumerated 'servants' would be removed. The surviving census schedules do indeed provide evidence that such alterations were made. Many such entries appear to have been crossed out and, in some cases, new occupations entered.

There would thus seem to be some grounds for believing that the national and district totals for the servant population do indeed represent 'servants' in the sense of living-in employees.

II. 'Servants' in Rochdale: the Validity of the Official Census Returns

In the case of Rochdale, however, confidence in the official census figures would seem to be misplaced. An examination of Table 6 shows that the numbers of persons over the age of 19 years in servant occupations in Rochdale in 1851 was very close to the official census figures for the same age group. Thus the figure of 1,425 servants in all, found in the census figures, was closely matched by the figure of 1,468 expected from the census sample of that year. In the case of housekeepers over the age of 19 years the correlation between the two sets of figures was almost exact. However, as is also evident from the same table, many of these 'servants' did not in fact live in the households of employers but with their kin. In fact, over 40 per cent of the 'servants' of the original sample of 1851 were not servants in the social sense used by F. R. Blatt. This is most clearly seen in the case of housekeepers, amongst whom only some 15 per cent of the sample were actually servants by occupation and by relationship to the head of the household in which they lived.

In 1861 there appears to be a slightly different pattern. (Table 7) The servant total suggested by the sample of households in 1861 was far in excess of the figure contained in the official census publications, although for the individual categories, with one notable exception, this is not necessarily the case. However, the removal of persons from the sample who lived with kin suggests that the actual figure for the number of servants in Rochdale was still smaller than that given in the official census publications. The most interesting category was again that of housekeepers. The sample suggested a total of 968 housekeepers in the district in 1861, over the age of 19 years, whilst the census tables only showed 253. However, the sample also suggested that the removal of all servants related to the household head by kinship would leave only some 68 housekeepers, a figure far below that actually recorded.

The situation in 1871 (Table 7A) was greatly confused by the fact that in this year it was decided not to tabulate servants and servant categories separately for large towns but to include them with other occupational groupings in a larger category defined ambiguously as Class 11, Order 5. This grouping included charwomen, innkeepers and their wives, beersellers and the officers of charitable institutions as well as domestic servants. It was thus necessary to reconstruct this grouping for the censuses of 1851 and 1861 so as to discover what proportion of such persons were actually servants in those years. The ratios for men and women found in the census of 1861 were then used to derive an approximate figure for the numbers of male and female servants over the age of 19 years in Rochdale in 1871. If correct, these figures seem to repeat the phenomenum found in the 1861 census. The sample total was far in excess of the assumed servant total inferred from the census tabulations. However, once 'servants' living with kin were removed the actual number of servants remaining was only half that suggested by the census.

Since the census reports only tabulate for Rochdale those persons who were over the age of 19 years we cannot be certain of the actual degree of misspecification. However, the comparison between the two sets of figures does seem to suggest that in 1851 the servants recorded as living in Rochdale actually included large numbers of persons who lived with kin and who were supposed to have been removed from the census totals. Similarly in 1861 and 1871 there may also have been a large degree of over-estimation, although there does appear to have been an attempt to remove a considerable number of such cases. If the 1861 census was typical then it would seem that an attempt was made to root out misspecified housekeepers, but that this was not done thoroughly, and that many general female servants who could have been removed from the census were not in fact so removed.

Conclusive proof of this proposition is provided by the initial examinations of all households in Rochdale district in 1851, 1861 and 1871 (Table 8). These show that the total number of persons with servant occupations in the district as a whole closely matched the populations expected from the census samples. However, they also show, in each case, that the number of persons living in house-holds as institutionalised servants was less than the figures given in the census reports for servants over 19 years of age. Since the census figures did not include servants under the age of 20, who represented something like 25 per cent of all servants in other northern cities (Table 9), this indicates that large numbers of the 'servant' class recorded in the census were in fact living with kin, and thus may have been working as 'home helps'. If indeed many such cases were removed from the census tabulations by the district or central census officials, then we must ask upon what criteria such a selection was made and with what degree of consistency was it performed in the case of the Rochdale enumeration districts.

There is also evidence that this process of misspecification was not confined to the Rochdale district. An examination of the numbers of housekeepers in the census tabulations for selected northern cities, in which figures for all age groups of servants are given, shows some remarkable fluctuations between the years 1851 and 1861 (Table 10). The numbers of housekeepers either moved in an opposite direction to the general trend or showed a wildly exaggerated form of that movement. It could of course be argued that individual servant categories would be likely to fluctuate more widely than the aggregate totals for all servants. This is indeed true, but it would seem that some of the observed fluctuations can only be explained as cases of misspecification, or as an attempt to remove such errors as had occurred in previous years. Thus in the borough of Oldham in 1851 we find no more than 48 housekeepers but a decade later this has increased to 146 housekeepers.[9] In the borough of Bolton in 1851 we find 369 housekeepers, a figure which had fallen to only 138 in 1861.[10] Perhaps the most extreme case is that of the borough of Blackburn; here housekeepers numbered some 733 persons in 1851 nearly 38 per cent of the entire servant population, but by 1861 the number of housekeepers recorded was only 51, or under 3 per cent of the servant total.[11]

In Table 11 the total number of servants over the age of 19 is given for the samples drawn from the Rochdale district in 1851, 1861 and 1871, and is broken down according to the percentage of servants in the differing

types of social category outlined in the Methodological
Introduction, i.e. into 'true servants', 'wrongly enumerated servants', 'possible servants' and 'out servants'.
These are then compared with the total number of servants
over 19 years old shown in the official census tabulations,
expressed as a percentage of the servant totals inferred
from the samples.[12]

If we can accept these figures as representative of the
pattern in each census then it becomes plain that the
quality of enumeration had in fact declined over time. The
total number of persons with servant occupations was
increasingly made up of persons who did not live as
servants in the households of their employers. Indeed by
1871 far more persons were housekeepers for their kin than
were actually servants, of all types, living as institutionalised domestics. Also the 'true servant' population
of all ages , as inferred from the samples, represented
only some 58 per cent of the census population in 1851, 65
per cent in 1861 and only just under 50 per cent in 1871.

Such errors if repeated in other areas would seriously
diminish the reliability of the mid-nineteenth century
censuses as indicators of movements within the servant
population and thus within the economy as a whole. Also
they might make it difficult to use servants as an indication of social stratification within local communities. It
is perhaps unlikely that such errors would occur on the
same scale in other parts of the country. However, in
agricultural areas we might well find large numbers of
servants who were kin helping on the farm. If the Rochdale
servant population given in the census account was too
large in 1871 by 100 per cent and this error was repeatead
nationally, then over 500,000 women would have been wrongly
enumerated in the census abstracts. Probably nothing on
this scale actually happened but this exercise should be a

warning to historians attempting to use the census abstracts in the field of local social history. Variations in the number of domestic servants cannot simply be considered as an indication of variations in social class within narrowly defined areas, they might equally imply changes in the method of enumeration and tabulation.

III. 'Out Servants'

There is certainly reason to suppose that a large number of the individuals who resided with kin and were enumerated as servants were actually helping in the home. It is perhaps best to consider the individual groups of such 'servants' in isolation so as to come to a fuller understanding of their relative social positions. Following the procedure outlined in the Methodological Introduction, these groups were defined as 'out servants', 'wrongly enumerated servants' and 'possible servants'.

The 'out servant' category was originally defined as households containing persons in servant occupations whose relationship to the head of the household was one of kinship or of lodging, but who were unlikely to be working at home. In practice this group was composed of males in occupations such as gardener, coachman and groom, as well as females recorded as general servants, housekeepers or nurses whose relationship to the head of the household was that of lodger.

It is almost impossible to come to any general conclusions about the males in this grouping since we cannot claim that men described as gardeners, coachmen or grooms were recognised in any sense as domestic servants.

34

Gardeners especially may not have worked as paid retainers but in municipal gardens, or as day labourers brought in at intervals on a contract basis. Henry Brierley, writing in 1923 about his childhood in the Rochdale of the mid-nineteenth century, recalls that his grandfather (1765-1833) worked as a gardener at the local vicarage. This 'gardener' spent £50 annually on labour and manure and went on to become a publican, corn merchant and partner in a cotton mill.[13] In this case the gardener was obviously a large-scale contractor rather then a personal servant. An examination of Tables 6 and 7 reveals that it is these categories of male 'servant' in the census samples which most obviously exceed the official census figures. This would indeed seem to confirm that these persons were often not regarded as domestic servants.

In the case of women living as lodgers it is equally difficult to distinguish between 'nurses' and mid-wives, or between 'servants' and charwomen. This group might also represent an attempt by householders to distinguish between domestic service as an occupation and as a social position. Thus the small number of 'housekeepers' who were described as lodgers may have been looking after the house in which they lived, but were not regarded by the head of the household as being in a position of institutionalised dependence.

IV. 'Wrongly Enumerated' Servants

An examination of those individuals classified as 'wrongly enumerated servants' is more rewarding and there is evidence that these persons were employed in their place of domicile. By far the largest component of this group were those women living in the home of their kin and who were enumerated as 'housekeepers'. The other members of this group, 'servants employed at home', represented 11 per cent of all 'wrong servants' in 1851 but a mere 0.5 per cent in 1871.

As can be seen from Table 11 this group of 'servants' became an increasingly large proportion of all the servants recorded in the samples taken from the census enumeration books, becoming the largest single category in 1871. The great increase in the number of such women takes place in 1861, and appears to be caused by a sudden increase in the number of wives enumerated as 'housekeepers'. Thus, wives as housekeepers represented some 23.4 per cent of the entire group in 1851, but 37.7 per cent and 40.4 per cent in 1861 and 1871 respectively.

In 1861 and 1871 some enumerators seem to have conventionally enumerated every housewife as a housekeeper, although such women appear in almost every district. It is perhaps unlikely that someone living in one household would have regarded themselves as a 'housekeeper' in another during the daytime, still less likely that such women should be concentrated in a few districts, and be the mothers of families.

This group was entirely female in each censal year. The women were often widows, although the number of married women increased as more wives were enumerated as housekeepers. There was also a tendency for this group to include an excess of migrants into the Rochdale district. Amongst women over the age of 20 years in the Rochdale control sample of 1851, 66.3 per cent had been born in Rochdale, whilst only 54.7 per cent of the contemporary 'wrongly enumerated servants' had been born there. In 1871 the corresponding figures were 57 per cent and 50.6 per cent. (Table 12)

A large number of these 'housekeepers' were the female heads of households, which accounts for the large number of widows amongst them. In 1851 females represented 41.3 per cent of all the heads of households in which 'wrongly enumerated servants' were to be found, compared to a mere 13.6 per cent amongst the control sample for that year. The corresponding figures for 1861 were 40.2 per cent and 8.6 per cent , and 36.4 per cent and 15.0 per cent in 1871. The overwhelming majority of these female housekeepers were widows heading households containing their kin. In 1861, for example, we find Alice Coupe living in High Street, Rochdale. Mrs Coupe was 69 years old and the widowed head of a household containing two of her daughters and her niece. One of her daughters was married and lived in the house with her husband and four year old child. Everybody was at work apart from Mrs Coupe and her grand-daughter. Thus, when we find that Alice Coupe was enumerated as a 'housekeeper', we can surmise that she was in fact looking after the house and her grand-daughter whilst the rest of the family were out at work.

From the figures contained in Table 13 it would appear that a woman from Ireland, when widowed, was more likely to stay at the head of her household, as a housekeeper, than was her contemporary who had been born in the Rochdale district. In 1861, for example, 48.9 per cent of all the housekeeper-heads in the sample were from the Rochdale district, compared with 61.0 per cent of the heads in the control sample. At the same date Irish women provided some 16.0 per cent of the housekeeper-heads, although the control sample showed only some 5.0 per cent of the heads in Rochdale as coming from Ireland. The causes of this difference may lie in the different cultures of the two groups, although it might be difficult to prove that Irish families were more 'matriarchal' than Lancashire families. Rochdale women could be expected to have more relatives in the immediate vicinity who might be willing to support them in the event of the death of their husbands. However, the Irish seem to have been less willing to depose a widow from her position as titular head of the household.

It would appear that such arrangements as have been discussed were more frequent in the towns of mid-nineteenth centure Lancashire than at any time before or since. In Table 14 the residence patterns of widowed persons, aged 65 or over, are shown for a sample of five communities in England prior to 1800; for a sample of households drawn from the 1851 census of Preston; and finally from Britain in the 1960's.[14]

If these figures have any general validity, they would suggest that families in the nineteenth-century industrial city were far less likely to break up on the death of one of the parents then in Britain in the pre-industrial age or in modern times. This may be further proof of Anderson's general thesis concerning the calculative nature of kinship bonds in society.[15] He suggests, on the basis of his work on nineteenth-century Preston, that the prevalent high degree of kinship support represented an intermediatory stage between 'welfare' in the pre-industrial period and in our modern Welfare State. In industrial Lancashire in the nineteenth century, the old were recruited into the households of kin (or headed households where different generations of the same family lived), providing assistance in the care of the house and children whilst other members of the family were at work. In earlier times, and in other areas, the level of family income was at subsistence level and a surplus was not available to support elderly relatives. In modern times these functions have come to be associated with the welfare services of the State. Thus,

38

in the nineteenth century, the large number of widowed household heads enumerated as housekeepers can be seen as fulfilling a special role within the working-class family in the early industrial environment.

On the other hand, the classification of housewives as 'housekeepers' was, in most cases, due to the particular conventions of individual enumerators. However, the heads of households containing such women appear to have been members of Social-Economic Groups 4 and 5, semi-skilled and unskilled workers. (See Appendix A, Note 7.) In 1851 such persons comprised 57.2 per cent of the household heads whose wives were enumerated as housekeepers, whilst such persons made up only 22.4 per cent of the household heads in the control sample of that year. The respective figures for 1861 were 40.7 per cent and 25.9 per cent; and 38.5 per cent and 30.0 per cent in 1871. (Table 15)

This pattern may simply be a coincidence, in that the enumeration districts in which the enumerators wrongly recorded such women might, by chance, have been the poorer areas of the region. However, this might also have represented, in part, the inability of the lower working classes to understand the instructions provided with the census schedules. This may have led household heads to wrongly classify household employment as a servant occupation. Alternatively, the poor quality of the returns from such low class areas may have encouraged enumerators to re-write the schedules and so to standardise them.

Some of the 'housekeepers' or 'servants at home' in this group were neither the heads of households nor the wives of the householders. This sub-group of daughters, cousins, nieces, aunts, mothers and other more distant relatives, appears to have declined in importance over the period but it still provided large numbers of such servants in 1871. (Table 16)   Many of these women appear to have been in

39

households headed by their single or widowed male relatives. Thus, despite the fact that many households headed by males must have included housekeepers who were in fact wives, the number of married male heads in the whole group was low. In the control sample of Rochdale households in 1851, 84.9 per cent of all male heads were married but this figure was reduced to 56.8 per cent amongst males heading households which contained 'wrongly enumerated servants'. (Table 17) The respective figures for 1861 were 88.9 per cent and 74.3 per cent, and 90.0 per cent and 78.3 per cent in 1871. This would seem to indicate that many 'housekeepers' in these households were relatives replacing wives and mothers.

There appears to have been a difference in the type of relative who fulfilled this role in houses headed by single men compared to those headed by widowers. Widowed male heads tended to have daughters and junior relations, such as nieces and grand-daughters, acting as 'housekeepers'; single heads tended to have elder relatives or their kin peers in this role. In the case of households containing daughters and junior relations as housekeepers, there was not a single case of a head who had not been married. In households containing elder relatives and peers, such as sisters and cousins, as housekeepers, the proportion of household heads who had ever been married was only 22.2 per cent, 43.5 per cent and 32.5 per cent in each censal year.[16] In the same years the households containing daughters and junior relations as 'housekeepers' had many widowed heads, over 80 per cent in each year, whilst the householders with elder relatives and their peers as housekeepers were less often widowed, 33.3 per cent, 17.4 per cent and 10 per cent in the three censal years.[17] These rather involved figures merely point to the fact that

40

daughters and other young relatives were replacing deceased wives, whereas sisters and elder relatives were 'huddling' with kin who had no children, for mutual support.

'Wrongly enumerated' servants are thus easily seen as working at home since they were either enumerated as 'working at home', or were housekeepers in households whose structure would suggest that these women would be working in the households in which they were enumerated.

V. 'Possible Servants': Nurses

There were, however, numerous 'servants' living with kin, here defined as 'possible servants', whose social standing or position within the household is more difficult to establish. For example, in 1851 we find the Bollitt family living in Yorkshire Street, Rochdale. John Bollitt was a hairdresser and he and his wife, Ann, had three children, all under the age of ten years. With the family lived Sally Howarth, who was Ann Bollitt's sister, and who was described as a 'general servant'. It is more difficult to gauge exactly where this 'servant' worked than it was in the case of housewives or widows described as housekeepers. It is only possible to note peculiarities in the aggregate characteristics of such women, or the households in which they lived, so as to infer their social position within the household. In the case quoted above we might note that the Bollitt's had a shop to run and would have needed someone to look after their young children; this would indicate that the household was particularly in need of extra help. We cannot say that Sally Howarth was definitely working at home, but there is a strong possibility that this household would have required someone like Sally because of its structure and functions. It is perhaps fortunate that such servants formed an increasingly small part of the census samples, since they were the group which was most difficult to interpret. (Table 11)

For the sake of convenience, kin who were enumerated as 'nurses' can be considered separately from the rest of this group. Such nurses, who were always female, numbered 38 in 1851, but only 22 in 1861 and 17 in 1871. No nurse in any sample was aged between 20 and 50 years and in no case was a wife or peer of the household head enumerated as such. These nurses were always young relatives such as daughters, nieces or grand-daughters, or elders such as mothers or aunts of the household head.

Households in which these nurses were found contained significantly large numbers of children under 10 years of age. In 1851, 27.8 per cent of these households contained three or more children under the age of 10, and this figure stood at 27.3 per cent in 1861 and no less than 52.9 per cent in 1871 (see Appendix A, Note 12). In the same censal years the control samples contained fewer households with that number of dependents under the age of 10; totalling only 16 per cent of the sample households in 1851, 16.3 per cent in 1861 and 15 per cent in 1871.[18] This suggests that these households would require someone to look after young children. This is especially likely since the households as a group were large, due, in part, to the large number of children which they contained. In 1871 no fewer than 94.2 per cent of all the households with kin enumerated as nurses contained more than four persons. In 1851 and 1861 the corresponding figures were 80.6 per cent and 77.2 per cent. The control samples showed that smaller household units were more typical, households with more than four persons in them accounting for only 46.3 per cent of the sample in 1851, 45.2 per cent in 1861 and only

37.5 per cent in 1871. If any women were likely to require someone to nurse children it would be the housewives in these homes .

These nurses were also associated with the textile industry. Thus, in 1851, 55.6 per cent of the heads whose families contained such servants actually worked in the textile trades, whilst such workers only represented some 41.6 per cent of all men aged over 19 years in the Rochdale district.[19] In 1861 the corresponding figures were 50 per cent and 40.7 per cent.[20] (Table 18) Such nurses were concentrated in the areas where textile workers lived. In 1851 58.3 per cent of all such nurses were found in nucleated settlements outside urban Rochdale (Appendix A, Note 28), although these areas contained only some 38 per cent of all households.[21] At the same time the control sample showed these settlements to have contained nearly 52 per cent of all textile workers in the sample.

Such nurses were most probably child-minders in their own homes, since in 1851 no less than 18 nurses out of a total sample of 38 were aged under 10 years. In 1861 such young children comprised 50 per cent of the sample. It is highly unlikely that girls of six or seven years of age could be doing any very responsible work, or be hiring out their services to middle-class employers. These children would be part of that vast army of 'child-minders' so familiar to students of the working-class household in nineteenth century Lancashire: children and old women left in charge of babies liberaly dosed with such opiates as Godfrey's Cordial, whilst the mothers of the infants were at work in the mill. This might have simply taken the form of an informal arrangement, part of the 'kindness existing between neighbours', as one report put it.[22] Alternatively, childminding could take on the form of a 'baby factory' with one person looking after babies from the households of whole working-class districts. Hewitt calculates that in certain districts in Lancashire between 16 per cent and 45 per cent of all cotton operatives were married and might thus have to leave their children to go to work.[23] There would thus have been plenty of work for 'baby-sitters' without this implying that such girls were domestic servants in any recognisable institutionalised sense.

VI. 'Possible Servants': Non-Nurses

Domestic servants who were day workers in the households of middle-class employers did exist in the nineteenth century. As one Midland factory worker commented in 1916, 'A servant has no trade after marriage. Up in the North there is a good demand for day service: there are so many works where girls are employed that even after marriage the servant can easily find work'.[24] Some of the women occupied as 'servants' and living with their kin may well have been day workers of this type. Certainly such women tended to live in areas with relatively high densities of servant-employing households. As part of the work on the Rochdale district in 1851, the whole area was divided into 100 yard grid squares and the number of households and servant employing households was calculated for each square. Of the 201 households randomly selected as a control in 1851, 159 households, or 79.3 per cent were situated in grid squares in which less than 10 per cent of the households contained 'true servants'. On the other hand, out of 79 households with 'possible servants' who were not nurses, only 54 households, or 68.4 per cent were situated in grid

44

squares in which less than 10 per cent of the households contained 'true servants'.[25] The households containing 'possible servants' were thus situated in slightly higher social areas than one would expect. There could therefore have been a demand for day servants in the immediate vicinity. (See Appendix A, Notes 28 and 29)

However these servants, and the households in which they lived, exhibited certain aggregate characteristics which suggest that the servants were often employed about the home. Contrary to the suggestion above, these women do not appear to have been married; they were much more likely to be either single or widowed. In 1851 just over 78 per cent of these women were single and 14.8 per cent were widows. The comparable figures for all women in the control sample were 60 per cent and 6.1 per cent. Similar differences were to be found in other censal years.[26] (Table 19)

These servants tended to be young, unmarried women or elderly widows. In 1871 51.4 per cent of all kin relations described as 'general servants' were aged between 10 and 29 years, compared with 40.9 per cent of all females in the 1871 control sample.[27] At the same date 23.6 per cent of such servants were aged over 50 years, compared with 12.4 per cent amongst the control population. Once again, similar patterns were to be found amongst the samples from other censal years.[28] (Table 20) These figures do not suggest married women doing day work to supplement the family income, but rather the labour of women prior to marriage, or during widowhood.

Such 'possible servants' were unusual in being additions to the normal nuclear family. In the Rochdale control sample of 1851, 84.9 per cent of all females were either heads of households or the wives and daughters of male heads. However, such persons made up only 53.4 per cent of all the servants we are dealing with here and the position

45

was similar in other years. (Table 21) There were thus more persons who were marginal to the 'normal' family in this servant group than might have been expected. These sisters, nieces, mothers-in-law and aunts showed many of the characteristics of being dependants of the households in which they lived.

Similarly, the households in which they resided might well have required someone to help with the household work. An unusually small number of the households contained married heads, 63.7 per cent in 1871, as compared with 76.5 per cent amongst the households in the 1871 control sample. The contrast was even more marked in other years. (Table 22) This would indicate that in the absence of a wife the household would require someone to work at home. This is made even more likely by the fact that these households tended to be large ones, despite there being so few married couples in the sample. Households with more than four persons in them comprised 57.1 per cent of the sample in 1851, 67.0 per cent in 1861 and 47.4 per cent in 1871. The corresponding figures from the control sample were, for each respective censal year, 46.3 per cent, 45.2 per cent and 37.5 per cent.[29]

It must also be noted that such households were not necessarily very poor ones. Indeed there appear to have been significantly large numbers of households in Social-Economic Groups 1 and 2, that is, amongst the capitalist, professional, farming and large retailing classes. Again comparing the households with 'possible servants' with those in the control samples, we find that in 1851 24 per cent of the heads in the former group were in Social Econo-mic-Groups 1 and 2, compared with 14.4 per cent in the control sample of that year.[30] This contrast was even more striking in the other censal years. (Table 23). A few examples will suffice to show the type of 'servant' we are discussing here. In 1861 the family of John Smith of Moorhouse comprised Smith, his wife Hannah, two employed sons in their twenties and three daughters, one of whom was described as a 'housemaid'. Smith did not employ any servants, although he was a woollen manufacturer employing 68 hands. Thomas Butterworth of Hamer Place, another woollen manufacturer employing 40 hands, had a family of two boys and two girls, all aged in their twenties; both girls lived at home and were described as 'servants'. At the same date the family of James Lord, a calico manufacturer employing 12 hands, lived at number 175 Broadoath Lane. The family comprised James and his wife, a daughter, two adult sons and Lord's 76 year old mother-in-law, who was described as 'House Cook'. It is surely unlikely that men such as these would have to send their daughters or aged relatives out to work at 'charring'.

Moreover, most of these households in the higher classes of Rochdale's society were headed by retailers and farmers, and were thus those which might require extra labour because of their productive functions. In 1851 34.3 per cent of all households containing 'possible servants' were headed by either a retailer or a farmer; the equivalent figure in the control sample was only 16.5 per cent. Similar figures could again be produced from the other census samples. (Table 24) It is unlikely that the relatives of these types of householders would have to go out to work to supplement the household income. If these women had to go out to work then it is unusual that they should have chosen an occupation that was dominated by migrant labour. As a group these servants tended to be local in origin, and it is difficult to see why they could not have gained alternative employment in factories or in the shops of their relations. In 1851 72.7 per cent of all these servants came from Rochdale compared with 69.9 per cent amongst the female population over ten years old in the control sample.[31] In later years the servants appear to have been more local than the female population of the control samples.[32] (Table 25)

There is thus a good deal of evidence to suggest that these women were working in the households in which they were enumerated on census night. Certainly the structure of the households in which they lived would suggest that extra labour was required in the home. It is also apparent that these women were not 'normally' members of households and show some characteristics which suggest that they were dependants of the households in which they lived. More conclusively still, these women, if day servants, would have been employed in what was basically 'charring', when many were related to householders of high social status.

Although it is impossible to say conclusively that nobody in this group went out to work as a servant during the daytime, it is more likely that the group as a whole was employed at home. It is best therefore to exclude this group from a discussion of service as an institutionalised relationship.

VII. Conclusion

It seems likely that many, if not most, of the persons in servant occupations who resided with kin in these samples were actually working in the households in which they were enumerated. This may reveal a significant difference in the manner in which some contemporaries viewed women's work in the home. Whereas modern scholars tend to disregard female labour in the home when discussing economic activity, some householders in the nineteenth century regarded such activities as definite occupations. An attempt therefore to limit domestic service to the relationship of the cash nexus, although necessary for the purposes of research, may merely reflect our own prejudices as to the scope of productive labour. Although in this work 'domestic servants' have been defined in terms of the cash nexus existing between servant and employer, it is plain that labour in the home by 'employees' or by kin, has much wider social implications. In practice it may have been difficult to quantify the various shades of social status which separated a paid employee, hired as a menial, from the old friend of the family, taken in when she fell on hard times, or from the distant cousin from the countryside who was paid pocket-money whilst she helped in the house. There would be even greater difficulties in separating the 'day servant' from the charwoman, and from Auntie So-and-So, who came round to help in a time of crisis, in return for payment in kind.

To undertake a study to embrace all these facets of labour in the home would be a immense task, given the sheer number of persons involved, and the notorious reluctance of the Victorians to intrude into the 'Englishman's Castle'. When they did intrude into the Victorian home, as with the census, it was plain that many were confused by the subtle variations which existed there. When the Registrar General's Office wrote to the local registrar of the Biggleswade area that,

> With respect to your question regarding the
> daughters of farmers who may assist in the house
> to some extent but do not assist on the farm, it
> is evident that they will have no occupation and

Column 6 may in their case also be left blank.[33]

they were stating their opinion as to how young women 'ought' to be employed, rather than how the household in which they lived saw the matter. For a family working and producing as a unit, a daughter employed about the house may have been seen as employed in a particular occupation - much as all the other members of the family. However, since this labour could not be directly exchanged for a cash equivalent, members of the middle classes who had to interpret this information were unable to regard the labour as an occupation. In this manner our definition of domestic service must be seen as one conditioned by our own conceptions of the organisation of labour. To do otherwise here would necessitate an examination of household labour as such, which would be an enormous task. By concentrating on the labour of hired servants in the households of the social elite we are thus concentrating our analysis on one sector in a much larger category of household work.

The 'uniqueness' of this type of labour did not lie in its tasks, or remuneration, but rather in its social implications. The work of the 'slavey' was not in itself especially onerous. It was rather the social relationship between 'master and servant' which marked this labour off from similar labour in the home. The domestic servant was part of the household of the Victorian middle classes but was not part of the family, and she appears to have represented an alien presence. Much of the following account of domestic service in Rochdale in the period 1851 to 1871 does not concentrate therefore on the servant and the employer as individuals who merely need to be described but rather on domestic service as a social relationship. An attempt will be made to link the type of servant which families chose to employ, with the type of social relationship which was supposed to exist between the two parties.

50

5. THE 'TRUE' SERVANT POPULATION OF ROCHDALE, 1851-1871

I. Defining the Population

The 'servants' to be examined in the rest of this work are
those who have been defined as 'true' servants. That is,
those persons in servant occupations whose relationship to
the head of the household in the census schedules was that
of 'Servant'. This is in no way a functional definition
since, as we have seen, many other women may have been
doing household labour of a personal nature. The true
difference lay in the fact that this labour lay outside the
world of kin relationships and was procured through a cash
nexus rather than through social pressures acting on kin.

In some cases relatives may actually have been
enumerated as servants with regard to their relationship to
the head of the household. It is conceivable that in the
case of remarriages some step-children might have been
retained within the household but refused admission into
the family as kin. It is unlikely, however, that this was
ever a very serious problem. Taking similarity of surname
as a measurement of possible misspecification of this type,
we find only 13 cases in 1851, out of a total of 296
servants. In 1861 the number was only seven out of 315
cases, and in 1871, 10 cases out of a total of 402
servants. Many of these cases involved coincidences of
very common local surnames such as Butterworth or Clegg,
and in no manner actually represent cases of the
suppression of kin relationships. In all probability such
relationships as were omitted from the census were very

few. A much more difficult question may be the exact social position of women enumerated as 'servants' to single male householders in the lower social-economic groups. Some of these women may well have been common law wives, or 'concubines', as one census report put it.[1]

In practice all persons whose relationship to the head of the household was that of 'servant' have been included in the various aggregate breakdowns of the total servant population. Servants employed by members of the lower working classes only made up a small fraction of the total servant population, so that their inclusion should not greatly affect the aggregate figures. In much of the discussion which follows these rather dubious 'servants' are often ignored, and only servants employed by the three highest social-economic groups are compared.

This is once again an arbitrary distinction which has been made, and it must not be assumed that such 'concubines' as did exist were not in fact engaged in household work. The assumption which runs through this work, and many other tracts on the subject, is that domestic servants can be dissociated from others performing household work on the basis of the absence of a kin relationship. This is not a functional division but one based on the distribution of remunerations in society. Both domestic servants and 'concubines' may have performed household labour, but only the labour of the servant produced a flow of cash as a money equivalent for labour performed. Thus, the definition of servant used here is social rather than functional.

II. The 'Typical' Servant in Rochdale

No better indication can be found of the extent to which paid domestic service has declined in this country than the popular stereotype of the 'typical' servant household. In popular literature the servant is portrayed as living in a large, well ordered household of servants in which strict functional demarcations and hierarchies of command existed. This impression has no doubt been fostered by the popularisation of works by upper-middle class authors of the day and by an examination of nineteenth-century books on household economy. Mrs Beeton, for example, was well aware that, on an income of only £150 to £200 per annum, a household could only afford a single maid-of-all-work and an occasional girl to help with the housework.[2] However, it is apparent that her Book of Household Management was aimed at a far higher social class than this. Out of sixty-five pages devoted in her 1863 edition to the description of the servant household, Mrs Beeton allocates only five to a discussion of the duties of the maid-of-all-work, whilst she gives seven pages to the footman, eight to the lady's maid and no less than 13 to the upper and under housemaids.[3]

In the Rochdale Registration District in the period 1851 to 1871 a very different pattern emerges from the census schedules. Throughout the period, households containing single servants predominted in the samples. In 1851 60.8 per cent of all servants were the only resident servant in the household in which they were enumerated. This proportion did decline over the next two decades but still stood at 53.0 per cent in 1871. From the samples it would appear that the most typical servant was therefore the maid-of-all-work. The impression of communal life 'downstairs' is a false one and the true servant was more likely to be solitary.

> One little soldier single-handed against a house
> and its wants, and the dust and the smuts, and
> the food and the inmates, and the bells, and the
> beds, and the fire, and water to be served up in
> cans, and stoves and plates. Atlas could carry
> the world upon his shoulder, but what was his task
> compared with poor little Betty's?[4]

The servant-employing household with only one resident
servant was typical of the country as a whole, although
Table 26 shows that there were distinct regional
differences.

These figures, drawn from 10 per cent samples of various
districts by Ebery and Preston, indicate that Rochdale had
relatively few large households. It shared this characteristic with other industrial towns such as Bolton and
Coventry. Ebery and Preston noted that the largest servant
households were in fact found in the rural areas of
Berkshire (Easthampstead, Bradfield, Cookham, Windsor and
Wokingham) and concluded that the size of households in a
region was dependent upon the wealth of the local middle
classes and the availability of alternative employment for
women.[5]

According to Ebery and Preston the average number of
female indoor servants per 1,000 families in England and
Wales in 1911 was 159. The industrial counties such as
Lancashire, Yorkshire, Derbyshire and Nottinghamshire stand
out as having very few servants; Lancashire having only
some 97 servants per 1,000 families. On the other hand,
agricultural counties such as Berkshire, Surrey and Sussex
showed much higher servant densities. Servants were scarce

therefore in industrial areas and plentiful in agricultural areas.[6] The reasons for this pattern lie in the supply and demand for servants in these areas. The lack of alternative employment for women in rural areas increased the potential supply of servants. At the same time the industrial areas appear to have had comparatively small servant-employing elites, which would reduce the effective demand for servants. (See Chapter 6, Section II)

It would appear that such small households were typical of other countries in this period. In France, for example, it has been calculated that out of 410 male servants and 2,211 female domestics in Versailles in 1872, 80 per cent worked alone or with one other servant. Similarly in Lyon at the same date only 3,179 servants out of a total servant population of 10,527, or 30 per cent, worked in households where more than one servant was employed.[7]

The small size of servant retinues is of considerable importance when discussing the quality of life experienced by servants in this period. The 'typical' servant was not part of an alternative society 'downstairs' opposed to the household 'upstairs'; she was more usually isolated in the household in which she worked. If she was lucky she would be counted as 'one of the family', perhaps on a par with the children of the household, but she might also find herself in the unfortunate position of being a lone outsider within the home of her employers. Such relationships would be an important determinant of the servant's conditions of work and her social standing in the community.

III. Types of servant employment

Given the small size of servant retinues in Rochdale in this period it was natural that there should be little functional differentiation amongst the servants employed. In 1871 some 67.7 per cent of all the servants in the Rochdsale sample were described simply as 'servant'. It is perhaps a mistake to take the servant occupations recorded in the schedules as conclusive evidence of the structure of households. Many persons in large households were simply described as 'servants' although they formed part of a relatively large retinue. Thus the household of John Bright at One Ash contained five servants in each censal year but all 15 of them were simply described as 'general servant' by Bright himself. However, it is apparent that the larger the household the greater the degree of specialization that was recorded.

As before, the work of Ebery and Preston can be used to put the figures for Rochdale into a national context. In Table 27 Ebery and Preston's breakdown of the types of servants employed in selected areas are given, along with comparable figures from Rochdale.[8]

Rochdale fits into the general pattern of industrial towns in this table. Since households in these areas had few servants, they tended to employ a disproportionately high number of general servants and few males. However, over the period 1851 to 1871, the degree of specialization and differentiation within the households in Rochdale had in fact increased significantly. Although general servants accounted for 67.7 per cent of the total in 1871, this proportion had been as high as 78.4 per cent of all servants in 1851. Over the two decades, cooks had increased from 1.4 per cent of all servants to 7.0 per cent, housemaids had risen from 2.7 per cent to 8.2 per cent and nurses had also risen from 3.7 per cent of the sample to 8.5 per cent. (Table 28)

This was directly linked to the increase in the size of servant households in the sample. Thus the households which appeared in more than one census and which increased in size, showed not only an increase in the number of servants but an increase in the number of different types of servant. In the first year in which they appeared these households contained nine general servants, one housekeeper and a man servant between them. On the second occasion they contained 10 general servants, three housekeepers, three housemaids, two nurses, a cook, a governess, a lady's maid and a footman.

A more detailed examination of this evidence reveals that the general servant was associated with single servant households. Thus in 1851 60.8 per cent of all servants were found in households which contained only one servant, but 67.7 per cent of all general servants were in such households.[9] This difference was much larger in 1861; and in 1871 69.9 per cent of all general servants were found in single servant households although only 57.1 per cent of all servants were resident in such families. Similarly cooks and nurses were relatively under-represented in single servant households in every sample, as were housemaids in 1861 and 1871. Some occupations, such as butler, coachman, lady's maid, kitchen maid and laundry maid, were only found in the largest households.

This indicates that the type of servant in the Rochdale district was undergoing a change in this period as the size of servant retinues increased. Single servant households would tend to employ only a maid-of-all-work, and add perhaps a housemaid, a cook and a nurse as their income rose. In only the very largest households does there appear to exist that hierarchical differentiation of labour which can be found in the pages of Mrs Beeton's work.

It is perhaps idle to speculate as to the exact duties performed by such servants. As was mentioned above, some employers appear to have been vague about the duties of their domestics. Thus, in 1861 John Bright employed five women as 'general servants' Four were in their twenties but one, Ellen Hemsworth, was aged 45 and was the first servant enumerated. It might be reasonable to assume that this woman had different duties from those of her fellow servants, although Bright gave no indication of this. Other servant employers were clearly conscious of the hierarchy of duties which existed within their households. For example, in 1871 William Shawcross, a cotton manufacturer, employed four servants: Annie Donough aged 24 was described as a 'housemaid'; Ann Corconnan aged 42 was described as a 'cook'; and there were two nurses, aged 38 and 14 respectively (the younger being described as an 'under-nurse'). The description of two servants in the household as 'nurses' can be explained by the presence of four children all under ten years of age, one being a baby of eleven months. This would appear to indicate a rigid occupational structure, although this may have varied between households.

The duties of general servants who were the only servants employed by households must have been numerous. Also, as will be suggested in Chapter Vl, Section VII, the duties of servants in retail establishments could include active participation in the productive labour of the family business.

IV. The Age Structure of the Rochdale Servant Population, 1851 to 1871

In the nineteenth century domestic service was part of the life-cycle of a large proportion of the female population. Whereas the daughter of a middle-class family could expect to pass directly from the house of her parents to that of her husband, her working-class contemporary might well expect to move out of her parental home into that of an employer, before setting up a household of her own. It was only in highly industrialised areas that young women could hope to earn enough to move out of the parental home and into lodgings whilst single. This must have greatly affected the expectations and outlooks of mill girls throughout the country as compared with their less independent country cousins.

In the mid-nineteenth century girls would enter service in their mid-teens and then leave in their mid-twenties to get married. This can be clearly seen in Table 29, in which female servants in particular age groups are represented as a percentage of the whole group. Thus, nearly a third of all females aged between 15 years old and 19 years old were in service, as were a quarter of all women aged between 20 and 24 years. After the age of 24 there was a sharp decline as women married.

This type of 'life-cycle service' has always been one of the distinctive characteristics of West European society, and is perhaps unique to it. Laslett believes that in most 'Western' communities prior to industrialization, servants, in the sense of living-in employees, comprised at least 10 per cent of the population.[10] These servants in Western communities in the pre-industrial age were also found in certain age groups which suggest that service was merely part of a normal person's life-cycle, as can be seen from Table 30.

It would be incorrect however to believe that this was in any sense the fixed pattern of service in the Victorian and Edwardian periods. As can be seen from Table 31, taken from one of the tables produced by Ebery and Preston, there was a considerable amount of regional variation in the age structure of servant populations in 1871.[11] The proportion of servants aged under 20 years in this sample of 20 settlements ranged from 14.3 per cent in Newbury to as high as 59.2 per cent in Wantage. Generally low figures for the proportion of servants under twenty years old are found in the industrial areas of Lancashire, in Bolton, Hulton and Turton, as well as in the sample from Rochdale in 1871. Some non-industrial areas, such as Hastings, had fairly elderly servants because of the large number of them employed in the upper levels of the servant hierarchy as housekeepers, cooks and ladies' maids. These figures suggest that the age structure of the servant population depended upon the availability of alternative employment for young women. Since some 42 per cent of all women in England and Wales employed in the manufacture of cotton were under the age of 20 years,[12] it is reasonable to assume that the low proportion of young servants found in the Lancashire towns was due to competition for young hands from the mills.

It is interesting to note, however, that such variations in the age structure of the servant population were also found on the national level through time. The relative rise in the servant population in the period 1851 to 1881 appears to coincide with a general reduction in the age of the servant population, whilst its stagnation and decline in later years was linked to a general ageing of the servant population. This process, shown in Table 32,

60

indicates that the growth in the servant population was directly caused by an influx of young women into this sector of the economy.

An explanation of the decline of the servant population in the late nineteenth century must explain why young women failed to enter the occupation, since it was the number of young women in domestic service which declined most rapidly. In 1871 50.2 per cent of those females in stated occupations in England and Wales, aged between 15 and 19 years, were in domestic service. In 1911 only 32.7 per cent of the same group were employed in domestic service, a percentage change of 17.4 per cent. During the same period domestic servants as a proportion of those occupied in the 20 to 24 year old age group in England and Wales declined from 46.5 per cent to 32.0 per cent. However, in the case of occupied women aged between 25 and 44 years, domestic servants only declined from 31.2 per cent to 25.2 per cent over the same period, a percentage shift of only 6.0 per cent.[13]

This would appear to indicate that older women were tending to stay within the confines of domestic service, whilst younger women were finding other work. It is probable that young women may have taken advantage of the alternative forms of employment which were becoming available at the end of the nineteenth century, whereas for older women only domestic employment was available. One could surmise that women who failed to find husbands whilst employed as servants would find it very difficult to get alternative employment, especially if they had little experience of work in commerce or industry. This raises the whole question of how working people changed their occupations in this period. We are today more used to the idea of changing jobs in middle life, as the pace of change increases, but it is difficult to discover to what extent people, especially women, changed their occupations in the past. As will be intimated below (Chapter 7, Section II), many people in the nineteenth century appear to have depended on their familes and connections for employment opportunities, and there was a considerable degree of occupational succession. In such cases a rural migrant who became a servant and then failed to marry, would be in a poor position to leave the family in which she was employed to seek a job elsewhere or outside domestic work. This would be the source of the numerous 'family retainers' found in large, well-to-do households.

The servant population in Rochdale in this period does not seem to have shown the same pattern of change as was found on the national level. Nationally there was a large increase in the proportion of servants under the age of 20 years between 1851 and 1861, and a slight increase in the following decade. (Table 32) In Rochdale, on the other hand, the proportion of such servants actually fell between 1851 and 1861, from 29.9 per cent to 21.6 per cent and then recovered to 30.1 per cent by 1871. This would seem to indicate a decline in new entrants in the first decade and a recovery in the second. (Table 33)

A more interesting pattern emerges if we look at the age structures of various sub-groups within the servant population. Servants from Rochdale itself appear to have become steadily older over the period, 34.5 per cent being under 20 years old in 1851 but only 22.6 per cent being in this age group in 1871.[14] At the same time, servants from English counties south of Lancashire and Yorkshire and from Wales, grew steadily younger as a group. In 1861 21.1 per cent of these migrants were aged under 20 years but this figure had increased to 33.5 per cent in 1871. (Table 34) The numbers of servants contained in these groups are not large enough to allow for a great deal of statistical significance but they suggest that the Rochdale servants as a group became older in the period 1851 to 1861, whilst the influx of young southern migrants did not take place until the period 1861 to 1871. In the 1850's therefore there appears to have been some difficulty in getting young, local servants, a problem which was overcome by an influx of young women who had migrated from the south of England and from Wales. Certainly these women become a much more important part of the servant population over this period.

Apart from this change over time it is also to be noted that in every censal year there appears to have been an excess of older servants from the counties of Lancashire (including Rochdale) and Yorkshire. Even in 1851, whilst 18.7 per cent of the servants from these counties were over 40 years of age, only 9.3 per cent of the servants from the rest of the United Kingdom were in the same age group. This pattern was repeated in 1861 and in 1871, when the proportions were 22.5 per cent and 6.4 per cent respectively.

Many of these older servants were spinsters. In 1861, for example, 57.6 per cent of all general servants over the age of 40 were unmarried; whilst amongst the women in the control sample of this age only 5.3 per cent were spinsters. (Table 35) We may thus assume that some of these northern servants were not simply employees but may have been regarded as dependants. It is interesting to note at this point that the only 'true' servant to appear in the same household in two different samples shows every sign of being more than a simple employee. In 1861, when she first appears, Helen Adams was aged 39 and was already old for a servant. Her employer, William Chadwick, was a woollen manufacturer aged 44 and both he and Helen Adams had been born in Scotland. Relationships such as this may have been based on something more than the cash nexus.

The age of servants was also linked to the type of work they performed. As one would expect, the more responsible jobs in service were dominated by older men and women. Thus out of the 20 cooks found in the 1861 sample, only six were under 25 years old. In the same year, out of 27 housemaids in the sample, 15 were over 25 years of age. This indicates that for some women service presented a career structure, through which they could rise as they gained experience. Thus in 1851 32.8 per cent of all general servants were aged under 20 years, but amongst other female servants only 11.4 per cent were in this age group. Over time, however, the age of such specialised servants actually fell as younger women became housemaids, and by 1871 23.6 per cent of the specialised servants were under the age of 20. (Table 36)

In general, however, the average servant in Rochdale in the period would be in her late teens or early twenties. Thus, in 1871, some 53.3 per cent of general servants were aged between 15 and 24 years. Comparatively few general servants were younger than this, only 3.3 per cent in 1871, and the number of servants in older age groups rapidly declined. The figures contained in Table 37, showing in detail the ages of general servants, would appear to con-firm the general hypothesis that domestic service was an occupation dominated by young women who had left home and were not yet married.

V. The Sex and Marital Status of Servants in Rochdale, 1851 to 1871

As was mentioned above, domestic service represented a distinct stage in the life-cycle of working-class women. In 'ideal' terms a young woman would move from the household of her parents into that of her employer; upon marrying, she would move into the home of her husband. This pattern would only be broken where there existed alternative employment for young women in the mills or in other forms of industrial production.

There is some reason to suppose that it was this type of servant who provided the upsurge in servant numbers in the mid-nineteenth century. As can be seen from Table 38, the increase in the relative size of the servant population can be linked nationally to an increase in the proportion of servants who were young and female.

Since the size of servant retinues was so small in Rochdale in the mid-nineteenth century (see above, Chapter 5, Section II), it is not surprising to discover that the number of males in domestic service was small. Thus out of a sample of 296 servants in 1851 only five, or 1.7 per cent, were males. In 1871 the corresponding figure was ten out of 402, or 2.2 per cent. These figures seem to be far below the national averages shown in Table 38.

Males tended to be found in certain specialised servant categories such as butler, footman, coachman and groom. Of the nine servants so described in the three census samples, none was the only servant employed in the household where they were resident. Similarly, of the 24 males who were simply described as 'servant' only eight were solitary servants. The fact that servants were very strictly demarcated according to sex, and that males were employed in households with large servant retinues, meant that male servants were very rare in Rochdale in this period.

The majority of servants were unmarried, as one would expect if service was in fact part of the female life-cycle prior to marriage. Of general female servants in the three samples, nearly 90 per cent were single. There appears to have been some difference between these servants in 1851 and women who had positions as housemaids, cooks, housekeepers, nurses and other specialised servants. Whilst some 92.3 per cent of the former were unmarried in 1851, the equivalent figure for the second group was as low as 68.2 per cent. Many more of the women in the second group appear to have been married or widowed. As they became younger in the period 1851 to 1871, however, so the percentage who were unmarried rose from 68.2 per cent in 1851, to 87.0 per cent in 1871. In the same period 88.5 per cent of all general servants were of the same marital status.[15] Thus over the whole period there was a general increase in the proportion of servants who were single.

In general it seems true to say that servants who were not unmarried were concentratead in the households in Social-Economic Group 3, that is amongst small shopkeepers and artisans. Thus if we combine the two highest social groupings we find that 94.4 per cent of their servants were unmarried in 1851 whilst the equivalent figure for Social-Economic Group 3 was only 83.9 per cent. Although there appears to have been little diference in the relative proportions in 1861, in 1871 we find that the corresponding figures were 91.8 per cent and 81.0 per cent.

VI. The Origins of Rochdale's Servants, 1851 to 1871

In the nineteenth century all urban centres grew by an influx of migrants rather than by a surplus of indiginous births over deaths. The period was one of vast population movements, both within national boundaries and across continents. This general stage of flux, caused by the establishment of a world capitalist economy, could be seen in microcosm in almost every town in the industrial north of England. According to the thesis propounded by Redford, much movement was over short distances, as individuals or families moved from one area of employment to another.[16]

However, in the case of domestic servants, there is some evidence that migration on a far larger scale was taking place. As can be seen from Table 39, servants in Rochdale in the years 1851 to 1871 tended to be born in places much more distant from the district than woman aged between 10 and 30 years in the control samples for the same years. (See Appendix A, Notes 37 and 16)

There were relatively few servants who had been born within the registration district of Rochdale itself. Not only were servants more likely to be migrants but they appear to have migrated over greater distances than was typical of most migrant women in Rochdale. Over time this pattern became more marked as servants born in the Rochdale district and within 30 miles declined, and as servants born in places over 30 miles away increased.

There is no way of telling how most of these women found their way to the Rochdale district, since such persons did not have accompanying children whose birthplaces might show the route of migration. However the fact that most of these women would have been under the age of 25 years, indicates that the distances migrated by them must have been large since they could not have been domiciled at many other areas in between their place of birth and Rochdale. There are other reasons to suppose that many of these migrants must have migrated directly from their place of birth to the Rochdale area. These include the desire of employers to hire non-urban women, especially those who had few relatives in the area, and some of the similarities which seem to exist between the birthplaces of employers and their domestics. As will be outlined below (Chapter 9, Section II), one of the principle desires of servant employers was to get servants who had no link with the immediate area, or relatives or 'hangers-on' nearby. In some cases connections can be found between the employers and their employees which suggest that employers actually recruited servants personally through contacts in other parts of the country.

As can be seen from Table 40, these migrants came from different areas in the different census samples. In the period 1851 to 1861, the proportion of servants from the Rochdale district fell from 38.2 per cent to 22.2 per cent, and remained constant in the next decade. Much of the shortfall appears to have been met by an influx of servants from Yorkshire in the years 1851 to 1861. However, in the next decade the percentage of servants from Yorkshire fell dramatically, and was more than halved. Over the same decades servants from Wales, and from England south of Lancashire and Yorkshire, accounted for 20.7 per cent of all servants in 1851, 24.7 per cent in 1861, and no less than 44.3 per cent in 1871. Thus, as a percentage of all servants, women from this area did not rise in the first decade,[17] but there was a prodigious increase in the period 1861 to 1871.

A more detailed analysis reveals that the increase in the number of servants drawn from areas south of the counties of Lancashire and Yorkshire was mainly due to increased recruitment from those counties stretching in a line from Caernarvonshire to Lincolnshire. These counties included Caernarvonshire, Denbighshire, Montgomeryshire, Flintshire, Cheshire, Shropshire, Staffordshire, Derbyshire, Nottinghamshire and Lincolnshire. This seems to indicate a progressive expansion in the area from which servants were recruited. As the number of servants recruited from the Rochdale area declined, so the 'catchment area' for recruitment expanded, first to the county of Yorkshire, and then outward to North Wales and to the counties south of Yorkshire.

It is to be argued here that this movement was due to an influx of servants from 'rural' areas. Information on the size of settlement where servants were born (see Appendix A, Note 18) can be used to indicate the type of background from which servants were drawn. Information so gathered (Tables 41, 42, and 43) can only be suggestive of the type of area from which servants came. Size of settlement cannot automatically be correlated with economic function, especially when the existence of so many settlements which could not be traced presents problems of statistical interpretation. In the case of Wales, Scotland, and Ireland, moreover, it was usual to give only the country of birth.

It is of interest that, in every sample, over 50 per cent of all servants were from settlements with more than 5,000 inhabitants, although this was always far lower than was usual in the population. It is thus not possible to maintain that servants were automatically from 'rural' backgrounds. Indeed many such women appear to have been migrants from other textile towns such as Bury and Oldham. It is difficult to give a full explanation for this phenomenon but the answer may lie in the fact that many may have come from families which did not have any access to employment for females. If we assume that a family's employment

69

in a factory was linked to the employment of the head of the household in that factory, then girls whose fathers were labourers or agricultural workers might be unable to gain industrial employment. This whole question is explored in greater depth in a later chapter (see Chapter 7, Section II).

Overall there appears to be as many servants from 'large' settlements in 1871 as there were in 1851. However, this was almost certainly a statistical illusion since the servant population was moving from areas with large numbers of settlements with more than 5,000 inhabitants, such as Rochdale and other towns in Lancashire, to areas in other parts of the country which showed a relatively small number of such settlements, What appears to have happened is that servants from Wales, Scotland and other areas in the U.K., who tended to give only their country of birth in 1851, gave more details in 1871, when they disclosed their place of birth as well. This meant an automatic increase in the number of 'large' townships recorded, especially since we might expect these to be most easily deciphered by the census enumerators. At the same time, there appears to have been a marked increase in the number of Lancashire servants from settlements with more than 5,000 inhabitants. In fact the proportion of servants from settlements with 5,000 inhabitants only fell from 59.9 per cent to 53.2 per cent over these 20 years.[18] If, however, we assume that Wales and Scotland returned no large towns in 1871, as was the case in 1851, and that the Lancashire returns were identical to those in 1851, then the figure for the proportion of settlements with more than 5,000 inhabitants in 1871 would have been only 42.8 per cent. This is in no way conclusive and these considerations show the difficulties of working with such imperfect data.

It would be unwise to use these figures as anything more than an indication of differences between regions. It seems admissible, however, to conclude that the servant population of Rochdale was increasingly being recruited from areas outside the industrial north, and that a relatively larger proportion of these immigrants were from rural settlements. If, from the sample of 1871, we take the figures for the size of settlements where Lancashire servants were born, and add to the proportion of settlements which could not be traced those which contained under 5,000 inhabitants, then the maximum percentage of servants from such small settlements in the county in 1871 could only be as high as 16.2 per cent. At the same date nearly 40 per cent of servants from Yorkshire and other English counties were from settlements with less than 5,000 inhabitants, not including any of the servants whose birthplaces could not be traced; it was from these counties, and from Wales, that the Rochdale servant population was increasingly drawn.

Indeed over the period 1851 to 1871 there is some indication that Rochdale, and Lancashire generally, were becomimg more 'urban'. As we have seen above (Chapter 3, Section II), the population of the Rochdale district was becoming increasingly concentrated in large settlements. In the same period the percentage of servants from Lancashire who came from settlements with over 5,000 inhabitants rose from 56.8 per cent of the whole group in 1851, to 82.8 per cent in 1871.

Within the broad category of servants from southern England there was a great deal of difference between the individual counties, especially with regard to the type of settlement from which servants originated. In Table 44 the servants from each English county in each census, excluding

71

Lancashire and Yorkshire, have been pooled, and the servants from counties providing more than 10 servants overall have been broken down according to their settlement types.

Of these counties, three, Derbyshire, Shropshire and especially Lincolnshire, seem to show an excess of servants from 'small' settlements, whilst servants from Cheshire and Stafordshire came on average from larger settlements. The result for Cheshire appears to be caused by fluctuations in the number of servants whose birthplaces could not be traced. Thus, in 1851, 40 per cent of all the birthplaces of servants in Cheshire could not be traced, whilst only 13.4 per cent of the servants could be recorded as coming from 'small' settlements. In 1871 the position had been reversed when the corresponding figures were 10.5 per cent and 42.1 per cent. Over the period the proportion of servants in Rochdale who came from Cheshire did not increase, but the proportion of these servants who came from 'small' settlements did.

The number of servants drawn from Staffordshire grew considerably in the period 1861 to 1871 and so the excess of servants from settlements with over 5000 inhabitants cannot be so easily explained. In 1871, of the 16 servants from Staffordshire who can be traced adequately, two came from towns in the Potteries, four from towns in the Black Country, two from the town of Stafford, and five from what might be described as agricultural areas. It is difficult to say why women should be moving from towns such as Stoke or Wolverhampton to be servants in Rochdale, especially during a decade which appears to have been a prosperous one for these areas. One might suggest that women were attempting to escape from the conditions in the brick yards of the Potteries, or were moving northwards with their parents as the Black Country coalfield passed its peak.

However this rise in the number of servants from Staffordshire should warn us against any simple attempt to equate servants with rural migration to the town, although this must have been taking place in many cases, certainly in the case of servants from Lincolnshire.

Many of the Welsh and English counties which appear to have become increasingly important for the recruitment of Rochdale's servants also appear to have been undergoing a relative population decline in this period. This especially so in the case of women aged between 15 and 24 years, the age when most girls were in service. This can be seen most clearly in Table 45, where the percentage increases between 1851 and 1871 for various female age groups, in selected counties, are compared with the percentage increases for the corresponding female age groups in England and Wales over the same period.[19] Of these 10 counties, which provided more than a quarter of all Rochdale's servants in 1871, only two, Cheshire and Staffordshire, appear to have had as rapid a population expansion in these various age groups as the country as a whole. Compared to other age groups the number of women aged between 15 and 24 years showed the slowest growth rate in all but two counties, Staffordshire and Lincolnshire, although in the latter case the rate of growth in this group was almost zero. With regard to the same age group, Denbighshire, Shropshire and Lincolnshire showed almost no increase over these 20 years, and Flintshire and Montgomeryshire actually showed a decrease. Similarly, whilst the national averages showed that the number of women aged between 15 and 24 years increased at the same rate as those aged between 25 and 34 years, this only happened in two of the ten counties we are here discussing. In the case of every county, apart from Staffordshire and Lincolnshire, the former age group showed a disproportionate decline.

Apart from Staffordshire and Cheshire it seems reasonable to assume that these counties were experiencing considerable outward migration in the period 1851 to 1871, and that this loss of population was most severe in the case of women aged between 15 and 24 years, the age of most domestic servants. These counties were not able to retain young women, presumably because of a lack of employment opportunities in industry, and they migrated to other parts of the country, many becoming domestic servants in the process.

Although the preceding considerations are very suggestive, and indicate that servants in Rochdale may well have had rural origins, it has not been possible to accurately describe the backgrounds from which individual servants came. This would only be possible if we could discover the occupation of a servant's father, as well as her place of birth. The census schedules of the mid-nineteenth century do not provide such information, but a record of the occupations of servants' fathers can be found in records relating to marriages. From parish registers, and from the certificates of marriage held by the local registry office, it would be possible to discover this type of information. Unfortunately it has not been possible to do this for Rochdale in the mid-nineteenth century. Having been refused access to the records of the local registry office, it was discovered that the parish registers for Rochdale did not record the occupations of brides, the standard procedure being to draw a line through the place in the record where the occupation of the woman was to be written. This is interesting in itself, since it indicates that women were automatically assumed to give up their occupations on marriage. However, it was possible to do a similar study of the marriage records of the parish church

74

of St John the Evangelist in Preston, since the registers were available on microfilm at the Manchester Central Library, and the occupations of brides were given.[20]

The marriages studied only included those involving women who had not previously been married, and excluded all persons described as 'housekeepers'. The categories used in the coding of the information drawn from the census samples (see Appendix A, Note 7), were employed to break-down the occupations of fathers of brides into social-economic groups, and then into occupational groups within these. The occupational information on fathers of women described as servants was then compared with that on the fathers of all other women, and the results are shown in Table 46. Of the 1,723 marriages recorded in the period from December 1851 to June 1856, some 237, or 13.8 per cent, involved brides who were described as 'servants'.

As can be seen from this table, servants tended to come from families where the head was employed in agriculture, or was described as a labourer. There was also a smaller tendency for the fathers of servants to be employed in the provision of dress, the working of wood, building and the production of building materials, and in transport. The term used for a worker in agriculture was 'farmer' but this probably did not denote a high social status given the small size of agricultural units in the area. Also, many of the men described as labourers may have been working on the land. Occupations in which the fathers of servants were not found included retailing and, above all, the production of textiles. We may conclude that servants tended to be recruited from amongst families which had either an agricultural background, or where the father was in a trade or occupation which was not open to females. If Preston saw the same change in the pattern of servant recruitment as took place in Rochdale in the 1860's, then we might expect the number of servants from agricultural backgrounds to have increased.

There is evidence that this pattern of servant recruitment was not unique, at least in Lancashire. As can be seen from Table 47, the town of Bolton in Lancashire appears to have had a similar recruitment structure. Servants were more likely to be long-distance migrants than were servants in most of the other towns for which figures are available.[21]

This suggests that in Lancashire generally it was more difficult to recruit servants locally then in other parts of the country. A study of Rochdale shows that this had not always been the case, and that the number of 'rural' servants in Lancashire towns was being maintained, if not increased, by an ever widening catchment area for recruits. The reasons for this unusual pattern will be discussed in a later chapter (Chapter 7), when it will be possible to examine both the supply and demand for rural domestic servants. However, it seems reasonable to conclude from the figures presented here that migrants, and especially those from rural areas, provided an unusually large component of the servant population of Rochdale in the period 1851 to 1871.

VII. The Wages and Conditions of Nineteenth-Century Domestic Servants

It will not be possible in the course of this section to give a detailed account of the wages and conditions of servants in Rochdale in the mid-nineteenth century. Since the work and lives of servants depended so much upon the personal relationships which they had with their employers it will always be difficult to speak of 'conditions' in any general sense. It would also be unwise to use uncritically many of the local sources which do exist, since they are usually derived from the households of the higher social classes. Many of the more humble servants, and the shop-keepers and tailors who employed them, have left few records.

This present section, therefore, is concerned primarily with a discussion, in general terms, of the hypothesis that the large number of rural migrants in the servant population of Rochdale, and in the country generally, was due to the harsh conditions of domestic service and low pay. It is assumed that only rural women, desperate for employment, would actually offer themselves on the market as domestic servants. An attempt will be made here to examine this hypothesis by an analysis of wage data on the national and local level and by a general consideration of food, living conditions and hours of work.

In Table 48 some crude wage rates are given for general servants and cooks in England in the period 1823 to 1907. These are averages, for particular dates, of wage rates recorded by W. T. Layton[22] and Horn.[23] The sources include the family records of Sir A. E. Bateman, advertisements in The Times and Christian World, and the account books of Hanwell County Asylum, Milton Manor (Berkshire), Lamport Hall (Northamptonshire), Englefield House (Berkshire), and the wages recommended in the various editions of Mrs Beeton's Household Management.[24]

In the same Table these crude wage rates (figures outside brackets) have been compared with annual wages paid to women in the production of wool and cotton textiles, and to a general average wage for women in industry, derived from G. H. Wood's essay, 'The Course of Women's Wages during the Nineteenth Century', published in 1903.[25] The latter are merely average weekly wages in these industrial categories multiplied by 52 weeks. They do not, therefore, take account of any stoppages, or time lost through lack of work, and are consequently maximum possible earnings rather than normal incomes.

These figures must not be regarded as in any sense definitive, since they ignore regional differences, and different wage rates acording to age and experience. Thus Miss Collet, in her parliamentary report of 1899, calculated that the average wage of a female domestic servant in London aged between 21 and 24 years was £17 10s 0d whilst a girl under the age of 16 years might only receive £7 18s 0d.[26] However, it can be seen plainly that the wages paid to domestic servants were far lower than those paid to women in industry.

Various documentary sources suggest that wage rates being paid in Lancashire were comparable with the national rate. This can be seen most clearly in Table 49, which gives the average wages being paid annually to servants and cooks at the County Lunatic Asylum, Prestwich,[27] at the County Asylum, Lancaster,[28] and in the workhouses of the Rochdale Poor Law Union,[29] as well as the wages quoted by employers in advertisements in the Rochdale Observer.[30] Compared with the national figures these results seem to be low in the period before the 1860's, and high thereafter,

78

although this appears to be less so in the case of advert-isements in the <u>Rochdale Observer</u>. This may reflect changes in the type and age of servants being employed.

The latter consideration is crucial since age affected wage rates to a considerable degree. Thus, we read in the diary of Agnes Blundell of Little Crosby, near Liverpool, on May 25th 1855,

> Elizabeth Young enters my service at £8 per annum and I am to find her tea, sugar and washing. Mrs Gailly at £20 per annum. Ann Barker at £9 per annum. Murphy at £18 per annum. Allen at £16 finding her tea, sugar and washing from the 29th October. Jannette at £6 her tea, sugar and washing from the 12th September.

Thus of six servants mentioned not one had the same wage although we may assume that some of them had similar duties.[31] In the light of such considerations it is best to accept the figures contained in Table 48 as the basis of further analysis but to regard them as only indicative of the very general levels and movements of wages paid to servants. It is unlikely that wages paid to servants in Rochdale would have fallen much below these levels, given the relative scarcity of servants in the area. It must also be remembered that the persons advertising for servants in the local newspaper would be quoting the minimum wages with which they hoped to attract servants, rather than the actual rate they had to pay.

We cannot regard servants, however, as poorly remune-rated since their money incomes were only one component of their total remuneration. Anderson in his study of family structure in nineteenth-century Lancashire has calculated that the cost of a minimum subsistence in lodgings would have been about 5s 6d per week, even when replacements for clothes and odd extra payments (for washing or an occasional drink, for example) were excluded.[32] If such a sum for subsistence were added to the money incomes of servants this would greatly increase their total remuneration. In Table 48 the figures in brackets represent the monetary wages of servants plus a subsistence allowance of 5s per week, reduced from Anderson's figure to take account of the lowering of food prices in the late nineteenth century. This subsistence allowance is without doubt far too small since it fails to include washing and clothing provided by the employer. These figures are more likely to represent the minimum total cost of servants to their employers. In the mid-nineteenth century, manuals of domestic economy regarded the cost of a female servant to be about £25 per annum,[33] whilst board wages paid to servants, when their employers left their country houses for the town, also came to 10s a week, or £24 per annum.[34]

It must also be recognised that there were other rewards to be had in larger households, such as tips and occasional gifts. In his diary, William Tyler, a footman in London in 1837, reckoned that his average annual takings from tips were between £10 and £15, and this was on top of an income which could have been no more than £40 per annum.[35] Even a maid-of-all-work, such as Hannah Cullwick who worked for a Kilburn beer merchant, could hope to collect £2 from 'Christmas Boxes' in 1863.[36]

There is evidence that the total income of servants was in fact regarded as quite good compared with that of other workers. In 1916 one cook-housekeeper of 31 years experience considered that,

we are better off than shop girls or factory girls. We may have our board and lodging free, also washing, which is equal to 12s or 14s a week. When the shop or factory girl pays for her food and lodgings she has very little.[37]

Similarly, in Paris about 1883 an estimate of the living expenses for a Parisian worker was set at 850 francs, which included rent, food, heating, lighting and some clothing. This would have made the true income of a Parisian servant about 1,350 francs, at a time when female cotton spinners in the Department de la Seine were earning approximately 780 francs per year.[38] Similarly in modern Peru, Margo Smith has discovered that domestic servants, who were predominantly from rural backgrounds, 'are actually better off than any other lower class working group'.[39]

The figures presented in Table 48 do not show as great a difference between the wages of women employed in industry and domestic service as is implied in the statements above. Indeed it would appear that although servants were better off than most female workers until the late 1850's, after this date they were less well paid than other women. This is undoubtedly untrue, since the wages of women in industry here presented were absolute maximum wages, whilst the incomes of servants only allow for the lowest subsistence diet, lodging and wages, without taking account of washing, any nourishment above the level of subsistence and occasional gratuities. It is also to be noted that the wages of more specialized servants, such as cooks, were almost always above the highest wages paid to other female workers, even allowing for only the barest of subsistence diets.

Although we cannot give an exact comparison between the wages paid to women workers and the incomes of domestic servants, we can say something about the relative trends of their wages. This has been done by converting the wage rates of private domestic servants found in Layton's work and Wood's wage rates for female workers in industry, into indices. The results, shown in Table 91, indicate that the movement of the wages of servants in the first half of the nineteenth century and until 1870 showed an opposite trend to that of women in industry, whilst showing a similarity in the period 1871 to 1900. Thus, between 1824 and 1845 the average wage rate of female industrial workers showed no rise, whilst that of servants rose from an indice of 42 to 59. However, in the 1850's and early 1860's the wages of servants rose comparatively little, whilst those of industrial workers climbed quite steeply. In the rest of the century the wage rates of both groups of workers rose, although the rate in service continued to rise in the 1880's and 1890's, whilst the wages of industrial workers stagnated.

Since the servant population was expanding, relative to the rest of the population, in the 1850's and 1860's and was in a relative decline thereafter, we may assume that the wages for servants were dependent upon the supply of servants. When servants were plentiful in the decades of the mid-century, wage rates stagnated, but they rose thereafter as servants became relatively scarce. This would appear to support the conclusion that women entering service in the period 1851 to 1871 could be regarded as 'cheap labour' from the countryside.

As was stated above, the true remuneration for domestic service did not simply consist of a cash payment but was also dependent on the fact that servants lived in the houses of their employers and had to be be fed and accommodated. Thus the actual 'income' from domestic labour depended upon the quality of board and lodging provided and also on the type of relationship that a servant had with the members of the household in which she worked. This type of qualitative remuneration is very difficult to measure, and all that will be attempted here is to discuss, in general terms, whether or not the domestic servant was more harshly treated than the girl who worked in the mill.

Perhaps the most crucial difference between work in industry and domestic service was that the servant was constantly at the beck and call of her employers. The mill girl lived in the factory for 10 hours a day, but the employment of the servant was continuous throughout the day, time-off and holidays being at the discretion of the employer. Hannah Cullwick, when employed by an upholsterer of Kilburn as a maid-of-all-work, was busy from 6.30 a.m. until 11.00 p.m. A description of a day in her life, recorded in her diary, will give some idea of her duties,

Opened the shutters and lighted the kitchen fire shook my sooty things in the dusthole & emptied the soot there, swept & dusted the rooms and the hall, laid the cloth and got breakfast up - clean'd 2 pairs of boots - made the beds and emptied the slops, clear'd & washed the breakfast things up - clean'd the plate - clean'd the knives and got dinner up - clear'd away, clean'd up the kitchen - unpack'd a hamper - took two chickens to Mrs Brewer's & brought the message back - made a tart & picked & gutted two ducks & roasted them - clean'd the steps & flags on my knees, blackleaded the scrapper in front of the house - clean'd the street flags too on my knees - had tea - clear'd away - washed up in the scullery - clean'd the pantry on my knees & scoured the tables - scrubbed the flags round the house & clean'd the window-sills - got tea at 9 for the master and Mrs Warwick in my dirt but Ann (a fellow servant) carried it up - clean'd the privy & passage & scullery on my knees - wash'd the door & clean'd the sink down - put the supper ready for Ann to take up, for I was too dirty & tired to go upstairs.[40]

This is a formidable list. However, to merely state that labour was hard is not to prove that it was harder than that performed by women in industry. In 1916 a report by the Women's Industrial Council claimed that servants worked fifteen and a half hours a day on average, but added,

Except in certain very hard situations or at times of special pressure, the work is emphatically not incessant throughout these fifteen and a half hours.....The work is, of course, done at much less high pressure generally than is that of work shops......[41]

What seemed to annoy servants most was not the hours worked, or the intensity of work, but the fact that, 'You are completely in the power of the lady, and can be called upon day or night'.[42]

The worst cases of overwork were probably to be found in households which employed only one resident servant. For, as Mrs Beeton herself remarks,

The general servant, or maid-of-all-work, is perhaps the only one of her class deserving commiseration: her life is a solitary one, and, in some places, her work is never done. She is also

84

subject to rougher treatment than either the house or kitchen maid, especially in her earlier career: she starts life probably a girl of 13, with some small tradesman's wife as her mistress, just a step above her in the social scale; and although the class contains among them many excellent, kind-hearted women, it also contains some very rough specimens of the female gender...[43]

However, in larger households the work was more specialized, and the mistress of the household might be less conscious of the need to assert her superior social status by bullying. In households situated in the countryside outside the town, there must have been many opportunities for servants to be sent on errands to buy supplies. This must have been a frequent task for 'Bella' who was a servant to Mrs Stopford of Upholland, near Wigan, in 1846. In her diary Mrs Stopford mentions that Bella went to Wigan (four miles away) on the 5th January; on the 14th January she went into Upholland, and she was again in Wigan on the 23rd of that month. On other occasions Bella went to Sandbrook, '... with some books' and went into Upholland to 'pay Mrs Walker for a cheese'.[44]

These points have not been made in order to present the lot of the servant as an easy one, but rather to contrast her life with that of the unmarried, female, mill operative. The latter may have worked shorter hours but her work may have been more intense. At the same time we must remember that many young girls who returned home after a long day at the mill were not simply at ease, and able do do as they pleased; they would probably have to help about the house and perform many of the functions of the servant, gratuitously. If the servant performed long hours of work in the household we can recognise this as hard labour for little remuneration, but we fail to recognise that the analogous functions were often being carried out in the home by working mothers and daughters for no extra income at all. Not until we can measure the amount of labour which working women performed in the home can we claim that domestic servants were comparatively overworked. This is very difficult to do, since, by definition, this labour fell outside the realm of monetary equivalents.

This problem of measurement is found again when one considers the diet of the average servant. It is probable, once more, that the food which servants ate in large, well-organized households was much better than that consumed in households where money was comparatively scarce. According to Booth, writing of London in the Edwardian period,

> The quality of food given to domestics, no doubt, depends on the liberality of the management, but is usually very good and in all but very rare cases greatly superior to that obtainable by other members of the working class families from which servants are drawn...[45]

Some servants in large households were conscious of this contrast. Thus, Margaret Powell, in her autobiography of her life as a servant in the 1920's and 1930's, remembers with anguish the amount of food which she and her fellow servants ate, and wasted, 'When I used to think of my family at home, where we seldom had enough to eat, it used to break my heart'.[46]

Some idea of the amount of food which could be consumed by a large household is given by Horn's study of the records of meat purchased at Bulstrode Parks, Buckinghamshire, in May 1887. For an average of five or six members

86

to the family, 20 servants and one 'extra', the daily consumption of meat per head was 1 lb. 12 and a half oz. During the 1890's it was calculated by D. J. Oddy that the average weekly consumption of meat in middle-class households was only 3.2 lbs. per head.[47] In any event, it is likely that many servants, at least in large households, ate well compared with most working-class women.

In a similar manner it is possible that domestic servants lived in better accommodation than their working-class contemporaries. Undoubtedly girls employed by shopkeepers or artisans slept in very poor conditions, often in the scullery or under the counter of the shop, but this may have been preferable to sleeping in a crowded bed at home. Even in more grand establishments the furniture and bedding provided for domestics would have been spartan compared with that used by their employers but these conditions would probably never be allowed to become too filthy or unhealthy for fear of spreading diseases to the employers. As the Women's Industrial Council claimed in 1916, 'it is no adquate defence of bad accommodation for servants to say, as is sometimes said, that in any case it is much better than they would get in their own homes.'[48]

Perhaps the worst part of life as a servant was not material conditions but her isolation within the household of her employers. The servant was isolated within the household by her inferior social position, and she was also isolated from the outside world by her long hours of duty, and often because she was living at a distance from her family and friends. The uniform the servant wore was a mark of her isolation and was rejected when possible. She was also at the mercy of the sexual drives of the male members of the household, although the author of My Secret Life, who delighted in tracking servants in 'out of the way

87

places', may not have been typical of all servant employers.[49]

Very few servants appear to have had members of their family living in the same household where they themselves worked. An attempt was made to discover if the kin of servants, usually recognised by their similarity of surname and birthplace, were resident in the same household as their servant relatives. Out of 296 servants in the 1851 sample, some 270 servants lived in households without any of their kin. This represented 91.2 per cent of the sample. Two servants had relatives who were non-domestic employees in the household, six had relatives who were lodgers, two had their children with them, 16 had sisters who were fellow servants. In 1861 and 1871 the percentage of servants who lived in isolation from their relatives had risen to 97.1 per cent and 95.5 per cent respectively.

This isolation might not be too onerous if the servant was accepted as 'one of the family', as could often happen, but it also left the young woman in a defenceless position if her employers should act unkindly or viciously towards her. The problems that such isolation could cause are exemplified by the inquest on the death of Ann McKie, which was reported in the Rochdale Observer in December 1859, the girl having been in the service of Mrs Sheperd of Townhead, near Rochdale, for two months. Elizabeth Sampson, a witness, described the condition of the girl, who was dying of dysentry,

On Wednesday between five and six o'clock, Mrs Sheperd went up with me when I took her tea up. I told Mrs Sheperd on Wednesday night the state the bed was in from the deceased's vomitings and purgings. I told her the bed was sopping wet, and she went up with me with the tea, but could not stop on account of the smell. The clothes were not changed before the deceased was carried away. When Whitworth said he could not remove her without a doctor's note, Mrs Sheperd said 'Then you'll send one up?'.......

The servant, who was 19 years old, was taken to the local workhouse where she died. The jury returned a verdict of death by natural causes but added that her death, 'had been hastened by want of proper attendance before she was received into the workhouse'. Her family in Scotland knew of her illness but were unable to help her because they could not afford the railway fare to Rochdale.[50]

Such cases were, of course, exceptional but exemplify, in the extreme, the position of the servant within the nineteenth-century household. Much depended on the personal relationship which existed between the employee and her employer, as well as on the size of house and family she had to serve and the number of other servants who were employed. This is evident in an examination of the advertisements contained in the Rochdale Observer of the mid-nineteenth century.[51] Frequently the advertisement states that the servant is required for 'a small family' and sometimes even gives the number of persons in the family, and whether or not there are any young children. It is also not unusual for mention to be made of the existence of other servants in the household with whom the work might be shared, and cooks might be told that there was 'no washing up to do', presumably because of the presence of a scullery maid.

It would be possible to continue in this manner but it is to be hoped that enough has been said about the general conditions of work in domestic service to allow us to come to some general conclusions. Taking wages, board and lodging together it is probable that many servants enjoyed a relatively high standard of living, although those working in the households of persons in the lower social classes may not have been nearly as well off. Also in the period which we are discussing, the relative standard of living of the servant class may have been in decline as their wages remained stationary whilst that of female industrial workers rose. In purely material terms the servant class cannot simply be described as 'cheap labour' from the countryside, although an influx of women from the countryside in this period may explain the relative stagnation of servant wages. There are some factors which suggest that rural, migrant servants were not simply employed because they were cheap, but because they would work in social conditions which were unacceptable to urban women.

This matter will be discussed more fully in a later chapter (Chapter 7) but two very important facts should be noted here. An examination of Table 41 will show that even in 1851, when servants were relatively well paid, migrant girls from rural backgrounds were already favoured as servants. Also, as can be seen from Tables 50 and 51, servants born in rural areas always tended to be concentrated in the highest social-economic groups, where pay and conditions were likely to be the best. It will be argued later that although rural servants were an economic advantage to servant employers, they were also favoured because they could be more easily disciplined within the social hierarchy of the household. The crux of the matter was not simply that urban women would not do the work for the wages asked, but that they would not take upon themselves the social stigma of service at that price.

VIII. Leaving Domestic Service—Servants and Marriage

As was claimed above (Chapter 5, Section IV), domestic service was usually a single stage in the life-cycle of working women and terminated when the servant married. Very few women were married and servants at the same time. Marriage, therefore, represented the termination of domestic employment. It has been claimed that the work experience of the servant had a crucial effect on the type of marriage she made and on the age at which she was betrothed. McBride, in The Domestic Revolution, has claimed that not only were English servants 'older than most women when they married',[52] but that they were prepared for upward social mobility through marriage by 'exposure to basic education, delay of marriage and the opportunity to save nearly the entire wage toward a future marriage or career or property investment.'[53] In short, the servant was a bridge between the middle and working-classes; she had acquired the bourgeois virtues of sexual abstinence, thrift, household economy and hygiene, and was thus a potentially 'good catch' for the improving working-class man.

McBride offers some statistical information to prove that women who were servants married later than their working-class contemporaries. She presents a table showing that 61.8 per cent of all servants in England in 1901 married before reaching the age of 24, whilst out of 1,000 working women in England at the same date some 73.6 per cent did so.[54] This would appear to support the hypothesis that servants delayed their marriages. However, since the source for this table is not quoted, it is difficult to measure the reliability of the figures. Also, it might be possible that servants were recruited from a particular section of the working population which was already practising such late marriage, in which case service was not a crucial determinant of this pattern. In addition, figures produced from England as a whole might hide very important local variations.

More detailed statistics can be obtained from the study of the marriage records of the parish church of St John the Evangelist, in Preston, which were used in Chapter 5, Section VI, to establish the occupational backgrounds of the fathers of servants.[55] These records give the ages of servants at the time of their first marriages, as well as those of all other women. Using the occupation of the bride's father as a basis for a division of females into social-economic groups, all servants and all other women were grouped according to their social class, and the average age at first marriage was then calculated for each group. It was thus possible to compare the average age at marriage of servants from different social backgrounds with that of other women from the same class. These results can be found in Table 52.

These figures do indeed show that servants married at a later age than other women from the same social backgrounds. Taken as a single group, the average age at first marriage amongst servants was higher than that found amongst any other group of women from every social class, except those from Social-Economic Group 1. Servants from Social-Economic Groups 2, 3 and 4 married, on average, some two years later than other girls from their own social class, whilst servants from Social Economic Group 5 were only some five months older. Servants in Preston at this period were thus marrying later than their working-class contemporaries and this may have been true of servants in Rochdale and the country generally.

However, this does not necessarily mean that servants in Lancashire at this time were rising in the social scale through advantageous marriages. Taking the same records from Preston, and comparing the social class of a bride-groom with that of a bride's father, it was possible to show that being a servant in Preston at this period was actually a disadvantage with respect to upward social mobility through marriage. As can be seen from Table 53 servants from every social-economic background tended to marry husbands in lower social-economic groups than other females from similar backgrounds. In the case of women whose fathers had been in Social-Economic Group 3, 30.8 per cent of the husbands of servants were from Social-Economic Groups 4 and 5, i.e. partly skilled and unskilled workers. Amongst other women from the same class, only 15.4 per cent of their husbands came from these lower working-class groups.

This does not automatically mean that being a servant in Preston, or in England as a whole, disqualified a woman from making an advantageous marriage. It is possible that the rather crude social and economic groupings used here conceal very important differences in occupational backgounds. For example, all retailers have had to be put in Social-Economic Group 3 because the parish registers give no information as to the number of persons a shop-keeper employed (Appendix A, Note 7). However, this cannot have been the case amongst servants and other women whose fathers were partly skilled or unskilled workers. There are, however, other problems with these data which make their interpretation difficult. We cannot be sure that the term 'servant' in the parish registers actually referred to living-in domestics. As we have seen, a servant could also be someone helping in the household of kin. Also, we are only dealing here with servants who came to Preston, or remained there, to marry. We can say nothing of the girls who returned home, perhaps to the countryside, in order to find husbands. Finally, we cannot be sure that a father's occupation did in fact correspond to the type of social background from which a servant came. We cannot tell from these figures the extent to which daughters were going into service because of financial difficulties at home, perhaps caused by unemployment or illness.

After making all these allowances, however, the uniformity of the results, in every social and economic category, is still extremely suggestive. Some servants who married in Preston were indeed rising in the social scale but their chances of doing so appear to have been less than other women from the same social-economic group. As will be suggested later (Chapter 7), being a servant in industrial Lancashire was in fact regarded by working people as a social disgrace, and this might well be the reason for the inability of servants in Preston, in this period, to make advantageous marriages.

There is also reason to believe that domestic service was not in any sense a 'training' for marriage. As Margaret Powell points out in her autobiography, a training in one particular branch of household service was not necessarily a good introduction to the running of a working-class home, where the family's income and needs might be very different. She goes so far as to suggest that on marriage she had to completely forget her old ways and learn how to keep house all over again.[56]

Similar, more detailed, studies will have to be undertaken before it is possible to come to conclusions about the effects of servant employment on the marital opportunities for women. However, this brief study does not indicate that domestic service led to social advancement through marriage; indeed it suggests the reverse.

6. SERVANT EMPLOYERS IN ROCHDALE AND THE FACTORS AFFECTING THEIR EMPLOYMENT OF SERVANTS

I. Domestic Servants and the Household Economy

According to Karl Marx the existence of a vast class of domestic servants in nineteenth-century Britain was an important vindication of his belief in the appropriation of surplus value by the capitalist classes. A million men and women were being supported out of surplus value to wait upon the needs of the bourgeoisie.[1] Much of the subsequent discussion of the subject of servants has focused on the servant as part of the 'paraphernalia of gentility'. The relationship between the servant and her employers has usually been discussed in terms of the personal relationship which existed between the servant and the mistress of the household.

Although the decision to employ a servant, and how many to employ, was obviously dependent upon a certain level of income, it is unwise to expect any simple correlation between the social standing of a servant employer and his or her demand for domestic servants. It must be stressed that a member of the bourgeoisie did not only employ a servant as a mark of social status, but also because the servant was domestically useful. It has always been difficult to include the work of women in the home when discussing active labour in the economy, since it cannot be expressed in money equivalents. However, the middle-class home was obviously a place of strenuous labour, as well as an expression of social status. To read a description of the duties of Hannah Cullwick[2], or the multifarious household tasks prescribed by Mrs Beeton[3], is to realise that the domestic servant was indeed involved in physical activity, creating use values for her employers. Many of the householders in Rochdale confirmed this when they described the household work of their relatives in terms of service.

The 'unproductive classes' in the home were certainly not the servants, but rather the females of the upper middle-classes, who were increasingly encouraged to lead a life of leisure. An individual's wealth did not, therefore, directly determine the number of servants he or she should employ, rather it determined how little work their female relations should do. It would also affect the size of house in which a family would reside, governing the number of amenities available, the number of guests who could stay, and the nature of the entertainments which could be offered, all of which would greatly affect the type and number of household tasks which needed to be performed.

In this chapter, therefore, no attempt has been made to give detailed breakdowns of the characteristics of the employers of servants. An attempt has been made to define which households employed servants, and to show how social status did indeed affect the number of servants a family employed. However, many of the characteristics of the heads of servant employing households, such as age and marital status, are only considered in so far as they affected the functions of the household. It is thus to be hoped that the functional role of the servant may be considered, as well as the servant's role in defining social status. The distinction made between domestic service as a symbol of status and as productive work within the household is, to some extent, a false one, since symbols of status such as large houses needed more labour to run them. It is necessary to separate the two, however, for the purposes of a statistical examination of the factors affecting servant employment.

II. The Social Status of Servant Employers

One of the principal determinants of the size of the servant population in any particular area was the composition and size of the local social elite. This is brought out by Ebery and Preston whose work is summarised in Table 54.[4] The 20 areas they studied were broken down into two groups, those in 1871 with percentages of servants to total population above the mode for the whole group, and those in 1871 with percentages below the mode. Table 54 shows the average percentage of household heads in different social-economic groups in these two sub-sets. The corresponding figures for Rochdale in 1871, and for the Bolton district are also given.

This reveals that the areas with most servants were those with relatively large numbers of heads in Social-Economic Groups 1 and 2, and comparatively few families in the upper working classes. This meant, in effect, that the areas with most servants were those with the highest potential demand, and also with the largest supply of women from lower working class backgrounds. Not only were families in the elite social classes more numerous in the areas with most servants but in proportional terms the professional class (Social-Economic Group 1) was more important. In contrast, the industrial towns of Rochdale and Bolton had very few persons in the highest social groups but a large number of household heads in the skilled labouring group and working in factories. It should be no surprise there-

97

fore that these towns had comparatively few domestic servants in the mid-nineteenth century, because women had access to alternative employment. The relatively large number of household heads in the lower social classes suggests an absence of factory employment in those areas with high servant populations. In fact many of these area, especially those in rural Berkshire, were predominantly rural communities, market towns or resorts, which had little factory production. Many of these householders, especially those employed in agriculture, would have been unable to find employment for their female children in their own occupations, and these girls might have been encouraged to enter domestic service. Certainly the servants in these towns appear to have been more likely to be local women than in industrial Lancashire (see Chapter 5, Section VI). These figures may, therefore, merely reflect the labour markets for women in these different areas.

It must not be assumed from these figures that servant employers were only to be found amongst the highest social classes. As can be seen from Table 55, it was Social-Economic Group 3, that is skilled manual workers and small shopkeepers, who provided the largest class of servant employers. Such persons individually did not employ as many servants as the social elite, but they still employed more than a quarter of all the servants in each sample. It should also be noted that some householders in the lower working class groups claimed to employ servants, although the social position of some of these women must be in doubt. Thus, we find in 1851 that Mary Diggle, aged 27 years, was living in the home of James Holt, aged 24 years, who gave his occupation as a 'factory labourer'. Mary Diggle appears to have been married but was living alone with Holt as his 'housekeeper', her relationship to him

98

being that of 'servant'. It seems unlikely in these circumstances that Mrs Diggle was living in the household of James Holt merely as a paid servant. These two people may have been living together as man and wife, or sharing the same house whilst Mary Diggle's husband was away. We have no way of telling if Mary was a hired 'servant', or whether the term was merely used to hide a socially unacceptable relationship.

Undoubtedly many of these 'working class' employers of servants were actually small shopkeepers but there still seem to have been many household heads who could be described as members of the 'aristocracy of labour'. E. J. Hobsbawm has attempted to define this amorphous group as those workers earning more than 40s a week[5], and it is perhaps no coincidence that in mid-Victorian England the minimum income regarded as necessary before a general maid could be employed was £100 per annum.[6] Many of the 'engineers', joiners, miners, spinners and weavers in Rochdale who consistently recorded themselves as servant employers must have fallen within this group and they were joined in later years by an increasingly large number of clerks and salesmen, representatives of a new 'labour aristocracy'. Thus in 1861 the employers of servants in Social-Economic Group 3 who were not retailers, included two joiners, two clerks and two salesmen, three textile 'overlookers', three cotton spinners and one wool spinner, two weavers, three power loom jobbers, a coal miner, a cotton warp beamer, a shoemaker, a reed-maker, a card-maker, a lathe-maker, a plumber, a currier, an 'engine driver' and a silk carder. The servant employers in this group in other years had similar occupations, as well as including watchmakers, blacksmiths, dyers and tailors.

It is difficult to assess what servant employment meant

to families in these social classes. The servants employed by these households appear to have been either generally younger or older than those employed by the professional classes. Thus, in 1851 only seven per cent of the servants employed by households in Social-Economic Group 1 were under 20 years of age. Amongst the servants in Social-Economic Group 3 households, 20.7 per cent were aged under 20 years. At the same date some 11.5 per cent of the servants in the former households were aged over 40 years, compared with 19.4 per cent amongst those in the latter.[7] Similar differences were to be found in other samples. (Table 56)[8] This meant that more of the servants in the lower class households had previously been married. In 1871, for example, 92.1 per cent of the servants of the professional classes were single, whilst in Social-Economic Group 3 the corresponding figure was only 81 per cent. (Table 57) As will be discussed below (Chapter 7, Section I), these 'working class' servant employers tended to employ more local servants than the higher social groups. This would seem to indicate that some of the women enumerated by this class as being 'servants' might have been aged dependants.

Such families may only have been temporary employers of servants. They may have hired servants to meet brief crises, such as illness or childbirth. Alternatively, their prosperity, based as it was on wage labour, may only have been transitory. Thus, of the 30 servant-employing households which appear more than once in the samples from the Rochdale district over 20 years, 14 were in Social-Economic Group 1, 12 were in Social-Economic Group 2 and only three came from the skilled manual worker/small shop-keeper class. Of the two households which appeared in all three samples, both were in Social-Economic Group 1. This might merely indicate, however, that the social elite in

100

Rochdale was less migratory than was the skilled manual class.

If we substitute an occupational grouping for that of social-economic groups (Table 58), it becomes plain that the most typical servant employer was not in fact the 'labour aristocrat', or the professional man, but a member of the retailing class, which provided a third of all employers in every sample. This group of shopkeepers, drapers, innkeepers, and restaurant owners employed numerous 'general servants' as well as persons described as shop assistants, waiters and barmaids, and it is clear that their labour was 'commercial' as well as domestic. This might also be true of the small number of servants employed by farmers.

It is probable that this pattern was general throughout mid-nineteenth century Britain. Horn, in a study of the rural market towns of Wantage, Thame and Fakenham, concludes that at this period approximately one household in six in these towns kept a resident maid, and that about two-fifths of the employers were small tradesmen, '...drapers, grocers, plumbers, coal merchants, corn dealers and the like'.[9] The popular belief that the 'typical' servant employer was a member of the social elite rests on shaky empirical foundations.

Since so many servants were employed in 'commercial units', or were the only servant in the household, it is unlikely that servants in Rochdale, in this period, could be regarded as mere 'flunkeys' hired for show. As will be pointed out below, domestic servants in Rochdale appear to have been carrying out productive work within the households of their employers.

The domestic servant in Rochdale must therefore be placed in a totally different social milieu than amongst the rich elite of London or county society. The typical employer was not a member of the titled aristocracy but someone like Jonas Beaver of 18 Yorkshire Street, Rochdale, a butcher from Yorkshire, who employed Margaret Whitworth of Rochdale as a general servant for his family of four. A servant such as this, living near Rochdale's market place, on a major street in town, might be expected to live a very different life from that of an under-parlourmaid in the upper middle-class suburbs of London or Manchester, or in the country mansion of a landed family. It is impossible to quantify the difference which this would make to the daily life and aspirations of a domestic servant.

III. Social Status and Servant Employment

Although servant employment in mid-nineteenth century Rochdale was found in all social classes, it is plain that there was a strong correlation between social position and servant employment. In Table 59 a calculation has been made of the percentage of households in particular social groups in the Rochdale district which employed servants in 1851 and 1871. This was done by using the control samples for these years to give a percentage of household heads in the various social groups. This was then converted into the total number of households in these groups using the figures for the total numbers of households in the district. Having gained an approximate figure for the size of each social group, it was then possible to compare this with the number of households in these groups with servants, which appeared in the census samples.

As can be seen, there was a very positive correlation between the employment of servants and social class, although it must be noted that in 1851 only a bare majority of even the householders in the highest social class employed servants. It should also be noted that the employment of servants appears to have actually declined in almost every social class between 1851 and 1871, although sampling error may have caused this pattern to emerge. It would be interesting if this was in fact a national trend, since it might show that the rise in the number of servants did not necessarily represent an increase in the number of middle-class families, or a relative increase in the pro-portion of all families who were middle class. Rather the increase could be explained in terms of an increase in the number of servants which existing servant employers employed. Also, it is plain from these figures that servant employment was not automatic amongst the middle classes, at least in Rochdale, and might even be becoming less common. In this sense servant employment might be seen not as an indication of middle class status but as a division within that class between those who employed servants and those who did not. To use servant employment, therefore, to measure the size of the middle classes in one area, or over time, might be a dubious undertaking.

The employment of servants was not, therefore, automati-cally asociated with even the highest social class, although someone in the professional class would be far more likely to employ a servant than would a labourer or even a member of the 'labour aristocracy'. Furthermore, it has been stated that the higher one rose in the social scale the greater the number of servants employed. Beeton, for example, directly relates the size of a family's servant retinue to its income, as follows,

About £1,000 a year - cook, upper housemaid,
nursemaid, under housemaid,

103

	manservant
About £750 a year	- cook, housemaid, nursemaid, footboy
About £500 a year	- cook, housemaid, nursemaid
About £300 a year	- maid-of-all-work, nursemaid
About £200 or £150 a year	- maid-of-all-work (and girl occassionally)

Banks has produced figures from mid-nineteenth century books of household management to show that as a family grew wealthier it was expected to spend an ever increasing percentage of its income on domestic assistance. Thus, in a manual of 1845 a family with an annual income of £100 was expected to spend 4 per cent of its income on servants; a family on an income of £250 was expected to spend 6 per cent; and a family earning £500 per annum was expected to spend no less than 15 per cent of its income in this manner.[10] It is difficult to say whether this was merely due to a desire to consume conspicuously, or whether the increase in servant retinues was necessary because of the assumed increase in the size, complexity, or number of the family residences. It was almost certainly linked to the extent to which the females of the household were expected to refrain from household labour.

This pattern was, however, only what certain authors thought desirable, or believed was the norm, rather than what might have been happening in middle-class homes. An attempt has been made to reconstruct the actual proportional expenditure on servants incurred by the families of persons who came before the Court of Bankruptcy in the period 1822 to 1833.[11] Persons appearing before this Court were usually in trade and were often required to hand in approximate calculations of their income and expenditure under various household headings in the period prior to their bankruptcy. The results of this work must be very tentative since only a sample of 26 households has been examined. By far the greater part of these refer to retailers in the London area, and represent, of course, families who might have been spending above their means. The results of this preliminary analysis are given in Table 60.

This gives some support to the belief that the percentage of incomes spent on domestic servants rose with the total size of middle-class incomes in the nineteenth century. However, the results are far from indicating any general social pattern since the group of households with an income of more than £1,000 per annum contained the household with the lowest proportional expenditure on servants, as well as the household with the highest proportional expenditure. This would appear to indicate that as incomes rose there was a tendency for servant employers to spend more on this item of household expenditure, but that this depended on personal tastes. At a low level of income there was little elasticity of demand since only one servant could be afforded, but as incomes rose householders could, and often did, increase the proportion of their total expenditure which went on servants. This was certainly not, however, a general rule of social behaviour.

As one would expect, in Rochdale in the mid-nineteenth century the number of servants employed by a family appears to have been influenced to a considerable degree by the social class of the household head. As can be seen from Table 61, a larger proportion of servant employing households in Social-Economic Group 1 had more than one servant than amongst the other major groups of employers. However, even in 1871 over 40 per cent of all the households in the highest social class made do with only one servant. A fuller breakdown of the number of servants employed by the different social groups is given in Table 62.

It is interesting to note that although proportionally fewer persons in all social classes in 1871 may have employed servants, those who did tended to employ larger numbers.[12] This was not the case, however, amongst servant employers from Social-Economic Group 3, who appear to have been unable to employ more than one servant throughout the period.[13] Those who did were usually shopkeepers. This meant, in effect, that there was an increasing division in social status between the households in Social-Economic Group 2 and those in the class immediately below them in the social scale. In 1851 single servant households were almost as common in the former class as in the latter,[14] but this was no longer the case twenty years later. This seems to indicate an increasing divergence of social status between retailers in this period. In 1851 the 25 retailers who are recorded as employing more than two assistants also employed on average 1.0 servants, whilst the 51 retailers with fewer than two assistants employed an average of 1.2 servants. Twenty years later, however, the 33 retailers in Social-Economic Group 2 employed an average of 1.7 servants, compared with an average of only 1.1 servants amongst the 68 retailers in the lower social class. This latter figure was equal to the average for servant employers from amongst the manual working classes, who employed on average 1.1 servants in 1871. We can see here the growing division between the class of shopkeepers who were still intimately connected with their working class backgrounds, and those who were attempting to establish a distinct social identity. The latter group might have been composed of those retailers who were resident,

.......in the main roads, rather than the back

streets - possessing some degree of solidarity, exhibited in the tradition by which shopkeepers made a public show of 'respect' on the day on which one of their number was to be buried, and frequently active in the affairs of the district in which they paid their rates, whether because of an inherited sense of obligation, or from more interested motives.[15]

This change can be seen clearly in Table 63 in which the average number of servants employed by households headed by persons in different occupational groups are given for 1851 and 1871. In the professional class, all the occupational groups appeared to have increased the number of servants they employed, especially the textile manufacturers and proprietors, the latter group including annuitants. In the 'intermediate' class, the servant retinues of small manufacturers and those providing industrial and commercial services appear to have declined in size. At the same time the number of servants employed by farmers went up, and there was a prodigious increase in the number of servants employed by large retailers. On the other hand, the servant employers in Social-Economic Group 3 do not appear to have employed any more servants over the period. This suggests that the growth in the number of servants employed varied between occupational groups as well as between social classes. The causes of these inequalities are difficult to pin down given the rather crude data used here. Why textile manufacturers should appear to have been increasing the number of servants they employed at a faster rate than other manufacturers is something of a mystery. The fact that the number of textile manufacturers appears to have declined over the period may indicate a process of industrial concentration, which was lacking in other industries.

Some of the figures in Table 63 are at first sight rather surprising. This is especially the case in 1851, where the small manufacturers, and those providing industrial and commercial services, were the largest employers. However, the figures for 1871 show very clearly the structure of servant employment in Rochdale, with the textile manufacturers as the largest employers, and large retailers and dealers approaching the status of the professional class.

As can be seen from Table 64, the pattern of increasingly dissimilar servant recruitment was repeated in the type of servants being employed by the different social groups. Over time the householders in Social-Economic Group 2 increased the number of servants they employed in specialised departments of the household economy. These servant retinues were not as specialised as those of the professional class in 1871, but contained more nurses, cooks and housemaids than the households in Social-Economic Group 3. This differentiation of household labour was a consequence of the increase in size and complexity of servant employing households.

It is probable that this pattern of servant employment was a national, if not international, phenomenon and domestic servants are still an important indication of social status in developing societies today. However, there were important regional variations in the number of servants employed according to the local conditions of supply and demand. In the metropolitan borough of Reading, for example, 59.5 per cent of the servant employers in Social-Economic Group 1 employed more than one servant in 1871 but only 38.1 per cent of the same class did so in the borough of Bolton. At the same date, 11.8 per cent of the servant employers in Reading who were in Social-Economic Group 3 employed more than one servant, compared with 2.2 per cent of the same group in Bolton.[16] The equivalent figure for the Rochdale district as a whole was 8.6 per cent. Since we are comparing servant employers of roughly the same social status, it would appear that such discrepancies must either be caused by differences in supply, or perhaps by the traditional consumption patterns of elites in different areas.

IV. The Age of Household Heads and the Employment of Servants

The employers of servants in Rochdale appear to have been were well established in the town's society. As can be seen from Table 65, there were comparatively few servant employers aged under 30 years. Thus in 1851 12.7 per cent of the employers of servants were under 30 years of age, compared with 18.4 per cent of the heads of the control sample for that year.[17] In other years the contrast was more striking.

This pattern could merely represent the differences in the compostion of the two groups of household heads. It has long been assumed that men and women in the highest social groups, which employed a disproportionate number of servants, married later than the other social classes of society. This would mean that the relatively small number of household heads in the younger age groups who employed servants could be explained in terms of different marital ages amongst the social clases. An examination of Table 66, however, reveals an unexpected pattern. Servant employers in Social-Economic Group 1 appear to have been younger than other servant employers in 1851, 44.6 per cent of them being under 40 years of age, compared with just over 30 per cent in the case of the other two main social groups.[18] However, over the next 20 years the proportion of such servant employers in this age group fell to 20.9 per cent, a smaller proportion than was found in either of the other social classes. From being the youngest class of servant employers in 1851, Social-Economic Group 1 had become the oldest by 1871.

This might reveal an increasing propensity on the part of the upper elite of Rochdale society to delay marriage. It cannot be due to problems in hiring domestic staff, as J. A. Banks has suggested,[19] since the wages of servants were not rising in this period. This pattern of delayed servant employment might not be caused directly by delayed marriage, but by changes in the family life cycle, or career prospects of the servant employers. If it was becoming more difficult for men to advance in the business world of the region, as the structure of the textile industry, or professional elite, matured, then young men might be less able to afford the 'paraphernalia of gentility'. On the other hand they may have married later, delaying having their children, and so required domestic assistance about the home at a later date. This again raises the question of whether or not the domestic servant was employed for functional reasons, or whether her employment can merely be discussed in terms of the economic status of her employer.

V. The Effect of Family Structure on the Employment of Servants

The aim of this section is to show that family structure affected whether or not a family employed a servant. Certain variables appear to have affected the choice of whether or not a family should employ a servant, others only affected the decision of how many to employ. Thus, in the case of some variables, such as marital status or family life-cycle stage (Appendix A, Notes 3 and 24), servant-employers appear to have been unusual in deviating from the Rochdale norm. In other cases, such as family size, (Appendix A, Note 9) servant-employing families do not appear to have been unusual, but conformed to the Rochdale norm, the variable affecting only the number of servants employed.

The life-cycle stage of servant-employing households was unusual in this period, compared with the control samples from Rochdale as a whole. The households in these samples were coded according to whether or not they contained a resident wife, and then as to the number of children, and working children within the household. Using this coding and pooling the results for 1851, 1861 and 1871, it was possible to see if the structure of servant-employing households was in any sense unusual. The results, given in Table 67, show that this was indeed the case. Servant-employing households in all social classes tended to be unusually concentrated in Life-Cycle Stage 0, or where there was no resident wife.[20] The servant employers in the first three social-economic groups were also concentrated in Life-Cycle Stage 3, where there were children at home, but none were in employment. On the other hand these same social classes do not appear to have been concentrated in Life Cycle Stage 5, where a majority of the children at home were in employment. Partly skilled and unskilled employers of servants appear to have been concentrated in the life-cycle stage where the wife was absent, but appear to approximate to the norm in LIfe-Cycle Stage 3.[21]

This would appear to indicate that one parent families or unmarried householders required domestic assistance about the house to replace a deceased wife or mother. However, households in the higher social classes also employed servants to look after young children. The difference can be explained in terms of the relative incomes of the social classes involved. Since a wife living at home had to be supported by her husband's income, her labour in the household producing no money equivalents, her replacement by a paid servant would inflict no extra burden on the householder. However, the employment of a servant to look after children, or to allow the woman of the house to do so, added an extra financial burden on the family, which assumed a certain level of income above basic subsistence.

This pattern appears to have been general in late Victorian England, at least with regard to the number of households which lacked married heads. Thus, Ebery and Preston discovered that in their 20 districts in 1871 some 73.9 per cent of the households in their samples contained a wife, but this figure was reduced to 60.9 per cent amongst the servant-employing households in these areas.[22] In Rochdale at that date, 75 per cent of the households in the control sample contained a wife, but only 61.7 per cent of the households containing servants did so.

It would be incorrect, however, to maintain that this was a consistent pattern in Rochdale in each of the censal years. An examination of Tables 68, 69 and 70 shows that there were an unusually small number of married male heads in 1861 and 1871, but that this was not the case in 1851.

112

Thus, in 1851 82.6 per cent of the male heads with servants were married, compared with 84.9 per cent in the control sample.[23] Twenty years later the corresponding figures were 77 per cent and 90 per cent. It would appear, therefore, that the absence of a wife was an important determinant of servant employment only in the later years of the period.

VI. The Effect of Family Structure on the Number of Servants Employed

As was mentioned above (Section V), some variables appear to have affected the number of servants employed, although they cannot have been responsible for servant employment in themselves. An attempt will be made in this section to show that large families, and especially families with large numbers of children under the age of 10 years, tended to employ more servants than smaller families. It would be incorrect, however, to maintain that servant-employing households were unusually large. There appears to have been no significant difference between the number of people or the number of dependents under 11 years old in the latter as compared to the Rochdale control samples.

However, it would appear that within the servant-employing class, these variables did indeed affect the number of servants employed. Multiple regression analysis was used to measure the effect of such variables on the number of servants employed.[24] Multiple regression is a general statistical technique through which one can analyse the relationship between a dependent variable and a set of independent or predictor variables. The analysis has been used to obtain a prediction equation that indicates how

scores on independent variables could be weighted and
summed to obtain the best possible prediction of the number
of servants in the sample households. In effect multiple
regression analysis has been used to tell how increases in
variables such as social-economic class, the total size of
the household, and the number of lodgers, affect the number
of servants which a family might employ.

A major problem with this regression analysis is that
the dependent variable was a discrete one. This means that
the observed number of servants in the household could only
be a few whole numbers such as 1, 2, 3, or 5. Thus, the
observed cases would not have been distributed in a random
manner but would be grouped in clusters, thus reducing the
range of possible differences between them. This in turn
affects the extent to which we can measure the statistical
significance of these results. When viewing the results of
this exercise in regression analysis we must regard the
figures given as indicative of the effects of certain
variables on servant employment, although there are
problems with the significance of the results. The regression analysis has been used because it gives a very clear
picture of the effects of various family characteristics on
the employment of servants. Other, more impressionistic,
statistics will be produced to substantiate the results.

An attempt was made to regress two sets of variables on
the number of servants employed in households in Rochdale
in 1851, 1861 and 1871. The first set of variables
included social-economic class (SEGH); whether or not the
wife was present in the household during the daytime, or
was dead, or at work (NOW); and the total size of the
household (TOTSIZE). These variables are described more
fully in Appendix A. In the regression equations given
below the total number of servants in the household in

114

represented by the variable NOSERV.

1851
$$NOSERV = 1.67 - 0.17(SEGH) - 0.18(NOW) + 0.009(TOTSIZE)$$
$$(0.06) \qquad (0.12) \qquad (0.025)$$

1861
$$NOSERV = 1.7 - 0.33(SEGH) - 0.11(NOW) + 0.09(TOTSIZE)$$
$$(0.07) \qquad (0.12) \qquad (0.03)$$

1871
$$NOSERV = 1.96 - 0.39(SEGH) - 0.04(NOW) + 0.09(TOTSIZE)$$
$$(0.05) \qquad (0.02) \qquad (0.025)$$

One can see from these equations that there is a negative correlation between the number of servants in a
household, the increase in the numerical coding of a
family's social class and the absence of a wife from the
household. There is a positive correlation between the
number of servants and the total size of the household.
This means that the higher one rises in the hierarchy of
social class, the greater the likelihood that one would
have more servants. Since the correlation was negative, a
family in Social-Economic Group 5 would have fewer servants
than a family in Social-Economic Group 2. At the same
time, the larger the family the more servants are resident.
On the other hand, if there is no wife at home during the
daytime then there will be fewer servants. Since the
number of servants appears to increase with an increase in
the total number of children in a family, we may assume
that this last variable indicates that a woman going out to
work would not have a young family to look after and would
therefore not require a large number of servants.

The equation for 1851 should be read as follows. The

number of servants kept by a servant-employing family in Social-Economic Group 1, with a resident wife with no occupation, and containing 5 persons, would be predicted as 1.545. That would be, 1.67 minus 0.17 (i.e. 0.17 x 1), minus 0 (i.e. 0.18 x 0 wives absent from the household), plus 0.045 (i.e. 0.009 x 5 members of the household). A family employing servants in Social-Economic Group 3, with a wife at work in the mill, and a total of 4 persons in the household would only be expected to employ 1.016 servants. This would be calculated as 1.67 minus 0.51 (i.e. 0.17 x 3), minus 0.18 (i.e. 0.18 x 1 wife absent from the household), plus 0.036 (i.e. 0.009 x 4 members of the household). It would be impossible to employ such fractions of servants, but these figures are only indicative of general trends within this population. The number of servants which would be predicted for other households and in other census samples can be calculated in the same manner.

An approximate calculation to show the statistical significance of these figures is provided by the standard errors for these variables, which are given below the values for the variables in brackets. Normally one can be 95 per cent certain that the true value for the variables will lie within two standard errors of the given value. Thus in the 1851 equation one can be 95 per cent sure that the value representing the effect of social-economic grouping on the number of servants employed lies between 0.05 and 0.29. The value thus given is positive and is thus significant. However, the same test shows that the value of the variable NOW could lie between -0.32 and 0.06 The result for this variable is not, therefore, significant at 95 per cent because the effect could have been positive, negative or zero. Because of the statistical problems outlined above, this test is not a truly reliable one for

116

statistical significance but it can be regarded as an approximation to such a test.

Having accepted this proviso it would seem that in 1851 only social-economic grouping was a statistically significant determinant of the number of servants employed. In 1861 and 1871, however, the total size of the servant-employing household also affected the number of servants which a family employed.

The changes in the values for the variables indicate that social class, and the size of the household, were both becoming more powerful determinants of the number of servants employed. Thus the negative effect of the rise in the coding of a family's social-economic group increased from -0.17 per unit to -0.39 in 1871. This is further statistical proof that the lower social-classes were not able to increase their servant retinues as the higher social classes did in this period. There was an increasing difference between the size of servant retinues employed by families in Social-Economic Groups 1 and 2, and those employed by Social-Classes 3,4 and 5. (See this chapter, Section III) The positive effect of a unit change in family size increased tenfold in the period, from +0.009 to +0.09. This would appear to indicate that family size only became a significant determinant of servant employment in the period after 1851.

A further regression was run on the data to see if the variable relating to the total size of the household could be broken down into its component parts. In this second regression the number of servants in a household (NOSERV) was again the dependent variable, whilst the independent variables included social-economic class (SEGH); whether or not the wife was present in the household during the daytime (NOW); the number of dependents under the age of three years in the household (DTWO); the number of dependents aged between three years and ten years (DNBAB); the number of unoccupied dependents over the age of ten years (DOLD); the total number of persons at work in the household (TOTWOK); and the number of lodgers (LODS). (See Appendix A for definition of variables.) The results for the regressions run on the servant-employing households in the three samples are given below.

1851

NOSERV = 1.66-0.17(SEGH)-0.14(NOW)-0.04(DTWO)+0.05(DNBAB)
            (0.06)   (0.12)   (0.09)   (0.05)

         +0.04(DOLD)-0.05(TOTWOK)+0.08(LODS)
         (0.06)   (0.04)   (0.04)

1861

NOSERV = 1.79-0.3(SEGH)-0.12(NOW)+0.04(DTWO)+0.14(DNBAB)
            (0.06)   (0.12)   (0.10)   (0.05)

         +0.17(DOLD)+0.05(TOTWOK)-0.09(LODS)
         (0.07)   (0.06)   (0.10)

1871

NOSERV = 2.13-0.38(SEGH)-0.12(NOW)+0.06(DTWO)+0.11(DNBAB)
            (0.05)   (0.12)   (0.08)   (0.05)

         +0.08(DOLD)+0.03(TOTWOK)+0.11(LODS)
         (0.05)   (0.05)   (0.70)

These equations should be read in the same manner as the first set, the value in front of the variable representing the change in the value of NOSERV caused by a unit change in that variable. The results from this exercise are more

118

problematic than those from the previous set of equations. Not only do we find that the values of the different variables change but that these values even change their sign from positive to negative or vice versa. Thus, in 1851 the total number of persons at work in a household appears to have a negative effect on the number of servants employed but has a positive effect in 1861 and 1871. The variables DTWO and LODS also change their sign in this manner, making these equations more difficult to interpret. To do so it would be best to describe the effect of the variables on the number of servants employed in each censal year, and then to state which appear to be statistically significant.

In every sample, social-economic class and the absence of the wife from the household have negative values; the further down the social scale one descends, or if the wife is absent from the home, the smaller the number of servants in the household. In 1851 only some components of the family appear to have a positive effect on the number of servants employed, that is, the number of dependents between the ages of three and 10 years, the number of dependents over the age of 10 years, and the number of lodgers in the household. In 1851 the number of dependents under the age of three years, and the number of persons in the household who were at work, appear to have had a negative effect on the number of servants employed. In other censal years all these components of the total family size appear to have had positive effects on servant employment, apart from the number of lodgers in 1861.

This would suggest that in 1851 servants were not required in large numbers in households where large numbers of the family were out all day at work, or which contained very young children. We must assume that a household in which there were few people at home during the daytime would require few servants. Also, a family with young children under the age of three years might not have been established very long and would not therefore have been very large. These variables are all interrelated in this manner which makes interpretation very difficult.

However, this problem is somewhat abated by the fact that only some of these values appear to be statistically significant. In 1851 only the variable relating to social-economic class appears to have a statistically significant effect on servant employment. In other years only the variable reflecting the number of dependents between the ages of three and 10 years was consistently statistically significant, although the variable for dependents over the age of ten was also significant in 1861.

We may tentatively conclude from this exercise that although social-economic class was the major determinant of the number of servants employed by families in Rochdale in the period 1851 to 1871, in 1861 and 1871 the number of persons in the household also affected the number employed. The major determinant of servant employment within the latter variable appears to have been the number of children in the household over the age of three and under eleven. Thus in 1861 it would appear that a household in Social-Economic Group 1 would tend to employ one more servant than a servant employer in Social-Economic Group 5, other things being equal. By 1871 this difference would have been 1.5 servants. On the same basis, in 1861 a family with seven children aged between three and ten years inclusive would employ one more servant than a family containing no such children, all things being equal.

These predictions about the effects of household size and composition on the employment of servants can be substantiated by an examination of Tables 71 and 72. In Table 71 the households in the three major social groups who employed servants are broken down according to the number of persons in each household in each censal year. This produces a number of cells for each year defined by the three social classes and by household size. The average numbers of servants employed by the households in each cell were then calculated, allowing us to see the effect of household size upon servant employment in each social class. Some of these cells included very small numbers of households, or were even empty, so these results are only illustrative. In Table 72 the same exercise has been carried out, substituting the number of children in the household aged under 11 years for the total size of the household.

These tables would appear to support the thesis that household size, and especially the number of children under the age of 10 years, influenced the number of servants being employed in these households. This effect does not appear to be marked in 1851, but becomes more evident in the later census samples. In 1851 there appears to be a tendency for the number of servants to rise with an increase in the size of the household and the number of children in it, but that after a certain stage any further increase in family size causes a decline in the number of servants employed.

The conclusion to be drawn from these figures appears to be that household structure and household size did have a significant effect on servant employment in Rochdale in this period. However, the effect of the loss of a wife, or the increase of family size, only appear to have become significant variables in the period after 1851. This conclusion is consistent with what we know about servants' wages in this period. As we saw in Chapter 5, Section VII, the wages of domestic servants appear to have been rising in the period prior to 1851 but were stable over the next decade and a half. We may thus surmise that the servant-employing classes of Rochdale in 1851 were generally only able to hire one servant, but that as their incomes rose over the next decades, whilst the wages of servants were not rising, they were encouraged to employ more servants according to the needs of their households. If we can generalise from these results to the national level we might argue that the mid-nineteenth century rise in the number of servants employed in England and Wales was due to servant-employing families taking advantage of cheap rural labour. Such employers could now employ extra servants to replace a deceased wife, or to look after a large family. This appears to have been the case in Rochdale in this period.

There is evidence that this pattern of servant employment by family size is not a social phenomenon confined to Rochdale in the mid-nineteenth century. Margo L. Smith has discovered in modern Peru that family size is a determinant of servant employment. Thus, amongst a sample of 2,355 servant-employing households in Lima in the late 1960's, only 8 per cent of the 278 households containing two persons employed more than two servants. However, amongst the 438 households containing five persons the corresponding figure was 12.3 per cent. In those households containing seven persons the proportion had risen to 21 per cent, and rose again to 30.5 per cent in those households which contained over nine persons.[25] This would seem to indicate that it is incorrect to view servant employment on an international level, merely as a symbol of elite status. Domestic servants must always be viewed in the context of the household as a functional economic unit.

It must be noted, however, that one cannot simply use the regression equations quoted above in order to predict

122

the number of servants employed by a particular family. The results represent general tendencies within the servant-employing population rather than hard and fast rules. A cross-census search of servant-employing households does indeed reveal some households which changed their servant retinues in accordance with their changing composition. Thus, a flannel manufacturer who had one child in his household in 1851, had four by 1861, and his domestic staff gained two nurses. Again, a female wine dealer had three servants in 1851, one of whom may have been a shopman, but only one in 1861. In 1851 she had two children at home but none in 1861, when she lived alone. However, there were also very striking examples of rigidity in servant retinues. John Bright, for example, employed five servants in 1851, 1861 and 1871, despite seeing his family grow up and leave home. In the same manner the Vicar of Smallbridge had two servants in each of the censal years although his family had also grown up and moved away during the period.[26]

VII. Domestic Service and Retailing

Perhaps no group of employers shows the functional role of the servant better than do retailers. As was intimated above (Chapter 6, Section II), retailers in one form or another, provided a third of all employers of servants in every census sample. As can be seen from Table 58, retailers and farmers always employed more than a quarter of all servants in the district, and usually over a third. If any group could be called 'typical' of servant-employers in this region then it would be this group.

These households were productive units providing goods

and services to members of the public. As such they were places where women would be expected to perform work other than that associated with household chores. According to the official Census Report, women, 'in certain branches of business at home render important services; such as wives of farmers, of small shopkeepers, innkeepers, shoemakers, butchers'.[27] This is an exact description of the group of employers we are discussing here. The number of women employed could be large. In Preston in 1851 it would appear that a third of all working wives were employed in non-factory occupations.[28] This must have been the case in Rochdale, where the average size of farm seems to have been so small. and where only a third of all retailers had two or more assistants.

In such circumstances it is probable that a wife would have worked in the shop, or on the farm, with her husband, leaving household work to the hired maid. Such a servant would not have been a burden on the household's finances since she was merely allowing a member of the household to help create products or services which the productive unit could exchange for a cash equivalent. On the other hand she may herself have been actively engaged in the productive process because there often appears to have been no distinction made between the work of the household and that of the shop. Since there was no distinction between the household as a place of residence and as a place of work, there appears to have been no distinction made between activity in one sphere or the other.

There is evidence that this overlap of duties existed in Rochdale in the mid-nineteenth century. Many young servants were recruited from the local workhouse, and the local Workhouse Committee of the Board of Guardians has left records relating to the hiring out of these young

124

girls.[29] These records reveal instances when the distinction between domestic servant and shopworker was evidently blurred. On 9th May 1851, for example, Lazarus Collinge of Market Place, Heywood, a confectioner, came before the Committee and applied for Elizabeth Holt from the Spotland Workhouse, 'to learn his trade and perform domestic duties'. On the 14th January, 1853, Rebecca Bowskill, aged 11 years, was allowed to work for Isaac Eastwood, a shopkeeper of Leavengreave,'to assist in domestic duties and to work in the factory'. The most interesting case is that of Catherine Garner, who, at the age of 13 years, was sent to work for Robert Whitehead of Hamer Place, a baker of bread. The Guardians appear to have kept a watch on their charges because on 11th May 1866 it was reported that,'Robert Whitehead of Hamer Place, Bread Baker, had a girl named Catherine Garner who was sent out to sell late at night and the relieving officer, Mr R. Whitworth was directed to enquire into the matter'. Catherine Garner had only been in the employment of Robert Whitehead a fortnight, but she had obviously been sent out to sell bread and cakes in the streets late at night on several occasions. Although Whitehead had employed her 'to be a servant', it is plain that she was also helping in the shop and in the business generally.

This was almost certainly the case with many of the males described as 'man servant' in the census schedules. Of the 14 men described as such in the 1851 sample, four were employed by beer sellers, two by innkeepers, and one each by a wine dealer, a carrier, a fishmonger, a 'merchant', a stone dealer, a stonemason, a cotton manufacturer and a woollen manufacturer. Similarly the employers of such men in 1871 included two innkeepers, a butcher, a draper, a baker and a loom tackler. Most of them appeared to be employed in households which were also productive units, which would require men as productive labour rather than as marks of social status.

If a quarter or a third of all servants were actually shop assistants, or allowed others to be so employed, in mid-nineteenth century Rochdale, then it would seem unwise to claim, as many have done,[30] that the decline of service in late Victorian and Edwardian England was caused by the rise of alternative employment for women in retailing. As will be discussed below (Chapter 10, Section IV), the rise of the number of such women workers in retailing could be seen merely in terms of the expansion of retailing chains, which replaced the shop as a household unit. The change in employment from domestic servant to shop assistant, might only represent, therefore, a change of nomenclature, as household production was superseded by the equivalent of factory production.

7. DOMESTIC SERVICE AND THE RURAL WOMAN

I. The Preference for Rural Women

An attempt has been made in Chapter 5, Section VII, to compare the wages and conditions of domestic servants with those of other working women. It was concluded that domestic service was probably not a poorly remunerated occupation, although more depended on the board and lodging provided than on the actual wage that was paid. It is probable that servants were comparatively better off at the beginning of our period than later, but that women in the households of the highest social class were probably in a favourable position at all times.

All things being equal therefore, one would expect there to be considerable competition for employment in the households of the professional elite. At the same time one would expect that employers would be equally interested in employing what might be expected to be 'cheap' rural servants. This should mean that the servants of rural origins would be evently distributed throughout the population of servant employers. However, as can be seen from Tables 73 and 74, rural servants were always more heavily concentrated in the highest social classes. Thus, in 1851, 23.6 per cent of the servants in Social-Economic Group 1 came from settlements with fewer than 5000 inhabitants, compared with 8.6 per cent of those employed by Social-Economic Group 3. This pattern was repeated in 1861 and 1871.[1] Similarly, in 1851, just over a quarter of the servants in the highest social grouping had been born within the Rochdale district, compared with nearly a half of the servants in households in Social-Economic Group 3. This pattern was just as marked in 1861 and 1871. The 'cheap' rural servant was thus employed by the householders who could afford the most expenditure, and where the standard of living would have been the highest. Rochdale women were far more likely to be employed by the lowest levels of Rochdale's servant-employing elite.

Some examples will show how the highest members of the local elite employed servants who were both migrants and rural born. Thus, Joseph Brierly, cotton manufacturer and magistrate, appears in two household samples employing a total of seven servant. Only one of his servants had been born within the district of Rochdale, the other six being born outside, one each in Yorkshire, Lancashire, Derbyshire, Scotland, Wales and Cornwall. Robert Cook, the perpetual Curate of Smallbridge, who appeared in all three samples, employed six servants in all, of whom only one was born in Rochdale. Of his other servants, one had been born in Yorkshire, in a settlement with under 5,000 inhabitants, one had been born in Scotland, and three in Wales. Similarly, John Bright employed 15 servants in the three census samples , and not one had been born within the Rochdale district. Of these 15 servants only one had been born in Lancashire, eight came from Yorkshire, two from Wales and one each from Middlesex, Surrey, Kent and Nottinghamshire. Of these 15 servants, six came from settlements with more than 5,000 inhabitants, eight from settlments with less than 5,000 and the birthplace of one girl was unknown. In one of the largest households recorded, that of William Barthemore, containing ten servants in 1851, not a single servant came from the Rochdale district. Five of his servants came from settlements in Yorkshire, three of which contained fewer than 5,000 inhabitants, and the rest came

from Essex, Shropshire, Staffordshire and two from Derbyshire.   Only two of his servants came from settlements
which could be shown to have contained more than 5,000
persons.[2]

This seems to indicate that rural migrants were actively
sought as servants.   It could be argued that the upper
levels of Rochdale's elite may have had more links with the
rural south of England and so employed more women from
those areas. As will be discussed below (Chapter 9, Section
II), servant employers in the higher levels of the social
elite do appear to have been southern migrants in 1851,
but this tendency declined over time.   This does not appear
to affect the number of southern servants which this group
employed.   Even if there was such a tendency in 1851, it
merely proves that such servant employers were actively
using such links to recruit servants, rather than using the
local population.

This preference was sometimes voiced in the advertisements for servants in the local newspapers.   For example,
in November 1861 an advertisement appeared in the <u>Rochdale
Observer</u> asking for a general servant, and adding, 'To a
person from an agricultural district liberal wages will be
given'.   On several other occasions the term 'one from the
country preferred' appeared in the advertisements.   Moreover, when a young woman applied for a post as housemaid or
nurse in January 1861, the principal asset that she
recorded was that she was 'from the country'.[3]

This preference for rural migrants as servants appears
to be universal.   According to Horn,

> In the small Lancashire cotton town of Colne, for
> example, the 1871 census showed that only a.....
> mere quarter of the Colne maids had been born in

Lancashire. Most had migrated from agricultural districts in Yorkshire, Cumberland, Westmorland and Wales. The same situation prevailed in larger industrial towns, including Preston, where the greater number of domestics were said to be immigrants from 'purely agricultural villages'.[4]

Similarly, in London in 1861, areas such as Bethnal Green, St Pancras and Clerkenwell, which contained comparatively few servants, all had populations of which more than 60 per cent had been born in London, over 80 per cent in the case of Bethnal Green. At the same date, in areas such as Hampstead, Kensington and Paddington, where servants accounted for over 50 per cent of all working women, the proportion of London-born persons was as low as 53 per cent, or just a bare majority. This might indicate that the social elite in London was itself a migrant one, but these figures must also reflect the employment of rural women in domestic service.[5] In France in the second quarter of the nineteenth century rural migrants appear to have dominated the domestic sector. Thus in the period 1825-1853 some 57.7 per cent of the fathers of servants marrying in Versailles were employed in agriculture, and in Bordeaux, over the same period, the equivalent figure was 52.8 per cent.[6]

It could be argued that the employers of servants sought rural women because those born in urban Lancashire were ignorant both of bourgeois morality and the very basics of household work. As one character in a novel set in nineteenth-century Lancashire claims, 'there isn't a small tradesman's wife would not think herself disgraced to take a factory girl as a servant'.[7] Urban women were known for their 'immorality' and for their supposed ignorance of basic household procedures. According to P. Gaskell, writing in 1833,

> The chastity of marriage is but little known or
> exercised among them: husband and wife sin equal-
> ly, and a habitual indifference to sexual rights
> is generated which adds one other item to the
> destruction of domestic habits.[8]

At the same time, according to Ashley,

> Out of 13 married females taken at one mill, it
> was claimed that only one knew how to make her
> husband a shirt, and only four know how to mend
> one. I have the evidence of several females who
> declare their ignorance of every domestic accom-
> plishment - the un-married declare - 'not a
> single qualification of any sort for domestic
> servants'.[9]

However, as Margaret Hewitt has attempted to show, these
were the claims of people who were afraid that the
Industrial Revolution, and the new social structures which
it engendered, were undermining the family structure of
society. She goes on to argue cogently that in these
respects the urban working classes were little different
from the rural population, and in some respects were a
great deal 'better'.[10]

It was the rural areas which had the highest levels of
illegitimate births, the highest levels in the nineteenth
century being found in Cumberland and Norfolk, with Lancashire having a generally low total.[11] In both town and
country the practice of sex before marriage, as part of
normal courtship, appears to have been widespread as far
back as the sixteenth century.[12] It was also not the mill

girl who was most likely to turn to prostitution in hard times but the domestic servant. Thus, according to the 1833 Factory Commissioners,

> the number of factory girls who are finally recruited to the ranks of professional prostitutes is perhaps small; at least out of fifty prostitutes who have entered Manchester Penitentiary during the last four years, only eight proceeded from factories, whilst twenty-nine had been in service.[13]

This probably reflected, of course, the inability of rural servants out of place to find alternative employment or to rely on local kin for support.

Nor was it likely that domestic skills were more widespread amongst rural women than amongst their urban contemporaries. According to Pinchbeck, in the nineteenth-century countryside,

> Cottage accommodation was often of the meanest; food in many homes was limited to oatmeal porridge, milk, bread, cheese and potatoes, with meat a rare luxury; cooking utensils were few and turf and furze were the common fuel used by the great proportion of the population. Brick ovens, although common in farm houses, were by no means general in use amongst the cottages, and iron grates only began to be supplied at the end of the eighteenth century after the expansion of the iron trade. In these circumstances it is inconceivable that the standard of culinary skill could ever have been higher, or that the training

of children in domestic affairs could have been much superior to that of children who spent their early lives in the factory.[14]

It is unlikely, therefore, that the widespread preference for rural migrants in domestic service could be explained by such women being of a superior 'quality'. Also, since conditions and remuneration in the households of rich employers may have been superior to those experienced by mill workers, we can only presume that this preference for rural women represented a social choice rather than a purely economic one.

If such a preference for rural servants did in fact exist, even though such women were not necessarily sought after as 'cheap' labour or as labour of a superior quality, then we must assume that there were non-economic reasons for the eagerness of the middle classes to employ such women and for the readiness of such women to be so employed. Since rural women were probably no better at domestic tasks than other females this preference must have been based on a consideration of their attitude to, rather than their aptitude for, the work. The contemporary literature on the subject of the 'Servant Problem' indicates that the real advantages attached to employing migrant women as servants, were social rather than economic. Migrants were more easily controlled and more 'biddable' than other women.

The Victorians expected employers to take a personal interest in the members of the working class whom they employed. The whole conception of 'stewardship' was the contemporary vindication of the political and social hierarchies which existed in society. Domestic servants, members of the lower orders actually living in the homes of the social elite, had to expect a good deal of interference

133

in their lives. According to Mrs Beeton,

> A lady should never allow herself to forget the
> important duty of watching over the moral and
> physical welfare of those beneath her roof.
> Without seeming unduly inquisitive, she can
> always learn something of their acquaintance and
> holiday occupation, and should, when necessary
> warn them against the dangers and evils of bad
> company.[15]

Contemporary descriptions of the lives of domestic
servants are often full of these examples of social
subordination, personified by the wearing of a uniform and
the vetting of acquaintances. There appears to have been a
constant attempt to discipline such women by stressing
their moral subordination to the authority of their
employers, by the regime of fines for misdemeanours, and by
the threat of refusing a 'character' on the termination of
employment. The deep distrust of the lower orders held by
the middle and upper-classes is shown here most clearly,
where the two groups met on the most intimate terms.

The imposition of such discipline was not an easy task
and often led to personal conflict rather than to the
establishment of hierarchical order. To be effective the
servant had to be isolated from external influences which
might diminish the authority of the employer. This meant
that local women were not suitable for domestic service.
There is also evidence that rural women were especially
easy to discipline, both because of their economic
dependence on domestic service and, possibly, because of
their greater willingness to defer to familial authority.

A basic prerequisite for such discipline was the
isolation of the servant from external aid. The presence

of relatives nearby could easily undermine the authority of an employer. This happened on several occasions to employers who recruited their servants from the workhouses in Rochdale. Thus, we find in the minutes of the Workhouse Committee of the Rochdale Board of Guardians for the 29th July, 1859, that,

> Robert Wrigley, of Brickfield (a shopkeeper) attended and informed the meeting that Elizabeth Conlon, a girl that had been let out to him by this committee in the month of November last, left his house on Sunday last and has not since returned....The brother of the girl attended the meeting also and stated that the girl came to him on Sunday night....The girl was also brought before the meeting and stated that she had nothing against her master or mistress, they both had been very kind to her and used her well but that she did not like her place and wanted to go and live with her brother and go to the factory.

Similarly, on the 12th July 1861 a Mrs Collinge brought Emiline Diggle, aged 10 years, before the Committee and asked that she should be readmitted into the workhouse since 'she has not done so well for her since two of her aunts called upon her'. Again, on the 14th November 1856 Mrs Smith of Rakebridge informed the Committee that Mary Walton, a girl the Guardians had allowed her to take, had actually been 'taken away from her service by her sister Betty Walton'.[16] It is no surprise, therefore, to discover one would-be employer advertising in the Rochdale Observer, on 8th May 1869, for a 'Girl for Housework...an orphan preferred'.[17]

Women without relatives in the vicinity, either because
they were orphans or migrants, could be more easily
disciplined. In the words of one author on the subject,

> If a girl were discontented with the conditions
> so decreed for her and threw up her post, she had
> no home to go to, no relations to tide her over a
> season of unemployment and so enable her to hold
> out for better terms.[18]

Similarly, one of Horn's informants, who was formerly a
servant in the Ewelme district of Oxfordshire, recalls that
it was usual for youngsters in her parish to be sent into
service at least 20 miles from home, in order, in her own
words, 'to discourage followers or to stop the girls
running home'.[19]

It was this type of isolation and discipline which
represented the true disincentive to joining the ranks of
domestic service rather than poor remuneration. As one of
the informants of the Women's Industrial Council, a hat
worker, stated in 1916,

> I was in a sanatorium in the South a short time
> ago, and met several servants there, and really
> those in good families had a splendid time, in a
> great many respects, but they have not the same
> independent outlook on life you meet among girls
> in workshops, and where men are concerned they
> gave me the impression that domestic service does
> not improve the morality of a girl: I suppose it
> is because of the repression.[20]

Servant employers were less willing to employ local
women because they had local connections which made

discipline difficult to uphold. Also, local women could spread gossip about local employers which might undermine a family's standing in the community, or an employer's authority over his or her other employees. This might have applied equally to migrants from other Lancashire towns, but an attempt will be made in the rest of this chapter to show that women from rural areas were especially easy to discipline, since they were less able to gain alternative employment, and were by their upbringing and background less likely to assert their independence.

II. The Rural Woman and Domestic Service-Economic Dependence

The rural migrant was especially sought after as a servant because she had to accept the isolation and discipline of her employer's household. This was not only because she was unable to gain alternative employment but because she was also more ignorant of the ways of town life than her urban contemporaries.

For rural women the financial aspects of servant employment must have seemed far better than they did to those born in the town. As we have seen above (Chapter 5, Section VII), the conditions and wages of domestic servants probably compared favourably with those of women working in the mill. However, in the countryside, where employment for women was so limited, the remuneration must have seemed far greater, and so encouraged them to put up with the restrictions of servant life. Under-employment was widespread amongst women in many of the areas which supplied Rochdale with servants in the mid-nineteenth century. This was brought out clearly in many of the rural replies to the Commission on the Poor Laws in 1834. At Yarm, in the North Riding of Yorkshire, in reply to the question 'Have you any and what employment for women and children?', a witness answered,

> We have no manufactures. Women are partially employed in the summer season, at 8d a day, in weeding corn and dressing fallows; in Hay Harvest at 1s, and in Corn Harvest at 2s, but they have no employment in Winter; and Children under 16 rarely meet with employment, until they are apprenticed to the various Mechanics, or go out to service, which they generally do at the age of about 12.[21]

At Dutton Township in Cheshire the answer to the same question was, 'Summer, but little; Winter, nothing; Harvest, according as they can work'.[22] At Llanamonyntal in Denbighshire, the answer was, 'Summer and Winter, nothing. Harvest, a few days, low wages'.[23] And at Aber in Caernarvonshire the reply was merely, 'Women are not employed'.[24] Such work as was available could hardly have provided much of an income in this period. Thus, the report of the Commissioners investigating the employment of women and children in agriculture in 1843, reckoned that the average earnings of women in agriculture in the Thirsk Union of Yorkshire were about £5 4s 0d per annum.[25] This was only half the wages paid to servants, excluding any consideration of the board and lodging which the latter received.

In these circumstances it is understandable why girls were encouraged to leave the land for employment in the town. As Flora Thompson puts it, in her portrait of rural life in Edwardian Oxfordshire,

> As soon as a little girl approached school
> leaving age, her mother would say, 'About time
> you was earnin' your own livin' me gal' or, to a
> neighbour, 'I shan't be sorry when our young so-
> and-so gets her knees under somebody else's
> table. Five slices for breakfast this mornin',
> if you please'. From that time onwards the
> child was made to feel herself one too many in
> the overcrowded home; while her brothers, when
> they left school and began to bring home a few
> shillings weekly were treated with a new consid-
> eration and made much of.[26]

It was plainly pressures such as these which brought many
young women into towns such as Rochdale seeking work. Mr
Ernest Gittins of Rochdale writes of his memories of rural
life at this time in a similar manner,

> I was born in Shropshire in a largish family con-
> sisting of six sisters and several brothers. I
> was the youngest child of the family,
> consequently my elder sisters had flown the nest
> to enter domestic service in various parts of the
> country. This was because around the late 1800's
> and early 1900's there was no work for females
> and very little for males in rural areas.[27]

His sisters went to cities such as Birmingham, Manchester
and Oldham to become servants. In the 1920's Mr Gittins
became a plain clothes policeman in Rochdale, attached to
the Warrants Office and Coroner's Office; his duties
included the supervision of the local employment agencies

and registries. As he goes on to say,

> I came across a great number of young women from
> quite a lot of counties who confirm what I have
> written earlier: they had to leave their origi-
> nal homes because there was no work for them to
> obtain and accommodation at their homes was over-
> crowded.

Domestic service would certainly provide these women with
an income far greater than they could receive at home.

Some would have us believe that domestic service would
also provide an opportunity for upward social mobility.
According to one employer interviewed by the Women's
Industrial Council in 1916,

> All my servants who have married after being with
> me many years have married tradesmen in good
> positions - some with property. Many servants in
> large establishments marry butlers, stewards,
> chauffers - I speak from personal knowledge -
> others, general servants, etc., marry trades-
> people.[28]

According to Flora Thompson, 'The Novelette of the
'eighties was a romantic love story, in which the poor
governess always married the duke....'[29] This cannot have
happened often in the nineteenth century, and was certainly
not happening in Preston in the early 1850's (see Chapter
5, Section VIII). However, it might be indicative of how
certain groups of women were encouraged to think.

For such rural migrants the environment of the town was
a strange one and they were poorly placed to gain any

employment except domestic service. In general, migrants, and especially those from rural areas, had fewer contacts in the town, less experience of urban work, and were thus unable to get work in factories. Anderson has discovered that in Preston in 1851, of the adult migrants born in Ireland 60, per cent were employed as labourers or in like occupations. Similarly, of adult migrants born in agricultural villages (in England, Scotland and Wales), 38 per cent were employed as labourers. But only 11 per cent of migrants born in towns were thus employed. Conversely, the proportion in factory occupations showed an opposite trend, being two, three and 32 per cent respectively.[30] This indicates that migrants, and especially rural migrants, found it difficult to obtain employment in the mills.

This was not surprising, given that employment in the mills appears to have been linked with the employment there of the family. Some employers had a policy of employing the children and relatives of their hands,[31] and the cotton spinners, power-loom weavers and other groups of workers certainly attempted to restrict entry into their trades to their relatives at various times in the nineteenth century.[32] In any case, the relatives of workers in the mill would be the first to know if hands were required. This can be confired by an examination of Table 75 which shows the extent to which occupied sons living at home in Bolton in 1871 were employed in the same occupational grouping as their fathers.[33]

This table is indicative of the extent to which sons followed their fathers into certain occupations. It is evident that there was little occupational succession in those occupational groups where rural migrants were most often found, that is, service and labouring. On the other hand, workers in textiles often appear to have followed their fathers into the work. No less than four-fifths of

141

the occupied sons of textile workers were also occupied in the textile industry. This is very strong evidence that family contacts were important in gaining employment in the mills.

There is evidence that this pattern of employment was also to be found in Rochdale in the mid-nineteenth century. Thus, the male heads in the three control samples of 1851, 1861 and 1871 who had been born outside Lancashire or Yorkshire, made up 9.1 per cent of all heads in Social-Economic Group 3, 11.0 per cent in Social-Economic Group 4, and no less than 26.0 per cent in Social-Economic Group 5. Rural migrants, and this often meant the Irish, found it difficult to get factory employment, and this appears to apply to female migrants as well.

If we again pool the results from the three control samples it becomes apparent that female migrants, and especially those from the countryside, were less able to get employment in the textile mills. Out of the 426 women in the three census samples with stated occupations who were born within the Rochdale district, 81.9 per cent were employed in the textile industry, compared with 54.5 per cent of the 121 migrant women from the rest of Lancashire and from Yorkshire, and compared with 49.4 per cent of the 83 employed female migrants from the rest of the country. Only 9.9 per cent of the occupied Rochdale women were employed in domestic service or 'charring', compared with 25.6 per cent of the northern migrants, and 33.7 per cent of the migrants from outside the industrial counties of Lancashire and Yorkshire.

Again, if we compare migrants from settlements with under or over 5,000 inhabitants with Rochdale women, we get a still greater contrast. As before 81.9 per cent of all occupied women from the Rochdale district were employed in the production of textiles, but only 45.6 per cent of the

142

employed migrants born in settlements with over 5,000 inhabitants were so employed. At the same time, however, only 19.2 per cent of the occupied migrant females born in settlements with less than 5,000 inhabitants were employed in the textile industry. This suggests that all migrants were at a disadvantage in getting factory employment, and that 'rural' migrants were especially disadvantaged. Migrants, and rural migrants in particular, gained employment in occupations which did not involve factory work. Thus, whereas only 9.9 per cent of the female workers from Rochdale were employed as domestics, 28.1 per cent of 'urban' migrants, and 53.8 per cent of 'rural' migrants were so employed. Similarly, whilst only 2.8 per cent of the female workers from Rochdale were employed in the provision of dress, that is, as dressmakers or milliners, 10.5 per cent of 'urban' migrants and 19.2 per cent of 'rural' migrants were so employed.[34]

Most female migrants from rural areas may never have intended working in the factories, coming to the city in search of primarily domestic employment. Once there, however, they would have found great difficulty in moving into the mills.

Female rural migrants seldom had any experience of factory work, which would allow them to compete for vacancies in the mills. This appears to be a general phenomenon of developing societies, for, according to Margo L. Smith, the female migrants from the rural highlands of Peru are even today at a distinct educational and cultural disadvantage when compared with their coastal counterparts, and even more so when compared to women born in Lima, the capital city. An examination of the migrant servants from the highlands, resident in Lima, revealed that 54.6 per cent of them had no habitual employment in the provinces from which they came, and 29.8 per cent had already been employed as private servants in their province of birth. Only 1.1 per cent of these migrant servants had been employed in offices or shops before they left for Lima.[35]

This pattern amongst rural, migrant workers was repeated in England in the past. Thus, few of the servants interviewed by the Women's Industrial Council in 1916 had experience of working in industry before becoming servants or between domestic positions.[36] It would appear that the group of women who became domestic servants was distinct from the group who entered industrial occupations.

Rural women also had fewer contacts with relatives within the towns, which meant that they would have less support whilst seeking a job and less access to information, especially since their relatives would be more likely to be employed in non-factory occupations, such as labouring, in which women were not employed. As Mr Gittins remarks, after a considerable acquaintance with the servant population of Rochdale,

> Country girls did not get work in factories or shops in towns as this would mean finding accommodation and having to pay their way, and then probably most of these girls had never been in a factory or a large town.[37]

Rural women, often desperate for employment, were unable to get jobs in the mills as their Rochdale contemporaries could, and were even at a disadvantage compared with fellow migrants who had experience of town life. The manner in which many migrants actually did find employment in Rochdale, or other industrial towns, has not been fully examined as yet. Many rural migrants and perhaps most of the urban migrants employed as servants may have travelled to Rochdale with their parents seeking work. However, there is some evidence that many rural women were actually recruited by their employers in the countryside and changed their place of abode at the instigation of their employers. This subject will be discussed in more detail in Chapter 9, Section II. However, it should be apparent that rural migrants would be poorly placed to reject the discipline of their employers and to assert their independence.

At this stage it is difficult to say which of the factors mentioned above was most important in keeping many rural women out of the factory. They may have been rejected by employers because of a lack of skills, or have had problems of access to the factory labour market, or were unfamiliar with the type of discipline required in factory production. It is likely that the problem of finding accommodation for a single women, unfamiliar with the area, was particularly difficult. Undoubtedly many rural migrants would not have come to Rochdale in this period with the intention of getting factory employment. As we have suggested, many rural migrants will have migrated to the area at the insti- gation of families who hoped to employ them as servants. However, once resident in Rochdale such women would find it difficult to find alternative employment if they were dissatisfied with their positions. They might also find it difficult to change households to find domestic work elsewhere if their present employers refused to give them a good 'character'.

III. The Rural Woman and Domestic Service-Habitual Deference

Rural women were generally regarded in this period as being more docile and easy to manage than their urban contemporaries, both in Britain and on the Continent. This may have been purely due to the economic dependence of rural women on domestic service and their relative isolation within the town. However, it might also be claimed that such women were habitually more willing to defer to the type of authority and discipline found within the nineteenth-century, middle-class household.

This habitual deference to authority amongst rural women is clearly brought out in Harrison's work on The Girls' Friendly Society in the period 1874 to 1920.[38] This Society, which had close links with the Anglican Church and the Conservative Party, saw itself as a bridge between town and country, and by 'befriending' young women hoped to preserve in the towns the old hierarchies of authority which had existed in the countryside. One of its principal aims was to isolate the rural woman who migrated to the town from the harmful influences of urban life. Thus, the G.F.S. arranged for girls arriving from the countryside to be met at railway stations, for, as one woman involved in the Society put it, 'there is a certain class of girls who lose their heads the moment they enter a railway station'.[39]

The Society, with its emphasis on the duty of the social elite to supervise the lives of the unmarried women of the lower classes, had its greatest following amongst domestic servants, who made up 57 per cent of its membership in 1891.[40] On the other hand, the Society found it almost impossible to recruit women from the urban working classes. A G.F.S. report from the Chester diocese in 1881 claimed

146

that mill girls were 'undisciplined, impatient of reproof and entirely wanting in self-control', and shop assistants and clerks evoked similar complaints.[41]

Similar attitudes were found amongst servant-employers in Britain and elsewhere. According to Eda Sagarra in her Social History of Germany, 1648-1914,

> After the (Napoleonic) war the numbers (of servants) rose again, at least in the more prosperous areas, but it was clear that the social origins of the domestic servant were changing. In the bigger towns they tended to come less from the vicinity than from the countryside, sons and daughters of small farmers or labourers, who would, it was thought, be biddable and hard-working'.[42]

These beliefs were also shared by the servant-employers interviewed by Margo L. Smith in Lima in the 1960's,

> The patrona might prefer to have a servant who had been born and raised in the highland provinces because highlanders are thought to be more docile and obedient than the arrogant girls born in Lima or along the coast..... Las serronitas (the little highland girls) know their place.[43]

This is reflected in an interesting correspondence between Mrs Munro of London and Mrs Cartwright of Wem, Shropshire, in the first decade of the nineteenth century. Mrs Munro, whose husband had a post in the customs Office, was eager to elicit Mrs Cartwright's help to get her a servant from the area around Wem.[44] She believed in London

147

there existed a class of 'lazy and vicious servants who walk about from place to place every six months'.[45] In a revealing passge she writes that she wishes to hire a servant,

> wholly unconnected with other servants who are
> now becoming a very lazy, corrupt class in this
> town. I am settled on the cook and impatient to
> get an uncorrupted country person if possible.[46]

It might be foolhardy to attempt to explain this 'docility' and readiness to conform on the part of rural women by any general social theories. Women from the countryside may have appeared 'uncorrupted' simply because they had more to lose by asserting their independence, since the urban environment was strange to them. As has been pointed out, rural women had great difficulty in getting alternative employment, and their comparative helplessness may have limited their desire to rebel against authority. Employers may also have been merely parroting the stereotyped conceptions of the characters of rural and urban women, which bore little relation to fact. However, some points could be made to indicate that rural women might have been more ready to accept the discipline of the households in which they lived.

As Obelkevitch has pointed out, the labouring classes of South Lindsey, an area from which Rochdale's rural servants were drawn, were used to deferring to the authority of the community in which they lived.

> .....the notion that church and chapel were
> equally legitimate, equally integral to the com-
> munity, was one that would have come most easily
> to the labourers, for whom the community was

148

> prior to the individual, to the family and to
> every other minority; they would have been the
> least eager to set themselves apart from their
> fellows by making a total commitment to a partial
> association. A related belief in the supremacy
> of the public realm over the private led them to
> prefer marriages by banns (though again finance
> was a consideration): it announced a private
> event to congregation and community, who, on the
> third time of asking, replied with their
> approval, 'God speed them well'.[47]

This may have been why the employers of servants were so eager to portray the household as an ethical community, as a substitute for the authority of the village.

It would be foolish to claim that rural men and women did not ever rebel against that which they regarded as unjust. This was clearly seen in the Swing riots of the 1830's. However, it must be noted that even in this period of social conflict, the agricultural workers involved believed that they were merely performing justice on those farmers and employers who had offended against the community of the land.[48]

Compared with their rural contemporaries the children of the urban working classes appear to have been far more independent of restraint by family or community. This might be seen as evidence of the effects of heightened class conflict in the cities, or as a function of the greater extent to which urban dwellers could act as independent agents outside the authority of any unified community or even of the family. In certain sections of his work on family structure in nineteenth century Lancashire, Anderson has attempted to show that urban children were far less dependent on their families and the local community for support.[49] In the town, work and employment were still to some extent dependent on the family but the acquisition of relatively high wages by young men and women made them independent of their parents. Lodgings presented an alternative to living at home which was not available in the countryside. As one contemporary put it,

> Children frequently leave their parents at a very early age in the manufacturing districts. Girls of sixteen, and lads of the same age, find that they can enjoy greater liberty, and if not greater comforts, that at least they can have their own way more completely in a separate house, and these partings cause little surprise or disturbance.[50]

Other partial associations also existed from which individuals could get support: neighbourhood friends, workmates and independent non-conformist churches, all of which must have increased the urban girl's sense of independence.

Whatever the reasons for such differences of temperament as did exist, there can be no denying the differences of outlook which existed between rural servants and their urban contemporaries. Many commentators directly contrasted the attitudes of the two groups. According to the Women's Industrial Council in 1916,

> It is very difficult to analyse the cause of the 'social stigma' (of domestic service). Clearly it does exist but by no means universally. In the country, as many mistresses point out when describing their former maids' marriages, the servants often represented the 'aristocracy of

150

the village'. In many towns, especially the small towns, the girl who goes into service does not lose caste, partly because there are so few alternative occupations for her. It is chiefly in the suburbs of large towns, and the industrial districts that the caste difficulty crops up.[51]

Similarly, in 1891 one contributor to the <u>Westminister Review</u> remarked,

The general servant of the North is too often an untrained factory hand turned loose upon the household, and she brings the traditions of factory life with her. In the south, among the sleepy villages of the agricultural counties, old traditions have lingered...[52]

Whereas Flora Thompson tells us that in Oxfordshire villages, servants home on holiday were regarded as objects for admiration and were encouraged to walk out in their town clothes 'in order to impress the neighbours',[53] a cook in Preston in 1916 could claim that, 'In this part of the country servants are treated very badly. They think that because we are in service, we spent our early days in prison'.[54] This would seem to indicate a total contrast in attitudes between the rural and urban working classes.

Many examples could be quoted of the low estimation in which working class women from the industrial districts held domestic service. These attitudes appear to have been well established in Lancashire before the 1850's. In his <u>Tour of the Manufacturing Districts of Lancashire</u> in 1842, Cooke Taylor recounts how he was present when a young Bolton man related his experiences in America to his working-class relatives and states that,

The accounts which he gave of the Americans seem
to have produced a very unfavourable impression
on his relatives for, on intimating an intention
to revisit the United States, his aunt said 'I am
sure, if I were in your case, I would do
anything, - I would even become a gentleman's
servant, rather than go back to such a place'.[55]

It was social attitudes such as these which meant that
urban women were found to be unsuitable for domestic
service. It was not economic considerations but rather
these social questions which encouraged urban women to seek
alternative employment for, according to the Women's
Industrial Council in 1916,

In the face of the persuasion of teachers and
mothers and outside 'social superiors' the most
promising girls are apt to prefer lower wages,
less material comfort and much less security of
employment in shop or offfice or factory work, to
the oft quoted advantages of domestic service.[56]

When the domestic servant class began to shrink with
increased rapidity during and after the First Work War, it
was these issues of 'caste' which were seen as the true
cause of the decline. The report of the Parliamentary Sub-
Committee on Domestic Service, published in 1919, recorded
that three reasons for the reluctance of women to enter
domestic service needed 'special attention'; the long hours
of duty, the lack of companionship and the loss of 'social
status by entering the profession'.[57] The first two are
perhaps of doubtful validity because they obviously failed
to deter women entering the occupation in the mid-nineteenth century. The third point is perhaps the most

crucial and refects the attitudes of a predominantly urban female population to domestic service. As the report continues,

> The fact cannot be denied that domestic workers are regarded by other workers as belonging to a lower social status. The distinctive dress which they are required to wear marks them out as a class apart, the cap being generally resented. It is sometimes stated that the differentiation in the quality of the food for the dining room and that for the servants' hall or kitchen is another class distinction which leads to a spirit of bitterness.
>
> The custom of addressing domestic workers by their Christian or surname is one of the causes of the superior attitude adopted by workers recruited from the same or even a lower social status.[58]

Where alternative employment for women existed, as in the Lancashire textile towns, servants were comparatively rare, and those that did exist were more likely to be migrants (see Chapter 5, Section VI). This reluctance to employ local women, and the reluctance of local women to be so employed, must have stemmed in part from attitudes such as those discussed above. The existence of alternative employment meant that urban women not only did not need to seek employment as domestic servants but that they were also less likely to endure the type of isolation and discipline which was imposed on servants in middle-class households. We can thus see alternative employment for urban women both as a factor limiting the supply of such women for domestic service and as a limitation to the demand for these women as servants on the part of servant employers. The mill girl had as much abhorrence of domestic service as an employer had of hiring her as a servant and these two attitudes reinforced one another.

8. THE EFFECT OF LOCATION ON SERVANT EMPLOYMENT

I. The Origins and Aims of the Study

The origins of this chapter lay in an attempt to measure the influence of the place of residence on the number of servants which a household employed. This was an attempt to check the hypothesis of John Foster that Nonconformist 'abstinence', as exemplified by the employment of small servant retinues, represented an attempt by employers living in working-class communities to hide the inequalities of wealth which existed between their employees and themselves.[1] Foster's analysis was based on a sample of employers in Oldham in 1851 who left more than £25,000 in their wills. As such, his data on wealth is far superior to the social-economic groupings used in this thesis, the basis of which is explained in Appendix A, Note 7. On the other hand, his division of these employers into two groups, 'rural' and 'urban', for the purposes of comparing how many servants they employed, appeared a crude geographical division. From an examination of the Rochdale registration district it had become apparent that a simple division between 'urban' and 'rural' was impossible, when the settlements outside the central urban mass of Rochdale included townships containing thousands of persons, as well as hamlets of two or three households and even isolated farm houses.

All the households in the Rochdale registration district in the censuses of 1851 and 1871 were placed in differing settlement categories, using the settlement typology set out in Appendix A, Note 28. This allowed all the households in the Rochdale registration districts in 1851 and 1871 to

155

be placed in distinct parts of the urban mass of Rochdale, and in various settlement types outside this central urban core. It was therfore possible to study the effect of area type on the employment of servants in greater detail.

In fact this analysis, although producing some interesting indications as to the effects of settlement type on the employment of servants, produced no results which could have been described as statistically significant. The division of the differing social-economic groups of servant employers into so many differing settlement types meant that the number of employers in each cell was too small to give anything more than some correlations which might be suggestive of important social phenomena. Also, when apparent differences did exist between the numbers of servants employed by households in the same social-economic class, this could have been caused by the wide variations in wealth that must have existed between members of these very crude categories. Thus, it would be no surprise to discover that a cotton manufacturer employing 30 hands had fewer servants than a similar manufacturer employing 700 hands, although both would be placed in Social-Economic Group 1 on the basis of the classification used here. The results of this exercise cannot be directly compared with Foster's results since his sample included households which did not employ servants. In the samples used in the present work only households with servants were included, which neglects a large number of middle-class households which did not employ any servants at all and are the most interesting examples of 'Nonconformist abstinence'.

II. Area of Residence as a Factor Affecting the Number of Servants Employed by a Household

In his work on Oldham, Foster finds links between employers living in out-townships, such as Royton, close to their employees and mills, and the practice of Calvinist religion and 'abstinence'.[2] He suggest that in the town, where the relationships of employer and employee were not so intimate, one finds less Calvinism and less abstinence on the part of the capitalists. He produces tables to show that employers resident outside of the town employed fewer servants than those of equivalent wealth who lived in Oldham itself. One of these tables, reproduced here as Table 76 would appear to indicate that employers in out-townships did indeed have fewer servants. Thus of the 28 employers who employed more than two servants in 1851, nearly 80 per cent lived in the town of Oldham. On the other hand, of the 30 employers who had fewer than two servants in 1851, only 30 per cent lived in the town, and 70 per cent lived in the 'rural' areas, that is, in the out-townships. We cannot calculate directly from these figures the relative number of servants employed by these two groups because we are not told the total number of employers who lived in the two areas. That group which employed two servants has not been given. However, these figures do indeed suggest that employers in out-townships did reduce the number of servants they employed.

However, a crude devision between 'urban' and 'rural' employers must hide as much as it reveals. Certainly in the Rochdale area some of the largest servant retinues were to be found in the isolated rural mansions which some of the large textile manufacturers inhabited. These would have to be included with the households of the employers who lived in out-townships as 'rural' households, even though their geographical and social setting was completely different. An attempt was therefore made to sub-divide the 'urban' and 'rural' settlements in the Rochdale district in order to show the differences which did indeed exist within these broader categories.

An examination of Tables 3 and 77, which show the occupations of persons in the control samples of 1851 and 1871 according to the settlement types in which they lived, reveals that industrial production tended to be concentrated in what are here termed 'large nucleated settlements', those with more than 50 per cent of their dwellings in a contiguous pattern of over 100 households. Thus although only 15.6 per cent of all households were resident in such areas in 1851, 23.9 per cent of all those employed in the textile industry were resident there. In 1871 such settlement contained 25.8 per cent of all households, but 35.1 per cent of all those employed in the production of textiles. Since textiles were the principal industry in nineteenth-century Rochdale, these townships can be seen as being distinctly 'industrial', although industrial production, and persons in industrial occupations, were to be found elsewhere in the area. It was in these communities, Foster suggests, with between 100 and 1000 households, that class conflict, based on the inequalities of wealth, must have been at their strongest. In the urban centre of Rochdale, in which the zoning of classes took place, the type of class confrontation to which Foster refers would not have been so evident. On the other hand, in smaller communities, of perhaps 20 households, such confrontations would have been on a small scale. Also, such small communities, and especially those which remained small, would probably not be 'industrial' in the sense of being communities formed around places of industrial production and containing a capitalist and his labour force.

These large nucleated settlements were evidently the most expansive settlements in the region, containing 15.6 per cent of all households in 1851, but as much as 25.8 per cent in 1871. More and more of the population of the Rochdale district was being concentrated in these settlements with the growth of the industries which they contained. Settlements which failed to grow would not be those based on industrial production. If Foster is correct it would be in these settlements that employers would attempt to hide inequalities of income by practising 'abstinence', including the reduction of the number of servants which they employed.

In Tables 78, 79 and 80 employers in the three main social classes which employed servants have been divided into occupational groupings and each of these has been subdivided according to place of residence. This produces a complex of cells for each class of servant employers, defined by occupational group and place of residence. A figure is given in each cell which represents the percentage of the employers in each cell who employed more than one servant. It is thus possible to see the effects of settlement type on the number of servants employed.

The figures in each cell are perhaps too small to give any significant results. Taking the totals for the social-economic groups as a whole, there does appear to be some evidence that servant employers in large nucleatead settlements tended to employ fewer servants than their social peers living in other areas. Thus, amongst servant employers in the professional class in 1871, only five out of the 12 living in large nucleated settlements employed more than one servant. At 41.7 per cent this is lower than the average for the group, which stood at 58.0 per cent.

In the intermediate class none of the employers who lived in large nucleated settlements ever employed more than one servant, which was unusual for the group. On the other hand, employers from Social-Economic Group 3 who lived in these settlements do not appear to show any such tendency, indeed they tended to employ more servants than was normal, although, as always, the number of cases involved is too small to be of any statistical significance.

It is perhaps more interesting that the clearest example of 'abstinence' shown here does not involve the class of large employers as Foster suggests, but rather the intermediate class of small manufacturers and large retailers. However, it is also interesting that in the highest social class it was the textile manufacturers who seemed to show the most distinct pattern of 'abstinence'. In both 1851 and 1871 the textile manufacturers who lived in large nucleated settlements were more willing to make do with only one resident servant than their fellow manufacturers elsewhere, as can be seen in Table 81.[3]

As was mentioned above, however, this apparent disparity could be explained in terms of inequalities in the incomes of these employers. It is possible that only small textile manufacturers remained close to the source of their wealth, whilst the larger employers moved into the 'suburbs' of Rochdale. Using the information contained in Table 5, it would appear that the average number of hands employed by textile manufacturers in this region in the period 1851-1871 was 186.2. Amongst the textile manufacturers who lived in large nucleated settlements in 1851 and 1871 the average number of hands employed, using the same method, was 195.3 hands. This suggest that these manufacturers were not, on average, smaller employers than those living elsewhere in the Rochdale area.

Although something of a pattern does appear to emerge

160

here, it would be premature to conclude that the intensity of class conflict, mediated by the social and spatial structure of settlement types, was a factor affecting the employment of servants. Although a pattern does appear to exist there are conceptual problems involved in its interpretation along the lines of Foster's thesis. The statistics produced here cannot prove Foster's hypothesis, rather we require Foster's arguments to give a conceptual explanation of this statistical pattern. Foster's argument rests on the belief that it was only in relatively small industrial settlements that the conflict between classes was 'face to face', and necessitated a concealment of wealth on the part of employers. We are to assume from this that in the town class conflict was not so obvious since the employers could live apart from their workers in 'safe' middle-class suburbs. This is in itself a geographical and sociological model which requires substantiation.

Although servant employers did appear to live in distinct areas in Rochdale, which could be designated as middle-class 'suburbs', we have comparatively little information as to the residence patterns of employers outside the urban centre. When enumerators gave the addresses of servant employers, or of other households, in out-townships such as Featherstall, Littleborough or Whitworth, they seldom gave any distinct information beyond the name of the township and perhaps the name of a street. The Ordnance Survey maps of this period seldom give us the street names of these settlements, so we are unable to accurately reconstruct the residence patterns of this group. At the same time we must be cautious of accepting the proposition that the middle-class 'suburbs' of a town such as Rochdale could in any sense represent a district in which the capitalists of the area could feel 'safe' from the surveillance of their workers. As can be seen from Tables 3 and 77, there were still numerous textile workers resident within the urban area of Rochdale who might have represented a threat to their employers. Even in 1871 the built-up urban area of Rochdale was only one and a half miles across at its extremes. Any part of the urban area could have been reached from any other part in twenty minutes, and usually within a quarter of an hour. We must not think in terms of the great middle-class districts of London when discussing the class structure of settlements such as these. Worker and capitalist must have lived in very close proximity to one another even in these urban areas. We need to know a great deal more about class zoning in such small urban centres before we are able to conclude that they enabled capitalists to relax any restrictions on their patterns of consumption. At this stage we are not even certain what constituted a middle-class 'neighbourhood' for such employers, or what was the minimum size for such an area beyond which they could feel that their employees no longer represented a threat to their safety or wealth. These questions, concerning the psychology of social and spatial perception, cannot adequately be answered by the type of statistics provided here.

Similarly, it could be argued that the immediate authority of the employer might have been far greater in the communities around the mill he owned than in the town. The employer's position as sole or principal employer, his ownership of shops and public houses, and perhaps his position as builder and landlord of the mill community, gave him considerable control over his workers.[4] In the words of a local historian of Rochdale,

It is interesting to recall the powerful position

162

of the mill owner's wife in this close-knit
industrial community (of Greenbooth, near
Rochdale) some sixty years ago, whose daily
custom was to inspect the school, scholars and
homes to ensure the inhabitants maintained her
own standards of cleanliness. Offending workers
were threatened by loss of employment and even
eviction, for rents were deducted from wages at
source.[5]

The whole question of class antagonisms and social controls
such as these, which may have varied over time and between
differing areas, is a complicated one and makes any simple
correlation between settlement type and the intensity of
class struggle a difficult one to establish.

It might also be argued that the whole question of class
struggle and 'abstinence' in this context is a false one.
Foster appears to assume that members of the bourgeois
class employed as many servants as they could afford, and
that any unwillingness to employ servants must represent a
desire to restrict necessary expenditure. In fact the
employers who lived in the urban centre of Oldham or
Rochdale, and who employed extra servants, may have been
the ones who were deviating from the norm. If the
statistics contained in Table 59 are correct, then it was
more common for householders in the highest class to employ
no servants at all than to employ more than one. Thus, the
'rural' capitalist who made do with only one servant, or
had his daughters running his household, was not res-
tricting his 'conspicuous consumption' but merely following
the social norm.

On the other hand, the employers concentrated in certain
sections of the town, and divorced from the capital and
labour which represented their function in society, could

have competed with each other in 'conspicuous consumption' in order to lay claim to social status amongst their peers; the nineteenth-century equivalent of 'keeping up with the Joneses'. An excess of servants would not therefore indicate a 'normal' expenditure pattern, from which 'rural' employers deviated.

We may conclude that textile employers in small settlements had fewer servants than their peers who lived in the town. The reasons for these inequalities, however, need to be examined with reference to psychological perceptions of space and social class, upon which little work has been done as yet. The patterns revealed by this statistical analysis cannot be used to 'prove' a conceptual hypothesis if alternative explanations for the phenomenon have not been investigated.

9. THE RECRUITMENT OF SERVANTS IN ROCHDALE, 1851-1871

I. The Size and Seasonal Structure of the Servant Recruitment Market in Rochdale

At any one time in Rochdale in the mid-nineteenth century there would probably have been over a thousand men and women employed as some sort of domestic servant. Since service was only a temporary occupation for most women, there must have been a continuous movement out of the occupation and a similar movement into it in order to keep the numbers stable. The normal duration of a woman's career in service would certainly have been less than 10 years, from leaving her parental home in her teens to marrying in her early twenties. Thus out of the 997 servants recorded in the households samples for Rochdale in the three censal years only 10 servants, traced by their names, ages and places of birth, appeared in more than one census. Only three of these were servants in 1851 and 1871. Many of the other servants may have moved out of the area, and still others may have only temporarily left the occupation to return later. However, this still represents striking confirmation of the belief that domestic service was merely part of the life-cycle of working women.

If we take 10 years as the normal length of time that women were servants, then every year approximately 10 per cent of the servants in the district would be leaving the occupation, other things being equal. This would mean that in 1861 some 126 women would have to enter the occupation to keep up the number of domestic servants. It is more likely that the average servant only remained so employed for six or seven years, in which case the annual replacement requirement at this time would be more in the region of 200 women.

But even women who were not intending to leave domestic service would not remain in the same household throughout their 'careers'. Servants might wish to move for a variety of reasons: to seek better posts, to escape harsh employers, or to avoid the boredom of routine. Miss Collet, in her Parliamentary Report of 1899, The Money Wages of Indoor Domestic Servants, collected survey data on 2,443 servants who were resident outside London. At the time of her survey, 35 per cent of the servants had been in their present households for less than three years; and only eight per cent had been in the same household for more than 10 years.[1] Similarly, Ebery and Preston have calculated that in Englefield House in Berkshire, in the period 1854 to 1894, the average length of time that a servant remained at the house was only 23.9 months, under two years. The average length of service by butlers was only five years, and upper housemaids only stayed an average of two and a half years.[2] Even in this country mansion there were very few servants who could be described as 'old family retainers'.

Even if we assume that servants remained in their positions for an average of three years, this still meant that every year approximately a third of all servants in Rochdale would have left their jobs to move elsewhere. In 1871 this would have meant some 500 servants changing their place of employment. These figures are very crude but they indicate that every year hundreds of men and women would be seeking domestic employment with middle-class householders, or would be sought by such families. On this basis there would have been nearly 700 men and women in 1871 who were either required to replace those who had left service, or who were changing their place of work. This must have represented a considerable movement of labour into the district and within its boundaries. If this was repeated on the national scale there would be an annual turnover of about half a million women in domestic positions, a prodigious figure. Such changes of positions amongst servants certainly did take place in Rochdale, for of the 10 servants who appeared in more than one census sample only two were found in the same household. The large and rapid turnover in servant employment in this period must have created a very widespread need for information about the labour market, which was reflected in the development of institutional arrangements for putting potential employers in touch with potential employees. The growth of newspaper advertising and the development of servant agencies were some of the first steps taken to establish an impersonal system of job placement within the urban employment market.

Since the majority of servants in the Rochdale Registration District in this period had been born outside its boundaries, this flow of labour must have represented a considerable component of the total inflow of migrants into the area. Many women who would find employment as domestic servants in Rochdale would not have migrated with the sole intention of taking up domestic employment, although many of the rural migrants may have done so, but domestic employment must have represented at least part of the pool of employment which attracted women. For many girls from agricultural backgrounds, employment as a servant was probably all they could hope for.

It is possible to do some rough calculations to show what percentage of migrants into the Rochdale district actually became servants. In the period 1861 to 1871 the population of the Rochdale district rose from 91,754 to 109,858 persons.[3] From the control samples of 200 households taken from the censuses of these years, we know that migrants into the district represented 33.8 per cent of the population in 1861 and 35 per cent in 1871. The number of migrants in the district thus rose from 31,013 persons to 38,450, a crude annual influx of 744 persons. If we allow an extra 20 per cent of the 1861 migrant total to compensate for those migrants who were resident in Rochdale in 1861 but who had either died or moved away in the subsequent 10 years, and so do not appear in our census totals, we get a total annual migration of 1,364 persons into the district.

According to the published census reports, over this 10 year period the number of males in the district rose from 44,484 to 52,249, whilst the number of women rose from 47,270 to 57,609.[4] Migrants represented 35.4 per cent of all males in the district in 1861 and 34.2 per cent in 1871, according to the control samples. The crude increase in the number of male migrants was thus 212 males per annum, and if we allow an extra 20 per cent of the 1861 male migrant total for deaths we get an annual migration rate of 527 men per annum. It is possible to do this calculation with the female population of Rochdale, which rose from 47,270 in 1861 to 57,609 in 1871.[5] Since the control samples show that the percentage of migrants in the female population rose from 32.1 per cent in 1861 to 35.9 per cent in 1871, this represents an annual immigration of 551 women, or 854 women if one includes the extra 20 per cent to cover deaths. It is interesting that this reveals a higher annual immigration amongst women than amongst men. This may reflect sampling error in the calculation of the percentage of men and women who were migrants. However, since the number of women in the district increased by 10,339 in this period, whilst the number of men only increased by 7,765, this would also appear to reflect a genuine predominance of female migrants, which might in part be linked to the demand for migrant servants.

The sample of servants in 1871 indicates that in that year there were 1,608 servants. If 79.1 per cent of these servants were migrants into the district, or 1272 persons, and we assume that a tenth of them left service annually then we can assume that some 127 migrants were required to enter service in Rochdale annually in order to keep the proportion of migrants in the servant population stable. This would represent 9.3 per cent of the annual migration rate of men and women into the area, and if we assume that all servants were females, then this represents some 14.9 per cent of all female migrants.

We can take this a stage further and divide migrants into two groups; those from Lancashire and Yorkshire, and those from the rest of the United Kingdom. Since comparatively few servants were Irish, whilst they represented a large proportion of the long distance migrants, Irish were included in the first migrant group with persons from Lancashire and Yorkshire. The total number of migrants in the Rochdale population was 31,013 in 1861 and of these the control sample shows that 81.7 per cent came from Lancashire, Yorkshire and Ireland. There were thus 25,322 migrants from this area, and 5,691 from the rest of the United Kingdom. In 1871 there were 38,450 migrants in the population, of which 74.5 per cent were from the counties of Lancashire and Yorkshire and Ireland, or 28,626 persons, with 9,824 migrants coming from the rest of the country. This indicates an annual influx of 836 persons from Lancashire, Yorkshire and Ireland, and 527 from the rest of the United Kingdom, allowing a 20 per cent margin for migrants in the Rochdale district in 1861 who had died within this decade. Since in 1871 migrants from

Lancashire, Yorkshire and Ireland represented 30.2 per cent of the 1,608 servants in the district, and other migrants equalled 48.9 per cent, assuming a 10 per cent annual turnover of servants, there would be an annual replacement requirement of 49 persons from the first group and 79 from the group representing areas other than Lancashire, Yorkshire and Ireland. Comparing this to the annual migration rates for these groups it would appear that servants would represent 5.9 per cent of the migrants from the norther counties and Ireland, but 15 per cent of all migrants from the rest of the United Kingdom.

In the same period the number of female migrants in the district had risen from 15,174 to 20,682. Since the percentage of these female migrants who were in the two area groups used above were similar to the overall proportions for migrants of both sexes, we may calculate that the annual influx of female migrants from Lancashire, Yorkshire and Ireland was 539 women, and 316 women from the rest of the United Kingdom, again allowing 20 per cent for deaths. Assuming that all servants were female this would mean that some 9.1 per cent of the migrants from Ireland, Lancashire and Yorkshire would be employed in the Rochdale district as servants, but no fewer than 25 per cent of all female migrants from the rest of the United Kingdom would be so employed. This indicates the important position which domestic service held in the structure of long-range female migration.

Since we lack crucial statistical information on birth and death rates in the district, and of movements into and out of the district, these figures can only be very rough indicators. Certain factors would tend to reduce the size of the percentages quoted here. An addition of 20 per cent of the base population in 1861 to cover deaths assumes a 50-year life span for all migrants, which is probably too long. If more migrants died, then Rochdale would have required more migrants to take their place and so the annual migration of persons into the district would have been greater, reducing the proportion that would have entered service. Similarly, we have only taken the 20 per cent as a proportion of the population in the base year, whilst the population was in fact increasing over time, so more migrants would have died in the inter-censal period than we allowed for. At the same time we calculated the annual relacement requirement of servants on the number of servants in 1871, which was far greater than it had been 10 years before. If we allow for this, fewer migrant servants would have been required to keep up the level of migrants in the servant population. However, this may be more than compensated for by the fact that we have assumed that only 10 per cent of the servants in Rochdale left service annually. Since the actual length of service was probably only six or seven years we might have calculated that some 15 per cent of the servant population left annually, which would greatly increase the number of migrants required to keep up the number of migrants in the servant population. Statistical problems such as these, and others which do exist, greatly reduce the significance of these results but the figures quoted still indicate, if in a very inexact manner, the extent to which domestic service provided employment for a considerable proportion of long-range female migrants. If this was the case in an industrial town in Lancashire one wonders what would have been the position in London or the south of England, where fewer women can have been moving into the towns in this period in search of industrial employment.

This considerable labour movement into and within the area did not represent a regular and even flow; there appears to have been a definite seasonal pattern. Such

171

seasonal movements of labour have had a long history in this country and go back, at least, to the seventeenth century. According to Peter Laslett, in the seventeenth century,

> Towards the end of summer every year, master and mistress, man servant and maid servant, all had to decide whether to go on with the engagement for a further twelve months......(servants) would seek another place, and the purpose of the statute fairs or mops which came on at Michaelmas time was to provide a public market for the purpose. In the North the day was November 11th, St Martin's day or Martinmas, and the autumn was certainly a time of general turn around amongst the community of employers and employed all over the country.[6]

In order to follow the seasonal fluctuations in the servant employment market in Rochdale, an examination was made of the advertisements for servants in the <u>Rochdale Observer</u> for the years 1856 to 1871[7] and of the number of girls being taken out of the Rochdale workhouses for employment in domestic duties in the period 1851 to 1871.[8] The cumulative number of advertisements in each month is given in Table 82, along with the total number of children in each month who were recorded as going out to service.

These two sets of figures do not show exactly the same pattern, the advertisements showing a distinctly low frequency in the months of spring and early summer, whilst the workhouse figures show some of these months to be the most busy of the year, although even here there is a distinct decline in April. However, both appear to show a decline in the months between July and December. The latter month appears in both cases to be the beginning of a winter climax in activity in this employment market. This appears to be at odds with the traditional picture of an autumnal climax in the market, as suggested by Laslett. It might be argued that people who resorted to the workhouse or newspaper advertising for their servants were actually those who had been unable to hire servants by more normal means in the preceding months. There might therefore be a time-lag between the peak period of activity in the servant employment market and the movements shown by these figures. It is certainly interesting that November, the month of Martinmas and the mop fairs, was in fact the month in which the least number of advertisements for servants were placed in the <u>Rochdale Observer</u>. This was the time of year when alternative modes of recruitment would have been available.

Whatever the exact monthly course of such movements it would appear plain that seasonal fluctuations did take place. The reasons for this are difficult to exlain since we can only guess at the causes of such complex social decisions. Was there any functional cycle within nineteenth-century households which could explain such movements? Perhaps the onset of winter meant extra labour, which encouraged dissatisfied servants to move on. On the other hand this may have simply been the effect of tradition which indicated certain months for changing occupations, perhaps a relic of rural life, when employment declined after the harvest. The general restlessness in the labour market would have encouraged other servants to move, since they could count on a large number of vacancies existing. It is interesting that when Margo L. Smith came to study the servant employment market of Lima in the 1960's she found a similar pattern of seasonal fluctuations, with the high periods of activity in April and then

August through to November. She found that the month of November had the highest average number of servants looking for new jobs.[9] This can hardly have reflected the oncoming of winter since in the southern hemisphere November is, of course, the end of spring. Thus, these seasonal fluctuations in the servant employment market may represent traditional patterns of labour movement common to the Christian world, from England in the seventeenth century to Lima at the present time.

The movement of servants on this scale must have presented serious problems for servant-employers, especially since, as we have suggested, the type of person sought after as a servant was a comparative rarity in the Rochdale district. Changing jobs must also have been difficult for servants since we can hardly imagine their employers being pleased at the prospect. We have a considerable amount of information about the means by which servant-employers hired new maids but we have very little information as to how servants themselves sought out new posts. Undoubtedly many will have heard of vacancies through tradesmen, or read the local newspaper, or listened to the conversations of their mistresses or other servants, and acted on this information in their spare time. Still others may have lost their places when their employers moved away, or through illness, and would have to seek employment through one of the servant registries. If we are to believe some stories of the time, some ladies actually 'poached' the servants of their neighbours. The rest of this chapter will be devoted to studying some of the means by which servants and would-be employers contacted each other, and the institutions and social forms which this created.

II. Private Forms of Servant Recruitment in Nineteenth-Century Rochdale

By the beginning of the twentieth century there were many institutions facilitating job placement for servants, especially servant registries and the advertising columns of local newspapers. These co-existed along with more personal contacts between would-be employer and servant. According to the 1906 edition of Mrs Beeton's Book of Household Management,

> One of the commonest ways of procuring servants is to answer advertisements or to insert a notice, setting forth what kind of servant is required. In these advertisements it is well to state whether the house is in the town or country and indicate the wages given. There are many respectable registry offices, where good servants may be hired. A good plan is for the mistress to tell her friends and acquaintances of the vacant place. A lady whose general relations with her domestics are friendly and fairly permanent, will seldom need to employ any of these methods. Suitable applicants will soon present themselves to fill the vacant places, generally friends of the domestic who is obliged to leave.[10]

The 1906 version of this work was virtually a copy of the 1863 edition, incorporating such information or corrections as were needed to bring it up to date. With this in mind it is interesting to find that the equivalent passage

175

in the first version is very different in emphasis from that quoted above. In 1863 the passage read,

> Engaging domestics is one of those duties in which the judgement of the mistress must be keenly exercised. There are some respectable registry offices, where good servants may sometimes be hired; but the plan rather to be recommended is for the mistress to make enquiry amongst her circle of friends and acquaintances, and her tradespeople. The latter generally know those in their neighbourhood, who are wanting situations, and will communicate with them.....[11]

In the mid-victorian period the emphasis was very much on personal contacts in order to hire domestic servants; the use of servant registries appears to have been actively discouraged and newspaper advertisements were not even mentioned.

The mid-Victorians did not like recruitment procedures which appeared to place servants and employers on an equal contractual basis. The emphasis was continually upon the mistress of the household seeking out servants herself and too much initiative on the part of servants was an undesirable personality trait. Thus, Webster and Parkes in their Encyclopaedia of Domestic Economy of 1861 warned their readers that,

> Registry offices, sometimes resorted to by those who are seeking for servants, have not of late been in much repute, because servants of indifferent characters more frequently apply to them for places than those of a better

description.[12]

Similarly, in the 1906 edition of Mrs Beeton's work even the written character was frowned upon and it was advised that 'it is better to have an interview, if possible, with the former mistress...'.[13]   Presumably servants who knew how to go about getting new places were not those who might easily be disciplined.

Although such strictures may not have been heeded in practice it would seem that many servant employers used links with friends and acquaintances in order to recruit servants. As early as 1805 we find Miss Lizabeth Appleton, governess to Mrs Walmsley of Castlemere, Rochdale, writing to her aunt in London, 'Mrs W. says she shall be obliged to you if you will continue your enquiries respecting a servant, if not French she must do with English but does not wish to advertize'.[14]   In the same manner, in 1837, John Cunliffe of Myerscough Hall wrote to Thomas Clifton of Lytham Hall that,

> I remember some time ago you spoke of the proba-
> bility that the boy who was then in your stable
> wanting a place and you gave him such a character
> as led me to think that he was likely to suit me
> if I had a vacancy. I am now on the look out for
> a groom, I should be glad to take him or any
> other person you could recommend for steadiness
> and sobriety.[15]

Contacts such as these must have accounted for a good deal of the long distance migration which servants under-took in this period. Male and female servants who had migrated into the Rochdale area in the mid-nineteenth century might well have been drawn there at the instigation of their employers, either by accompanying them as the whole household moved to the district, or by the use which Rochdale residents made of their personal contacts with other parts of the country to recruit servants.

There would appear to have been a correlation between the birthplace of the heads of servant-employing households in Rochdale and the birthplaces of their servants, which indicates the importance of personal contacts in recruitment. An examination of the statistics contained in Table 83 reveals that there was a tendency for employers to employ servants from their region of birth. Thus in 1851 employers who had been born in Rochdale itself employed 50 per cent of their servants from the district of Rochdale, whilst the figure for all employers was only 38.2 per cent. Similarly, employers born in areas of Lancashire beyond the Rochdale district hired 29.4 per cent of their servants from those areas, whilst the figure for all employers was 15.2 per cent.[16] The same held true for employers born in Yorkshire,[17] and for those employers born outside Lancashire and Yorkshire.[18] In 1861 and 1871 the pattern was not so well defined, especially since all the servant-employing groups began to employ increasingly large numbers of servants from areas outside Lancashire and Yorkshire. However, it still seems true to say that in these years, and excluding servants from outside Lancashire and Yorkshire, that servant-employers tended to recruit more servants from the areas where they had been born and where they presumably still had contacts.

This analysis can be extended to discover the extent to which servant-employers recruited servants from areas in which they had once lived. Taking only those servants who had been born outside the counties of Yorkshire and Lancashire, we can calculate what percentage of them were

178

employed by households in which one member had been born in the town or county where the servants had been born. Thus, if a servant had been born in Chelmsford, Essex, and one of the children of the household head had been born there, then we might conclude that the servant had been recruited by the household when it was resident in that town, or through personal contacts which members of the household still had with the area. In 1851 9.2 per cent of these servants, 8 out of 87, were resident in households in the Rochdale district in which one member of the employing family had been born in the town, or county, where the servant had been born. In 1861 the figure was 15 out of 116, or 13 per cent, and in 1871 it was 18 out of 207, or 8.7 per cent. There appears to have been a decline in the closeness of these links as the number of township pairings on this basis actually declined. In 1851 some 4.6 per cent of the servants in Rochdale who were born outside the counties of Lancashire and Yorkshire were resident in households which contained a member of the family who had been born in the same town as the servant. The equivalent figure for 1871 was only 0.5 per cent. These links were thus increasingly between counties of birth rather than actual settlements of birth.

Figures such as these undoubtedly underestimate the number of servants who were recruited through such personal contacts, since information on place of birth does not necessarily give a true indication of contacts which Rochdale families had with the rest of the country. It should be no surprise, for example, to discover that a Member of Parliament such as John Bright should employ a domestic servant from Acton in London in 1851.

Some occasional coincidences give us an insight into the type of contacts which servant-employers in Rochdale used to recruit their servants. A most interesting example is

provided by the information on the household of Edward
Whitehead, cotton manufacturer, which resided at The
Grange, Rochdale, in 1871. At this date Mr Whitehead was
employing two servants, both of whom had been born in
Longnor, an agricultural village in the north east of
Staffordshire. There was nothing to link the Whitehead
family with this area since Mr Whitehead had been born in
Facit within the Rochdale district, as had his only child,
Gertrude, while his wife had been born in Cragg in
Yorkshire. However, on the night of the census the White-
heads had visitors, none other then the Vicar of Longnor,
Staffordshire, the Reverend John Crowther, and his family.
Crowther had been born in Cragg in Yorkshire, and his wife
had been born in Facit. Edward Whitehead was aged 52
years, 10 years older than Priscilla Crowther, the Reverend
Crowther's wife, but still not too old to have been this
woman's older brother. At the same time Phoebe, Mr
Whitehead's wife, was only four years older than Priscilla
Crowther's husband, and might thus have been his sister.
Whatever the exact relationship between these couples it is
probable that the Whiteheads had used their contacts with
the area to recruit both of their servants. It is
interesting in this context to recall the important position which the clergyman and his wife held in the rural
community as providers of servant places for the female
children of their parishioners.

Many of the long-distance migrants in this area who
were, or had been, domestic servants may well have come to
Rochdale through such recruitment channels, although it
would be impossible to give any exact figures for the
numbers involved. Once in such employment rural migrants
might be able to use other methods, such as newspaper
advertisements and registries, to get new places if they
were dismissed, or grew dissatisfied with their work.

Given the poverty of rural migrants and their ignorance of urban ways it is very unlikely that young women could have migrated over considerable distances on the off-chance of finding work in Rochdale, unless they had relatives there who had preceded them. But even then it is unlikely that the relatives of such migrants would house and feed them, unless they already had a place to work.

As is indicated in Table 83, however, the apparent coincidence between the servants' birthplaces and those of their employers appears to have declined over time and this was due to the divergence in the georgraphical areas from which these two groups were drawn. In contrast to the servant population, the heads of households which employed domestics became less of a migrant group in the period 1851 to 1871. In 1851 some 64.7 per cent of the heads in the control sample came from Rochdale, compared with 57 per cent amongst servant-employers.[19] This contrast appears to have been stronger in 1861 but had vanished by 1871.[20] (Table 84) As can be seen from Table 85, employers from Social-Economic Group 3 did not show a strong tendency to be migrants,[21] in contrast to the other social classes. The professional class tended to be migratory in 1851 and 1861,[22] but not one of the three principal servant-employing classes showed themselves to have an unusually large migrant component in 1871.[23]

The professional class appear to have been recruited, in part, from outside the industrial north in 1851 but this became less so over time. In 1851 some 77 per cent of this group had been born in either Lancashire or Yorkshire but this figure had risen to 88 per cent in 1871.[24] This tendency was the opposite of that revealed in the control samples. In the control sample of 1851 some 91.6 per cent of the household heads had been born in Lancashire and

Yorkshire but this had dropped to 85.5 per cent 20 years later.[25] The main reason for this decline of migrants in the professional claass appears to have been the reduction in the number of persons from English counties to the south of Lancashire and Yorkshire. (Table 84) This area had provided 16.7 per cent of the servant-employing households in the professional class in 1851 but only 6 per cent in 1871.[26] An important component of this decline was the absolute reduction in the number of employers in this group who were born in London or 'Middlesex'. Seven had been born in this area in 1851 but only two in 1871.

This suggests a gradual change in the social elite of the Rochdale area. In the earlier period of growth and development the social elite included a number of migrants from the south of England, who may have provided financial and professional expertise. However, they may have been gradually replaced by men from the north as the economy and society of the region matured. On the other had, since we are only dealing here with households which actually employed servants, this might represent a change in social habits. In 1851 local members of the social elite may not have employed servants, perhaps because of traditions of 'abstinence', whilst migrants had no such inhibitions. Twenty years later such local traditions may have declined and so the proportion of migrant servant employers would have declined without the composition of Rochdale's social elite having in fact changed.

This development was in complete contrast to the proportional increase in the number of long-distance migrants in the servant population. It could be argued, therefore, that there would have been a decline in the number of servants who were recruited personally by their employers and a greater need for employers, and servants, to resort to institutionalised channels of recruitment, such as servant registries. This is not necessarily so since we are assuming that servant employers who had been born in Rochdale had no links with other areas of the country. This was not the case with Edward Whitehead, as mentioned above, who certainly had contacts with rural Staffordshire. There would be every reason to suppose that a group rising in power and prestige, such as the manufacturers and professional classes of Lancashire, would be extending the contacts and friendship networks they had in the rest of the country, If there was a divergence between the birthplaces of servants and of their employers, then this might not reflect a decline in the use of personal recruitment channels but rather that employers were having to go farther afield in order to find suitable servants, and so used a different set of contacts to achieve this.

Over this 20 year period there was a marked increase in the number of newspaper advertisements for servants and the number of servant registries recorded in the newspapers, but this does not necessarily indicate a decline in the importance of personal contacts in hiring servants. We cannot be sure of the extent to which the apparent increases in these institutionalised forms of servant recruitment merely reflected movements within the Rochdale servant market from job to job, rather than means to facilitate the migration of servants into the area. Young rural servants may have gained their first jobs in the area through personal contacts and then taken advantage of other methods of job placement after they had migrated to the area. The increase in these forms of servant recruitment might merely reflect an increase in the turnover rate in servant places within the Rochdale district.

In connection with this matter it is interesting to note that the number of advertisements in the <u>Rochdale Observer</u>

and the number of registries advertising, showed a dramatic leap in the years after 1867, which could be seen as evidence of a crisis in the Rochdale servant market. This also appears to have coincided with a rise in the wages paid to servants, which might suggest a reduction in their supply. The institutionalised recruitment channels and the 'crisis' in the Rochdale servant market will be examined in the remaining sections of this chapter.

III. The Recruitment of Servants from the Rochdale Workhouse, 1851-1871

People who could not find servants through their friends, or who did not have the necessary contacts, might turn to other recruitment channels and even public institutions for help. Thus one of the most interesting sources of servants in the Rochdale district were the children and orphans of the local workhouses. Although the number of girls involved was not large, the rapidity with which many of them changed their employers, and the identity of the householders who sought them, makes a study of this subject historically revealing. The evidence presented here only pertains to the recruitment of servants from the workhouses within the Rochdale Poor Law Union and may thus underestimate this source, since many servants may have been recruited from workhouses in other areas. Many rural workhouses exported their charges to work in the towns, thus relieving the ratepayers of the cost of their upkeep and hoping to provide their charges with a 'start in life'.

In the Rochdale Poor Law Union, and presumably elsewhere, would-be employers could apply for children from the workhouse at meetings of the Workhouse Committee of the Rochdale Board of Guardians, after having selected a suitable child at the workhouse. Usually the girl was let out on a month's trial and then brought back before the Committee. At that stage the girl might be returned if the employer was not satisfied. Thus, on the 25th February, 1853 Mr Schofield of Milkstone returned such a child to the Committee, since 'in consequence of her being almost idiotic he could not keep her as a nurse....'.[27] Alternatively, if both parties appeared satisfied, the girl could remain, 'as long as they could both agree'. It was never stated what this 'agreement' amounted to, and there was certainly never any mention of the payment of wages.

Although the minutes of the Workhouse Committee give the appearance of a system of mutual agreement, it is likely that such arrangements were at the pleasure of the employer. Girls were frequently allowed to remain on this basis but soon reappear in the minutes with other employers. Girls who ran away from their employers were returned. Thus, on the 20th January, 1865 Ellen, wife of George Taylor of Haugh, appeared before the Committee with Ann Bentley, a girl she had had on a month's trial, and she was allowed to keep her 'so long as they could agree'.[28] But on the 3rd March, 'The wife of George Taylor of Haugh called and said that Elizabeth Ann Bentley had run away and the girl was produced and cautioned and was sent back again'.[29] These young girls, one of whom was four years old, could hardly have had much say in the matter of their employment.

Such a system of recruitment could degenerate into a form of temporary employment which was damaging to the child. Thus, in April 1855 Violet Marsden was allowed to go to Mr John Clarkes of Limefield, 'to assist in household work'.[30] However, by the 23rd May, Violet, who was 12 years old, was back in the workhouse and was applied for by a small-wares dealer of Yorkshire Street in Rochdale.[31] She was brought back a month later, 'in consequence of her being too young....'.[32] On the 8th February of the following year Violet was given to a joiner in Wardleworth on a month's trial,[33] but on August 8th 1856 the Joiner's wife appeared with the girl, 'and stated that she had run away and Mrs Hollingworth not appearing willing to try the girl again she was ordered to the Marland workhouse'.[34] Violet Marsden did not remain there because on the 3rd October a butcher of Yorkshire Street applied for her,[35] but on the 29th May, 1857 the relieving officer reported to the Committee that, 'Violet Marsden a girl let out by this Committee to Mr John Handley, butcher, absconded on Monday 25th last, taking with her some clothing which had but recently been granted her'.[36] She does not appear in the minutes of the Workhouse Committee again.

The Workhouse Committee was not totally uninterested in the welfare of its charges. Under the Apprentices and Servants Act of 1851, where any 'young person under the Age of Sixteen' was hired out as a servant from a workhouse 'so long as such young person shall be under the Age of Sixteen', he or she was to receive at least two visits from the relieving officer a year.[37] The relieving officer could act to protect the child, as when Elizabeth Holt, who had been working for a confectioner of Heywood, was brought back to the workhouse after the relieving officer reported that she was 'very badly treated and beaten many times a day'.[38]

Some selectivity appears to have been practised in deciding whether or not a girl should be allowed to go out to a particular employer, although there does not appear to have been much consistency. On the 27th November 1863, for example, the wife of Peregrine Pilling of Bagslate, a publican, was refused permission to employ a girl 'owing to her keeping a Beerhouse',[39] but in February 1864, John Mitchell, a publican, received Alice Holt Manley on a month's trial.[40]   Matters such as this may have depended on the changing composition of the Workhouse Committee.

The number of girls involved in the Rochdale district was fairly small, with never more than 18 girls recorded as going out to employment in any one year.   There were probably omissions, since many girls we do have information about were only recorded when they were brought back after a month's trial.   The numbers involved, shown in Table 86 reveal a considerable degree of variation from year to year, with high points in 1851, 1864 and 1870.[41]   Apart from the high level in 1851 it would appear that the number of girls so employed increased over time, and was at a higher level in the late 1860's than in the previous years. The apparent decline in the number of girls being employed in this manner in the years 1866, 1867 and 1868 appears to have been caused by the policy of the Workhouse Committee. The committee wished to restrict such employment since it was having difficulties in hiring servants for the workhouses.[42]   No doubt these young girls were required to undertake work about the workhouses and external employment was only a secondary consideration.

The number of girls in external employment was often less than the number of employers in any one year since one girls might have more than one employer in any 12 month period.   In all, 97 girls appeared only once in the records, 24 had two employers, eight had three employers, two had four employers and one had six in the period covered by the records.   The vast majority of these girls, 109 out of 140, only appeared as servants in one year but 14 appeared in two years and 16 appeared in three or more years.[43]

The ages of the girls about whom we have information ranged from four to 18 years. Most of these girls were, however, in their early teens; 70 out of 103 being aged between 10 and 14 years. At the same time, 22.3 per cent of were aged under 10 years old. Overall the average age of this group was 11.3 years, which is very low compared to the average age of servants in the Rochdale district.[44]

The employers of these young children who gave their occupations were predominantly members of Social-Economic Group 3, as can be seen from Table 87. Out of the 70 employers placed in this class, 28 were members of the retailing and dealing group, who had to be placed here because of lack of information as to the number of shop assistants they employed. This means that nearly half of all the employers whose occupations could be traced were members of the industrial manual class; factory operatives, joiners, weavers and the like.[45]

It is impossible to tell if such 'working-class' employers regarded their servants as cheap labour, or whether this represented a form of adoption. The rapidity with which many of these girls passed from employer to employer suggests that the former was true in many cases. This reveals a certain contradiction in the attitudes of members of the working classes to the workhouse; for some it was a hateful instrument of oppression but others regarded it as a useful source of household labour. There was plainly more than one proletarian reaction to the characteristic institutions of Victorian England.

IV. The Rochdale Press and the Recruitment of Servants

Although the history of advertising for labour in the press goes back to the seventeenth century,[46] there appears to have been a great increase in this form of servant recruitment in the nineteenth century. Thus, on 3rd January 1832, The Times carried advertisements in which places were offered to, or sought by, 19 servants in seven different categories. Thirty-eight years later, in the issue of The Times of 10th January 1870, there were 177 offers of places, or requests for employment, in 33 separate categories of servant employment.[47] This indicates a prodigious increase in this form of servant recruitment, although we cannot be sure of the extent to which this represented a means of attracting migrants to areas of servant employment, or whether it indicates movements within the job market of a particular area.

In the period 1851 to 1871 there was a considerable expansion of newspaper activity within the Rochdale district, ranging from the brief career of the Rachde Kronikul un Workin Man's Lantrun in the winter of 1852-3, to the founding of the Rochdale Times in December 1871. Over this period there were no fewer than 10 newspapers produced within the district, although only four of these continued in publication for over a year. Only one newspaper, the Rochdale Observer, was printed continually, from its founding in February 1856, throughout the period. Its main rival, the tory Rochdale Pilot, had a chequered history, being founded in March 1983, running through until 1867, and appearing intermittently afterwards.[48] Only the Rochdale Observer, therefore, gives us an uninterrupted picture of the development of newspaper advertising within the Rochdale district. The other newspapers, of which few copies remain, carried similar advertisements, although the

189

continuity of the _Observer_ enabled it to attract most business.

The number of advertisements placed in the _Rochdale Observer_, either by would-be employers asking for servants, or by servants looking for places, can be seen in Table 88. There was obviously a considerable increase in the use that was made of this newspaper by servant and servant-employers. The increase in the number of advertisements placed followed a three-year cycle starting in 1859 but excluding 1862, the year of the Cotton Famine. The years 1859, 1865, 1868 and 1871 all saw a sudden jump in the number of 'Wanted' notices being placed. It is difficult to say if this represented a cycle within the Rochdale employment market. Alternatively, this might reflect the trade-cycle, with depressed figures in boom years when other employment opportunities were good.

There are other patterns in these figures which are equally difficult to interpret. The number of times that an employer had to advertise for a particular servant varied over time. In 1864, for example, the average advertisement for a servant was placed in the newspaper twice, whilst in 1871 it only had to be placed once. This would appear to indicate that it took longer to get servants by this method at some dates than at others, especially in the periods 1858 to 1860, and 1863 to 1867. In the other periods it was only necessary to advertise once on average. These periods of increased difficulty in recruitment may reflect restrictions on the supply of servants, or ease of recruitment in certain years may reflect the willingness of servants to change their jobs when such restrictions of supply placed them in a 'seller's market'.

The servants sought by employers, and those advertising for jobs were not 'typical' of those employed in the

Rochdale area, as can be seen from the figures in Table 89. In comparative terms, servant employers were advertising for relatively few general servants. They tended to be more interested in hiring nurses and men who would be useful as coachmen and gardeners. Similarly, of the servants who advertised for places in the period, very few described themselves as general servants, and there was an excess in the number of housekeepers, nurses and men seeking work in the garden or coachhouse. This suggests that the 'Wanted' columns of the Rochdale Observer tended to be used to hire, or sell, the more specialised domestic services, which might be difficult to obtain by other methods.

Of the advertisements offering positions, 51.8 per cent gave an address at which prospective servants were to call, 40 per cent advised would-be applicants to apply to the office of the newspaper or the printers, 6.4 per cent gave a post office box as a means of contact, and 10 notices gave the addresses of shops at which further enquiries could be made. This indicates that large numbers of the people who used the press as a means of recruitment were wary of revealing their true identities in the newspaper, presumably because they wished to be able to vet applicants before they came to their homes.

Some of these employers may have lived outside the region, or deep in the countryside, and so used the shops they frequented as convenient places to meet servants but many others must have been unhappy at the prospect of 'servants of indifferent characters' coming to their houses. Although an increasing number of employers were thus using the Observer to recruit servants, many of them must still have felt unhappy at the prospect of recruiting servants in such an open manner.

The wording of the advertisements over this period

indicates some of the problems of recruiting servants, and the criteria by which servants were to be chosen. In general the conditions of employment were only vaguely described, the wages paid being seldom mentioned. There was no strict definition of the post being offered, although a position for 'an active girl for housework' obviously referred to a general servant. However, it was not unusual for definite positions to be quoted followed by an indication that suitable applicants were to 'make themselves generally useful'. Employers gave very little away in their notices, no doubt wary of having their hands tied when it came to bargaining over pay and conditions with their employees.

What was most frequently mentioned was the type of household in which the servant was expected to work. The exact position of the dwelling place, whether in the town or in the country, was sometimes given, and occasionally the type of business carried on there. Allusions were often made to the size of the household, especially to it being a 'small household', and occasionally even the number of persons resident was given. On other occasions a reduction of the workload in a post would be indicated by a reference to the presence of other servants, as in the following, 'Wanted. A Cook and a Housemaid where a man-servant is kept'.[49] Information such as this, designed to attract servants, or particular types of servants, indicates the extent to which workload and possible duties were important considerations for servants. Service was not merely a question of status fulfilment, it was also a physically exacting occupation, especially if the ratio of household members to servants was high.

Nationality was often an important factor mentioned in the advertisements, either by a stated preference for 'English' servants, or by the bald statement that 'No Irish

192

need apply'. This type of discrimination may have reflected a desire by employers to acquire servants of a particular religious background, and to exclude the employment of Roman Catholics, although it might also have been a simple reaction to the widely-spread belief in national stereotypes. This would have been especially true in cases where the servant would be in charge of young children and would be responsible for many of their early ideas about religion. There was certainly one case where a nurse was required and had to be an 'English Protestant'.[50]

As was indicated above (Chapter 7, Section I) these advertisements expressed a preference for women from the rural areas of the country, and there were other indications that servant employers wished to employ inexperienced or isolated women who might be more easily disciplined. As was mentioned before, one advertisement for a 'Girl for housework' sought a girl with no relatives, and stated 'an orphan preferred'.[51] Yet another advertised for a nurse and added, 'One that has not been out before preferred'.[52] These requirements, which were only occasionally voiced, may have been in the minds of other employers, who nevertheless omitted them for fear of reducing the number of women who might apply.

This examination of newspaper advertising in the Rochdale Observer indicates the increasing importance of this form of recruitment in the Rochdale area. However, we cannot tell if this growth indicates an increased turnover in the servant market, an increasing problem of supply, or a movement away from the use of personal contacts. It is perhaps unlikely that the advertisements in this newspaper could have attracted long-distance migrants from outiside the area of circulation. Such advertisements must have been of most importance for the movement of servants within the Rochdale district.

V. Servant Registries in Rochdale, 1856-1871

This section presents an examination of servant registries derived from an examination of advertisements by these businesses in the Rochdale Observer in the period 1856 to 1871.[53] This is only a partial study since it concentrates on those businesses which actually advertised their services. It might be expected, however, that commercial enterprises such as servant registries, which depended on public knowledge of their services, readily availed themselves of the opportunity of advertising in the newspapers of the area. Figures showing the number of registries advertising, and the frequency with which they did so, may reflect changes in the advertising practices of these agencies but must also give some indication of the number of registries and the amount of activity in them. Much of the information gleaned from these advertisements, with regard to the origins and spatial distributions of the registries, is of use and is not distorted by the problems outlined above.

In Table 90 the number of registries advertising their services in the Rochdale Observer and the frequency of their notices, are given for each year between 1856 and 1871. Assuming that all registries actually advertised in the press, these statistics indicate a generally stable number of one or two registries throughout the period from 1856 to 1868, and a prodigious growth, both in advertising and numbers, in the years 1869, 1870 and 1871. These figures are comparable with those for individual newspaper advertisements. The latter show that in the period 1858 to

1860 the number of times that individuals advertised for servants rose, as did the number of times that the registries were advertising. In the period 1863 to 1867 the average number of times that individual newspaper advertisements were placed rose again, and the figures for the number of times that the registries were advertising also show some high levels, although there were also years of comparatively low rates. However, in the last years of the period, the number of times that individuals advertised in the Rochdale Observer fell very markedly, whilst servant registries were placing increasing numbers of advertisements.

It is difficult to interpret these figures since we do not have sufficient information about the workings of these recruitment chanels to tell if high levels of newspaper activity represented a high turnover of servants or general restrictions in supply. However, the prodigious increase in the number, and apparent activity, of servant registries at the end of the period would suggest that the number of persons looking for work, or seeking servants, had greatly increased. The general increase in wage rates in this area, and in the country as a whole, at this time, coupled with the relative national decline of the servant population after 1871, would indicate a short supply of servants which might encourage domestics to seek better positions in different households. An increase in the turnover within the servant market of Rochdale would increase the potential business of servant registries, and so increase the number of businesses entering the market. Thus, of the seven registries advertising in the Rochdale Observer in 1869, five had never done so before.

The advertisements placed in the Rochdale Observer were of three types. Occasionally a registry simply advertised its services, as in an advertisement of 30th November 1861

195

stating, 'Ladies supplied with respectable servants at Mrs Barker's Registry Office'.[54] More usually the registries placed advertisements on behalf of servants seeking places, carefully pointing out that they were 'disengaged'. Most frequently of all, the registries placed notices asking for servants to come to them, presumably for jobs they had on their books, as when an advertisement of 7th January, 1871 stated, 'Wanted. Plain cooks, General servants, Housemaids and Nurses. Apply Mrs Asquith, 44 Mill Street, Freeholdings'.[55]

The advertisements give the impression that the registries were not institutions for placing migrants from the countryside in their first jobs; they appeared to deal with vacancies within the Rochdale region, rather than facilitating long-range migration. The advertisements often quoted the number of servants required, '2 Cooks, Housemaids, young girls, and 15 General servants',[56] which gives the impression of recruitment for actual vacant positions. Most of these registries seldom advertised for more than one year and appear to have been short-term ventures. It is therefore unlikely that they could provide facilities for housing and maintaining young migrants from the countryside seeking their first posts. This class of servant must have gained their first jobs in the area by other means. These agencies would be much more likely to act as clearing houses for vacant jobs, and for servants out of places, or seeking a change of employer.

The origins of these registries can be gauged from the wording of many of the advertisements in the Rochdale Observer. Of the 26 registries, defined by a separate address, only four were not headed by a woman with the prefix 'Mrs'. One was simply referred to an 'Vernon's & Co.', another was headed by two 'Misses' and the other two only gave an address at which servants should call. It would seem, therefore, that these businesses were being run either by married women or, more probably, by widows who were attempting to support themselves. Such registries were normally situated in high-class areas. This may merely have been to be close to potential customers but it might also reflect an attempt by the widows of high social class to support themselves on the death of their husbands. Such a woman, perhaps a servant employer herself, and with contacts amongst other servant-employing families, might find this a suitable, and profitable, means of support.

If the evidence from the Rochdale Observer can be trusted, it would appear that many of these registries were short-run affairs. This would fit in with the picture of 'amateur' commericial enterprises entered into by people with little commercial experience or capital. Thus, out of 20 individual registries advertising in the press in the period 1856 to 1870, nine only advertised in one year and then disappeared and seven of the remainder only advertised in two years. This is not a very reliable test since one registry which advertised in 1862 did not insert another notice till 1868, although this might indicate the refounding of an enterprise. However, it is interesting that of the 16 registries advertising in the Rochdale Observer in the comparatively hectic period of 1869 to 1871, only two had previously advertised in the press. This would not suggest the domination of the market by large, well-established concerns.

There is evidence, however, that some of these busi-nesses were established on a larger scale than the parlour of a respectable widow. Some women may have operated from more than one base at the same time. One Mrs Taylor was operating a registry from 42 Drake Street in 1869; another Mrs Taylor was operating in Manchester Road in 1871 and in the same year yet another Mrs Taylor was resident at 14 Penn Street. These may have been three separate women, or one business rapidly moving its place of operation, or it might have represented one concern with more than one base of operation. At least one building, 37 Toad Lane, was used by two registries, Mrs Handy taking over from Mrs Greenwood in 1870. This indicates that at least one address was a recognised place of business. Also, in the years 1870 and 1871, two registries, that of Mrs Sumner and that of Mrs Barker, were operating from the same address, 16 East Street, which indicates that this was more than a private address.

Other information in the advertisements suggests that some of these agencies developed from retailing businesses. In the newspaper advertisements would-be employers sometimes left their addresses with grocers, perhaps those with which they habitually traded, and this may have been the basis of the activities of the registries in the Rochdale area. Some registries still retained their retailing functions, as when Mrs Greenwood advertised herself as a 'Confectioner and Registrar for Respectable Servants, 37 Toad Lane'.[57] When a Mrs Handy began to operate from this same address in 1870 she still described herself as a 'confectioner',[58] implying that she had taken over both branches of the business. The registry run by Mrs Redman, which advertised in the Rochdale Observer in 1864, had even closer links with household work since it was described as a 'Baby Linen Establishment and Family Register Office'.[59] For an enterprising shopkeeper it would be only a small step from selling baby linen to expectant mothers to putting them in touch with potential nursemaids, and this might lead eventually to acting as a recruitment agency for all types of servant.

On the basis of this source we cannot go much further in

our description of the workings of these employment agencies. We cannot say directly that a rise in the number of advertisements placed represented a rise in commercial activity, although the sudden expansion of such notices in the years from 1869 to 1871 would strongly suggest an increase in competition within the area. The nature of these businesses and their essentially limited scope would not suggest that they were channels of long-range servant migration but must have facilitated movement between jobs within the Rochdale servant market.

VI. The Channels of Servant Recruitment and the Rochdale Servant Market, 1851-1871

In the first section of this chapter it was claimed that hundreds of servants within the Rochdale district would be moving their place of employment every year. Over time there would also be an increase in the number of servants who migrated into the area from distant 'agricultural' counties, and that this would represent a considerable component of the total female migration into the district. A question which has continually arisen is the extent to which the means used to recruit servants from within the existing pool of household labour in the Rochdale area were the same as those used to recruit servants into the district from other parts of the country. This problem becomes more pressing once we note the manner in which servant employers became less of a migrant group over time. It is difficult to judge to what extent this affected the links which such employers had with other parts of the United Kingdom.

An examination of the advertisements in the Rochdale Observer in this period, including those placed by servant registries, does not give the impression that such 'institutionalised' methods of servant recruitment could have facilitated the migration of servants into the district from other counties. If contact had not already been made between a servant and her employer it is unlikely that registries could have supported servants whilst they found places. It might have been possible that would-be employers, or registries acting for such persons, placed advertisements in newspapers in other parts of the country in order to attract rural migrants but the type of organisations involved do not appear to have been sufficiently large or well-established to do so, although this might not be so in other parts of the country. Probably rural migrants would have found their way to Rochdale through personal contacts which their employers had in their place of birth. However, after this initial entrance into the servant market these women might have availed themselves of other channels of servant recruitment if they wished to change their place of employment.

At the same time, however, the number of migrants entering the district might directly affect the servant market in Rochdale. A relative decline in the number of women willing to be servants in the area would encourage existing servants to attempt to improve their conditions of work by moving their place of employment. The creation of a 'seller's market' for servants would encourage domestics to seek new positions, the method by which such women could increase the value of their remuneration. Such a change of place might not entail a higher rate of pay for equivalent services. It might involve a change of occupation, a rise from under to upper housemaid or, alternatively, a move to a smaller household where the work-load would be less.

There is evidence on the national and local level to suggest that such a 'crisis' did take place in the servant employment market in the late 1860's and 1870's. The first signs of such a restriction in the relative supply of servants were found in the minutes of the Workhouse Committee of the Rochdale Board of Guardians in 1866. In April of that year the wife of Richard Diggle, a joiner and builder of Blue Pits, was refused permission to take a 13 year old girl from the workhouse since, 'the Guardians cannot allow any girls to go out to service until the workhouses are better supplied with servants'.[60] Table 86 shows that the number of girls going out of the workhouse to be servants declined markedly in 1866 and 1867 and this appears to reflect the problem of getting women to work as servants.

This led the Guardians to increase the wages paid to servants in the workhouse in order to attract labour. In the period 1859 to 1866 the annual wages paid to servants in the Rochdale Workhouse had never risen above £7 16s 0d,[61] which appears to have been the standard rate. In August 1866, however, one Esther Hardman was hired at a wage of £12 per annum, an increase of 54 per cent on the previous highest wage paid.[62] By 1873 the Guardians were paying wages of £16 to some of their servant,[63] and this had risen to £20 by 1879.[64] Much the same happened in the County Lunatic Asylum at Prestwich. In this establishment the annual wages paid to housemaids in the period 1851 to 1867 had never risen above £12 10s 0d, and in most years wages paid varied between £7 for young girls and £11 11s 0d for older women.[65] In the years 1865, 1866 and 1867 housemaids at Prestwich were paid £10 per annum,[66] but in 1868 this rose to £14, and to £17 in 1876.[67] This would suggest a general rise in servant wages in this period after more than a decade of little change.

This appears to have been a national phenomenon, as can be seen from an examination of the figures contained in Table 91. The indices of the wages of private domestic servants rose from 59 in the period 1843-7, to 63 in the period 1863-7, an increase of 4 points. In the same period the wage indices of women in industrial occupations rose by 16 points. In the following twenty years, however, from the period 1863-7 to the period 1883-7, the indices of servant wages rose by 25 points, compared with an increase of 19 points amongst females industrial workers.

This rise in wage rates was directly related to the beginning of the relative decline in the servant population. According to figures presented by W.A. Armstrong, the domestic service sector of the economy of England and Wales (defined here as the number of indoor domestic servants, coachman, grooms and gardeners) grew as a percentage of the total population, and of the occupied population, in the period 1851 to 1871 and declined thereafter.[68] These figures, some of which are reproduced in Table 92, suggest that in relative terms the servant population of England and Wales began to decline at approximately the same date as the servant 'crisis' in the Rochdale area. This decline, or rather the failure of the servant population to increase at the same rate as the rest of the population, is evidence of a reduction in the potential supply of servants, resulting in the rise of the wage rates in the industry.

If this was happening in Rochdale at this date then it would explain the apparent increase in the activities of servant registries in the area in the period 1869 to 1871. Employers were less able to employ servants and were willing to pay higher wages. This may have increased the fluidity of the labour market and encouraged a higher

202

turnover of servant positions. Within the Rochdale area this may well have been linked with the decline of migration into the district which occurred at this period. As we have seen above (Chapter 5, Section VI), migrants were becoming an increasingly important component of the Rochdale servant population in the period between 1851 and 1871. Such women would have been part of that large influx of migrants which kept the decennial increase in population in the Rochdale district above 15 per cent throughout the period from 1801 to 1871. As can be seen from Table 2, the average decennial increase in population in the Rochdale district over this period was in fact 22.5 per cent. However, in the period 1871 to 1881 Rochdale's population only grew by 7.7 per cent, which was half the previous lowest rate of increase in the century. In later decades the decennial increase was even less. We cannot assume that there had been a prodigious increase in the death rate, and although there probably was an expansion in the use of methods to control conception much of this decline must have been due to a reduction in the rate of migration into the area. Such a decline, if it affected the supply of servants in the area, might have produced the type of 'crisis' in the servant employment market which we have been discussing here. If such a 'crisis' affected other local servant markets, and there is some evidence that this was so, we would be able to trace the decline of the domestic servant population in late Victorian and Edwardian England, in part, to a relative decline in migration from the countryside to the towns.

In this chapter we have dealt with the differing forms of servant recruitment separately in order to examine the structure of the servant recruitment market as a whole. Individual servants, however, would have experienced more than one of these placement channels in their careers. The author's mother, who was a servant in Ulster in the period from 1934 to 1940, experienced several forms of servant recruitment in the four places which she had in seven years. Her first job, at the age of 14 was at the local manor house, a position she obtained through the good offices of the local vicar. She heard of her second job through her brother-in-law, who was the milkman who served the house of her next employer. She later acquired a position in a rectory by applying at an agency and only moved from there when a friend, who worked at the house of a local manufacturer as a charwoman, managed to obtain a position for her.[69] She therefore passed through most of the recruitment channels we have been discussing here and, as in the nineteenth century, personal links were still of paramount importance.

10. DOMESTIC SERVICE IN NINETEENTH CENTURY ROCHDALE: SOME IMPLICATIONS FOR CONTEMPORARY HISTORICAL RESEARCH

I. A Spacial Perspective for Writing the History of Domestic Service in the Nineteenth Century

Domestic service in the nineteenth century is currently receiving a great deal of attention from historians and sociologists after a period of almost total neglect. Pioneering works on the subject, such as Theresa McBride's The Domestic Revolution,[1] and The Rise and Fall of the Victorian Servant by Pamela Horn,[2] have examined the servant population of the whole country. In doing so they have drawn on the national census reports, contemporary manuals of domestic economy and the reminiscences of servants and their employers, with little attempt to provide a link between the aggregate and the particular. Thus, changes in the size of the total servant population have been noted from the published census reports, and the means by which servants were recruited have been reconstructed from personal recollections and household manuals. Little attempt has been made, however, to show the effects of changes in the supply of servants on the turnover of servants and the channels of recruitment. It has been possible to look at service from the point of view of individuals, and as a macro-economic structure, but it has not been possible to see how changes in the national servant population have reflected changes within differing households and within differing geographical areas.

This tendency to omit a consideration of local or regional factors, and to concentrate on the individual household and the national servant population, is understandable when attempting to examine relationships within households on a national scale. Students of domestic servants have had to deal with individual households as their unit of anlysis but have often attempted to see service as a national phenomenon. This has meant that the social context of servant employment has been obscured. Thus, householders who have left us records of their employment of servants have tended to be members of the upper and middle classes, so the rise in the number of servants in the national census figures has been interpreted as evidence of a rise in the relative wealth of the members of these groups.[3] Until recently there has been little attempt to see to what extent servant employers were actually from these classes, or indeed who was the 'typical' employer.

Questions such as these can only be answered on the national level by sampling all servant-employing households in England and Wales, a formidable task. However, some preliminary conclusions can be reached by sampling local servant-employing populations. By comparing local servant populations, as Ebery and Preston have done in their recent work,[4] we can examine regional differences which would be obscured in the national aggregates. Local studies, such as that attempted here, by limiting the total number of households involved in the analysis, allow us to link changes in the local servant population with actual conditions in individual households and with the actual social, economic and institutional structure of the region. Since our aggregate statistics are based upon an examination of individual households we have a direct link between these two conceptual levels and we are able to examine local institutions and employment patterns which would have affected these actual units of analysis. Such local studies will enable us to see domestic service as a concrete social and economic relationship.

Although by definition such local studies must be restricted in their geographical scope, it is hoped that by revealing the social and economic context of service, and servant employment, they will raise questions concerning previously held assumptions on the subject. Such insights into the actual social relationships underlying national aggregates must help us to understand change more fully. Such social processes as are posited must remain conjectural, however, whilst the analysis is restricted to only one geographical area.

II. The Problem of Sources in Modern Studies of Service in the Nineteenth Century

An examination of domestic service in a local context raises doubts about the use of particular sources in other studies on the subject. The use of sources drawn from individual households, such as letters and diaries, or the reminiscences of individuals, have been used without an attempt to discover if these households or individuals were 'typical' of the servant, or the servant-employing, class. Similarly, literary sources, such as household manuals, have been used to describe actual social practices, although they may merely have represented ideals which could seldom be achieved. Perhaps most serious of all, figures drawn from the national census publications have been used to calculate the relative size of the servant and servant-employing populations, without a consideration of the ambiguities contained in the published reports, or of the differing interpretations which can be placed on the patterns revealed.

Since many students of domestic service on the national level have been unable to study, in detail, the structure of households which contained servants, there has been a tendency to quote sources from households which were far from typical. Account books, letters, diaries and autobiographies concerning the households and lives of members of the landed aristocracy and 'upper-middle classes' have survived in large numbers and have been used to reconstruct the relationships which existed between servant and master. It is probable, however, that such servant employers were far from typical.

Thus, in the work of Pamela Horn, of the servant employers mentioned whose social standing may be inferred from their title or occupation, no less than 46.8 per cent were members of the titled aristocracy.[5] Similarly, of the 22 employers mentioned in the servant autobiographies collected by John Burnett, and published in his work Useful Toil, 45.5 per cent were also members of the titled aristocracy.[6] A more detailed breakdown of the occupations of the employers mentioned in these two works is shown in Table 93. This reveals a very different population than that found in Rochdale in the mid-nineteenth century. (Table 58) Rochdale contained no servant employers who were members of the titled aristocracy, far fewer members of the professional class, and far more employers from the world of commerce and retailing and from the manual/artisan class.

It is probable that Rochdale was not unusual in this matter. Thus, David Chaplin, taking a 1 per cent cluster sample of the London Metropolitan area in 1851, discovered that out of 858 servant-employing households, in which the head's occupation appeared at least five times, members of the professions accounted for only some 11.2 per cent of servant employers, whilst those occupied in commerce or retailing represented 34.6 per cent of the sample, and those who appear to have been occupied in artisan work accounted for 23.1 per cent. Those describing themselves as 'Gentleperson' accounted for only 1.7 per cent of the entire sample.[7]

The tendency to reconstruct the work of the domestic servant from accounts and sources left by aristocratic households has led to the popular belief that servants lived in a world dominated by the internal politics of large servant retinues, formal dinner parties and the comings and goings of London and County Society. This was very far from the reality of nineteenth-century Rochdale, and even of metropoliatan London where the employers of servants were more 'typically' members of the commercial and retailing classes. Chaplin discovered that in 1851, out of the 1,190 households in his sample which contained servants, 55.7 per cent contained only one.[8] This was not very different from the situation in the district of Rochdale, in which 60.8 per cent of the servant-employing households in the 1851 sample only employed a single domestic. This indicates distortions introduced by relying too heavily on sources which may be biased towards particular social classes.

Much the same can be said about the use made of domestic manuals, such as Mrs Beeton's famous Household Management, in the historiography of this subject. As was mentioned above , such manuals were obviously aimed at a far higher social class than the 'typical' servant employer in Rochdale, or in the country as a whole. Patricia Branca has shown conclusively that the 'normal' middle-class servant retinue, comprising a cook, parlourmaid and nursemaid, would have been out of the reach of most members of the middle classes'.[9] According to Patrick Colquhoun's Treatise on Indigence, published in 1803, the middle-class family can be defined as a household earning more than £100 per annum. On this basis only 20 per cent of the whole class earned over £300.[10] Similarly, R. D. Baxter, in his 'National Income' of 1868, calculated that of those families earning £100 or over, only about 20 per cent had incomes of over £300 per annum.[11] A 'normal' middle-class household, such as that mentioned above would have spent £56 annually on the wages of servants, or between 20 per cent and 50 per cent of the annual income of the majority of middle-class households, earning between £100 and £300 a year. This does not take account of the considerable cost of board and lodging for the servants.[12] In reality servant-employing households spent a far smaller proportion of their total annual income on domestics, as can be seen from Table 60.

A more 'typical' middle-class household would have been that described by Mrs Warren in her book How I Managed My House on Two Hundred Pounds a Year, full of the agonies of making ends meet, stringent economies and infant mortality.[13] The domestic manuals, containing advice on how to organise the summer ball, or the maintenance of the wine cellar, or the duties of the butler, did not reflect the running of most middle-class households. Such works as Mrs Beeton's Household Management were probably bought for the recipies they contained, or as wedding presents. They did not represent how most middle-class families lived, although they may have represented ideals to which house-wives could aspire.

Perhaps the most important historical source which has been used in writing the history of domestic service in the nineteenth-century has been the statistics and tables con-tained in the published census reports. Indeed such has been the use to which this source has been put, in certain works on the subject, that one might assume that domestic service was a purely nineteenth-century phenomenon. One book has been explicitly called The Rise and Fall of the Victorian Servant.[14] The servant had existed since the Middle Ages, and Gregory King certainly regarded servants as representing 10.5 per cent of the population of seventeenth century England.[15] 'Service' in this sense included agricultural and industrial workers who lived with their employers but we must recognise that the domestic servant population of Victorian England and Wales was merely the remains of an institutional relationship between master and servant which had once been far more important. If, as we have suggested in Chapter 6, Section VII, servants working in the households of retailers were actually taking part in the commercial labour of the household, then the traditional 'servant', in the sense of a living-in employee active in commercial work, still existed in Victorian England.

It has long been recognised that there is a distinctive pattern within this data in the period after 1851. This involves a relative rise in the size of the servant population, followed by a period of relative decline which has continued to the present day. However, the dating of this 'Rise and Fall' of the Victorian servant has often been inaccurate, due to a failure to recognise the differing methods of compilation in the census reports. According to Deane and Cole the number of persons shown in the official census publications as being employed in the Domestic and Personal Sector of the British economy, rose from 13.0 per cent of the total labour force in 1851 to 15.8 per cent of the total British labour force in 1891, and declined steadily thereafter.[16] Theresa McBride has used these figures to claim that, 'The total number of servants (both male and female) in England and Wales increased from

908,138 in 1851 to 1,549,502 in 1891, and then began to decline only in percentage terms'.[17]

According to W. A. Armstrong, however, the apparent rise in the relative size of the servant population in the decade between 1881 and 1891 was caused, 'by a perverse decision to include with domestics all those female relatives and daughters returned as 'helping at home', 'housework', etc.'.[18] He suggests that one must use Booth's system of occupational groupings to reconstruct, from the census records, the true number of persons employed in domestic service.[19] Using this 'Booth-Armstrong' allocation scheme, Ebery and Preston have calculated the percentage of occupied men and women employed in domestic service in the decades from 1851 to 1951. Their figures show that the Domestic Service Sector of the economy of England and Wales employed 40.4 per cent of all occupied women in 1851, a figure which rose steadily to 46.4 per cent in 1871, and then declined gradually after this date to 37.7 per cent by 1911.[20]

The 'Domestic Service Sector' in these calculations included persons employed by clubs and hotels, as well as charwomen, porters and laundry workers, but their figures are still very suggestive. If we take the tables produced by Armstrong in E. A. Wrigley's Nineteenth Century Society,[21] and sum the numbers of those men and women who in Booth's scheme were employed as indoor domestic servants, coachmen, grooms and gardeners, we can produce figures for the total number of private domestic servants in England and Wales, in the period 1851 to 1891. These totals are reproduced in Table 92, with calculations of the percentage of the total population and occupied population which they represented. The total number of servants continued to increase in the period 1851 to 1891, but at a decreasing rate after 1871, and this latter date represents the relative peak of the servant population as a percentage of the total and occupied populations.

This dating of the relative peak of the servant population in England and Wales is substantiated by work carried out by Jill Franklin on the planning of English country houses. According to her, in the early Victorian period the servant wing of country house,

> was planned with immense elaboration but after 1870 it began gradually to shrink. By 1900 it was rare to find one as large and lavish as in the 1840's, even in the grandest new houses.[22]

Part of this decline she explains by the decrease in the number of servants employed.

> Many hereditary landowners in their great mansions needed to cut expenditure in the face of falling rents, thus expressing the decline of landed power. Owners of new houses had them planned on more labour saving lines partly because of their awareness of the Servant Question (by which they meant the decline in the numbers and quality of new entrants), and partly because there was less social cachet to be had than formerly from an outsized establishment.[23]

Statistical arguments, such as that of Armstrong, still assume, however, that the official census reports differentiated between relatives working at home and servants who were related to their employers by the cash nexus alone. As we have seen in Chapter 4, in Rochdale in the mid-nineteenth century many men and women who were probably working in the homes of their relatives were incorporated into the official census publications as 'housekeepers', 'nurses', 'servants', and so on. There are signs that this was also happening in other northern cities. If this is the case, and if such mis-classifications were extensive enough, this might invalidate any attempt to reconstruct the relative size of the servant population from the evidence of the official census publications alone.

If the inaccuracies in the census reports were of the same magnitude over time, it would still be possible to argue that the figures they contain represent a true picture of general trends in such employment, even if they fail to provide accurate totals for the numbers so employed. In the absence of any examination of census schedules on the national level this might be accepted as a working hypothesis. However, it is perhaps disturbing that some of the most suspect servant categories, such as 'housekeepers', show rather large fluctuations over time, Thus, 'housekeepers' accounted for approximately 6.1 per cent of all domestic servants in the census reports of 1851 and 1861, but no less than 12.7 per cent of the same group in 1871.[24]

The official census reports, Franklin's work on the size of servant wings in country houses and the evidence of a 'crisis' in the Rochdale servant market in the late 1860's (Chapter 9, Section VI), which appears to have been reflected in servant wage rates across the country, all point in the same direction. On this evidence we can tetatively conclude that the servant population of England and Wales reached its greatest extent, as a proportion of the entire population, in the late 1860's and early 1870's and declined thereafter. Since the occupational breakdowns in the census reports prior to 1851 are suspect, we could

214

conclude that domestic servants were becoming relatively more numerous in only two decades of the nineteenth century, between the years 1851 and 1871. On this evidence it is even possible to argue that domestic service was on the decline throughout the nineteenth century, with a comparatively brief expansion at the mid-century, and that the extinction of the servant class in the twentieth century was only the culmination of a process which had been going on for at least a hundred years. Such a conclusion may be incorrect but is a useful corrective to the general assumption that the domestic servant was a peculiarly Victorian character.

III. Domestic Servants as an Indication of 'Middle-Class' Status

Many historians and sociologists have examined the census statistics relating to the size of the national and local servant populations in order to use such figures as a proxy for the size and wealth of the 'middle classes' in their area of study. By doing so they are merely following the example set by the authors of the 1901 census report, who coined the phrase 'standard of comfort', this being the number of domestic servants per hundred separate occupiers or families, excluding hotels.[25] Domestics have been used to calculate the wealth of the 'middle classes' and the 'rich' on the national level, as well as to measure the social status of areas within local studies. Harold Perkin, for example, claims that,

The number of servant increased faster than the

population, from 600,000 in 1801 to 1,300,000 in 1851 (and to two million in 1881) - a clear indication that the rich could afford to buy more of the labour of the poor, and so of the widening gap in income distribution.[26]

Similarly, in Class and Religion in the late Victorian City, Hugh McLeod uses the number of female indoor domestic servants per 100 familes, as well as the percentage of the population counted in tenements of eight or more rooms, as a definition of the social character of the 28 metropolitan boroughs and 23 outer districts of London.[27]
It may be perfectly legitimate to use the number of domestic servants in this manner but the evidence for the Rochdale district would suggest caution in this matter. As we have mentioned above, the published census reports cannot be regarded as completely reliable sources for the actual number of resident domestic indoor servants, both nationally and locally. Certainly the censuses before 1851 are not reliable indicators of such numbers, since the occupational categories given were so vaguely defined.[28] A critical examination of the census reports after this date indicates that the number of servants increased faster then the population in only two decades, the 1850's and 1860's. As such, the rise in the number of servants at this period might not indicate a widening gap in income distribution but merely the effect of temporarily static wage rates for servants in these years, probably the result of an increased influx of rural migrants. This might indicate a change in supply within the servant market, rather than a shift in income distribution towards the 'rich'.
Nor can one use the rising number of domestic servants as an indication of the expansion in the number of servant-

employing families. An examination of Table 59 shows that the average number of servants that each household employed in the Rochdale district increased over time. This means that the rise in the number of servants might not necessarily indicate a rise in the numbers of servant employers but rather the ability of servant-employers to hire more servants in a period when wage rates were static and thus in decline compared with the general trend of all incomes.

The ambiguities found in the census reports on the national level are repeated within local districts, which may reduce the accuracy of servant numbers as an indication of changes in local social structure, or as a means of measuring the social status of a particular area. The published census reports indicate that the number of servants aged 20 years or over in the Rochdale Registration District rose from 1,425 in 1851 to 2,292 in 1871,[29] representing a slight rise from 1.96 per cent of the district's total population to 2.09 per cent. However, the household samples show that the actual number of 'true servants' in this age group only rose from 828 in 1851 to 1,136 in 1871, representing an actual decline from 1.14 per cent of the entire population to 1.03 per cent At the same time, the number of households containing such servants in the Rochdale district declined from 6.0 per cent of all households to 4.9 per cent. The published census figures would appear to indicate that the servant class, and by inference the class that employed them, actually increased its size relative to the rest of the population of the district, whilst an examination of the census schedules indicates that the opposite was in fact the case.

It would also appear from the evidence of Rochdale, and of other areas, that it is doubtful if servants can be used to indicate 'middle-class' status. J. F. C. Harrison, amongst others, has claimed that servant employment 'played

217

an essential part in defining' the middle classes.[30]   Such
claims ignore the fact that many servant employers appear
to have been artisans and manual workers, both in Rochdale
and probably in London as well. The most 'typical' servant
employers were not members of the professions, manufacturers, nor large-scale proprietors, but members of the
retailing and commercial classes, many of them little
removed from their working-class origins. If we thus
extend the term 'middle class' to members of the 'petite-
bourgeoisie' and the 'aristocracy of labour', we may be
consistent in our approach, but we would also be fundamen-
tally altering our conception of the class relations of the
period.

It could be argued that servant employment was not
'typical' of these working-class groups but it is also
plain from an examination of Table 59 that in 1871 the
majority of all social classes may not have employed
servants. Foster, in his study of the bourgeoisie of
Oldham, certainly found examples of large-scale manufacturers who employed no servants at all and relied upon their
daughters to perform household work.[31] This was also the
case in the Rochdale district. In 1871, for example,
William Clegg, a widowed flannel manufacturer employing 80
hands, lived with his two sons and his step-daughter, the
latter being the 'housekeeper' of the family.[32] At the
same date John Wilson, 'Surveyor and Architect' lived in
Co-operative Street with his two young children and his
sister-in-law, who was also described as a 'housekeeper'.[33]
Similarly, in 1861 Henry Crosskill, his wife, and their
family of two daughters and three sons, lived in Yorkshire
Street. Crosskill was a 'Bookseller, Printer and Sta-
tioner', employing seven men and three boys but he had no
servants except his eldest daughter, Elizabeth, who was

218

described as a 'housemaid'.[34] Such individuals were
undoubtedly members of the 'middle classes' but used their
relatives to fulfil the domestic functions of the household. Thus 'middle-class' status was not defined by the
employment of servants in this area, although conditions
may have been different elsewhere. These households may
also have depended on charwomen and other out-workers to
perform necessary domestic tasks.

Domestic service, therefore, does not give us an automatic register of the number or wealth of 'middle-class'
households in an area, nor is it an infallible indication
of a certain social status. It is only within the context
of an examination of individual census schedules, and a
reconstruction of the households that they portray, that we
can understand the social implications of the term
'servant'. In the official census publications, servants
employed by members of the 'middle classes' are confused
with other men and women in servant occupations, which
reduces the validity of pronouncements on social structure
based on this source. At the same time, servant employment
may have been more common amongst the members of the
'middle classes', but it was not confined to this group,
nor did all members of the professions, or large employers,
employ servants, at least in industrial Lancashire.

IV. The 'Rise and Fall' of the Victorian Servant: Towards an Interpretation

The decline of the domestic servant population in England
and Wales, from approximately 1871 onwards, is arguably one
of the most important changes in our society, given the
vast numbers of persons involved, and the fact that this

obliterated one of the factors defining the 'Western' family unit (see Chapter 1, Section I). To what extent this was due to a decline in the demand for servants after this date, or a decline in the relative supply, has been a question which has interested all students of the subject. Usually an attempt has been made to see the decline as a product of both factors, without giving any indication of the relative importance of the social processes involved. There has also been little attempt to link the forces underlying the relative growth of the servant population in the early Victorian period, with those processes which led to its relative decline after 1871.

The information gained by this discussion of domestic service in the Rochdale district and the country as a whole can help us to come to a fuller understanding of the processes involved. An attempt will be made in this section to put forward a theoretical framework within which the phenomenon of the relative rise and decline of the servant population can be discussed. It will be suggested that the changes in the supply of servants were the most important factors in the changing dynamics of the servant market. It will also be argued that both the mid-Victorian expansion of servant employment, and its relative decline after 1871, can be linked to the course of migration from the countryside to the town, although other factors, such as the spread of compulsory education and changes in employment terminology, may also have had an effect.

The suggestion has been made that for various reasons the demand for servants was declining in the late Victorian period, and that this was part of the reason for the decline in servant numbers. Such theories fail to explain why the wages paid to servants in the late nineteenth century were rising at a faster rate than those earned by women in industrial employment (see Chapter 5, Section

VII). If the demand for servants was on the decline one would hardly expect such a pattern of rising wage rates, especially after a period of static rates during the middle decades of the nineteenth century. This rise in the wages paid to servants seems, in Rochdale at least, to have been associated with difficulties in hiring servants (see Chapter 9, Section VI), which suggest that this was caused by a relative contraction of supply. If there was a decline in the demand for servants in the last decades of the nineteenth century then the voluminous literature of the period bewailing the lack of suitable servants would become incomprehensible.[35] The fact that for the employing class the 'Servant Question' was a topic of deep concern, indicates that servant employers did not see domestic servants as less important for the preservation of their way of life.

Of the various individual factors seen as producing a relative contraction in the demand for domestic servants two themes have been stressed, the 'economic crisis' of the bourgeoisie in the late nineteenth century, and the desire of the middle classes to 'privatise' their lives. According to Theresa McBride,

> The decline in the demand for servants may have resulted from the economic crisis which English middle-class families faced in attempting to afford the 'paraphernalia of gentility' which were increasingly expensive, as John and Olive Banks have argued.[36]

It is difficult to substantiate this argument given the calculations of the real incomes of the middle classes over this period shown in Table 94. These figures, taken from

J. A. Banks' Prosperity and Parenthood,[37] suggest that although the rate of increase in the real incomes of the middle classes slowed during the 'Great Depression', it was still increasing throughout the late Victorian and Edwardian periods. Also, the rate of increase in the real incomes of this group was very low during the 1850's, when servant numbers were rising relative to the total population, and peaked in the 1870's, when domestic servants began to decline as a proportion of the entire population. There is also a logical inconsistency in attempting to argue that the rising cost of the 'paraphernalia of gentility' encouraged employers to reduce the number of servants they employed when, as Banks suggest, servants were a fundamental part of that 'paraphernalia'. If the cost of employing servants was rising in relative terms then this does not suggest that servant employers were demanding fewer servants. Banks did not suggest that servant employers reduced the number of servants they employed in order to afford other middle-class trimmings, but rather that they limited the number of children in their family, thus saving on the costs of educating their children and gaining positions for them. In this manner they gained resources to spend on other symbols of 'gentility', such as domestic servants.[38]

However, this decline in the size of the middle-class household could have led to a reduction in the number of servants employed, since, as Banks points out,[39] there was then less work to be done and employers could save on the rising costs of servants. As we have seen in Chapter 6, Section VI, the number of persons in a household, and especially the number of children, had a direct effect on the number of servants employed and one would assume that a reduction in household numbers would have this effect. However, as the regression showed, the number of persons in a household was not as important a determinant of servant employment as social status, and members of the higher social classes were employing increasingly more servants in the period 1851 to 1871, although there is no evidence that their households were increasing in size. The thrust of Banks' argument is not that family limitation amongst the middle classes reduced the number of servants employed, but that the rising costs of raising a family, including the cost of servants, encouraged householders to limit their families to make do with fewer servants. Banks' argument therefore presupposes a rise in the wages paid to servants, which appears to have been associated with a relative contraction in the supply of servants.

The continued rise in the wages paid to servants throughout the late nineteenth century does not suggest, however, that the reduction of the size of the middle-class household had any overwhelming effect on the forces of supply and demand within the domestic service market. Nor is it possible to date the decline in middle-class fertility accurately enough to show a positive correlation between falling household size and the relative decline in the number of servants. According to J. W. Innes, in his Class Fertility Trends in England and Wales, 1876-1934, there is some evidence that the decline in fertility began in the 1850's amongst certain social classes,

> ......that there had been some decline (in ferti-
> lity rates) by 1851-1861 in the higher social
> classes seems to be implied by the fertility
> differentia existing at that time. The inference
> is rendered a bit precarious, of course, by the
> fact that for this date the material is none to
> plentiful and by the possibility that variations
> in the marriage age distributions within the

223

five-year periods have affected class-fertilities.[40]

According to the figures contained in the Report of the 1911 Fertility Commission the average size of completed families of women in the 'Professional and Higher Administrative' class, who married in the period 1851 to 1861, was only 86 per cent of the average for all classes at that period.[41] J. W. Innes' guarded conclusion was that,

This strong confirmation of 1877 as the date of the inception of the fall in birth rates was qualified only by the existence of some inverse aassociations between fertility and status even for marriages contracted in 1851-1861, which may have signified a somewhat earlier decline among the higher ranks.[42]

It is therefore possible that middle-class households were practising family limitation in the 1850's and 1860's, when the wages of servants were not rising and when servant numbers were rising in comparison to the rest of the population.

Whatever the changes in the relative size and income of the middle-class family there is no indication that the number of such families was in fact declining. Jill Franklin has suggested that the number of middle-class families can be measured by the number of people who could keep their own coach, horses and coachmen. The figures she produces, which are summarised in Table 95, indicate that the number of coachmen, grooms and motor car attendants was increasing at a faster rate than the population as a whole, and certainly faster than the number of female servants.[43] Although not conclusive, this evidence would appear to suggest that the number of 'carriage folk' was not on the decline in the last decades of the nineteenth century.

Theresa McBride has also offered the hypothesis that the middle-class family was attempting to exclude outsiders from the household, which led to a reluctance to hire servants,

> The middle-class inclination to employ a live-in maid after 1880 was lessening. The middle-classes wanted to privatise their lives and had begun to feel that live-in servants were obtrusive.....the motivation for this decline in demand could also have been due to a growing intimacy within the middle-class family and a wish to be closer to and to provide better care for one's children. This wish produced an increased exclusiveness by middle-class families towards outsiders, and in particular, a movement to eliminate intermediaries like servants who might come between parents and children.[44]

Apart from the failure by McBride to provide any evidence for these presumed changes in the outlook of middle-class families, it is unlikely that such processes led to a decline in demand for servants. One of the principal reasons for employing servants had always been a desire to exclude outsiders from the home. Leonora Davidoff suggests that the domestic servant was the principal means of 'privatising' the lives of the middle classes since she was employed to answer the door and run messages for the household. To exclude the maid from the household would have removed an outside presence, but it would also have forced the middle-class woman to do her own shopping and to meet her friends more openly.[45] As will be suggested here, the decline in the number of servants may actually have encouraged the middle classes to adopt a more open style of life, since they could no longer count on the 'protection' of their servants. Similarly, it is unlikely that the late Victorians or Edwardians were actively dispensing with the services of the nurse or nanny. According to Gathorne-Hardy, in his study of The Rise and Fall of the British Nanny, the number of nurses recorded in the census reports remained a fairly static percentage of the total servant population throughout the late nineteenth century and into the twentieth century.[46] He continues,

> What happened to the Nanny during her relative decline (as regards the total population) from 1901 to 1939? At the top of the scale very little. Grand houses and rich parents continued to live much as before. But as we go down, common sense and the evidence of letters and interviews suggest a loosening of the structure. Certainly, Nanny would be one of the last of the servants to be relinquished. Along with cooking, children were by far the most demanding of household tasks. The Nanny custom was by now firmly established. Mothers panicked at the idea of looking after the children and were in any case probably less fitted for it than at any other time in history. What happened was that Nanny had to help out in the home.[47]

This rather lengthy discussion of the factors which supposedly caused a decline in the middle-class demand for servants indicates that, at best, there is no conclusive evidence that such a decline took place, and that most of the reasons suggested for this decline would be difficult to substantiate. The evidence suggest that a relative contraction in supply was the most direct cause of the relative decline of the servant population. Various reasons have been suggested for this contraction of supply, including the spread of full-time education, the rise of alternative employment for women in shops and offices, and the decline of the relative size of the rural population. Each of these factors will be examined in turn, but emphasis will be laid on the decline of the rural population as the key factor in this process, the other factors being unable to explain the change fully.

Undoubtedly the introduction of compulsory education in late Victorian England must have reduced the potential supply of very young servants. However, this could only have affected very young girls, and cannot explain why fewer women in older age groups were employed in service. In 1871, according to Ebery and Preston, 50.15 per cent of all employed females aged between 15 and 19 years were employed in private indoor service. By 1911 only 32.73 per cent of this group were so employed. Similarly, in 1871 some 46.48 per cent of all employed females aged between 20 and 24 years were employed in private indoor service, but by 1911 the proportion had declined to 31.97 per cent.[48]

Rather than working in domestic service, women were increasingly being employed in other occupations. In Table 96, taken from the work of Ebery and Preston, the decennial changes in the percentage of occupied females in nine occupational sectors are given for the period 1851 to 1911.[49] The changes in these occupational sectors, which are based on Booth's occupational classification, suggest that in the last decades of the nineteenth century women

227

were increasingly more likely to be employed in dealing, and industrial and professional services, than in domestic service. In every decade after 1871 the percentage of employed women in the domestic service sector declined, whilst larger proportions of the female workforce found employment in shops and offices. According to Ebery and Preston,

> These figures, of course, reflect the movement of women from domestic service, agriculture and manufacturing into such areas as urban transport, retail services, including the new marketing system of large chain stores and, especially, office employment. The fundamental characteristic was the replacement of the servant by the shorthand-typist, the cook by the conductress.[50]

Stated in this simple form, these changes in the employment structure of the nineteenth-century economy totally lack any historical perspective. The simple assertion that women were finding alternative employment to domestic service in the late nineteenth century assumes that women who would once have been servants were now becoming shop workers and typists, and that only employment opportunities had changed. The whole structure of British society, however, was changing rapidly in this period as the population became concentrated in large urban settlements. The women who were getting jobs in service in the 1850's and 1860's tended to be rural migrants, for the reasons set out in Chapter 7. This was certainly the case in the Rochdale district, where the number of servants from 'rural' settlements remained constant, or even increased, whilst the population of the area was rapidly becoming concentrated in 'urban' settlements (see Chapter 5, Section VI). By 1900,

228

however, the female population was, to a far greater extent, an urban one, having a higher level of education than 50 years before. It was these women, with different aptitudes, qualities and outlooks who were becoming shop-workers and typists. These women had no interest in becoming domestics and were recognised as being unsuitable for domestic employment, as was pointed out in Chapter 7, Section III.

If the employment structure of the British economy had altered in these 50 years then this may have been directly due to the decline in the number of rural women in the population, the concentration of population in the cities, and the acquisition of urban education and modes of thought. According to Durkheim, the division of labour in society, including the differentiation of differing functions out of the household, is a consequence of the increasing density of human interactions within the city. In the Division of Labour in Society Durkheim put forward the theory that the 'moral density' of society, that is in effect the network of interrelationships and interactions of individuals, is intensified through its concentration in the urban milieu. Individuals in similar occupations come into greater competition with each other, and the weaker can only survive by concentrating their efforts on one part of the functions which they previously performed.[51] Durkheim sees economic processes as an escape from competition; the differentiation of functions and the expanding scale of all economic enterprises being an attempt to avoid direct competition, or to assimilate potential competitors.

The increasing scale of all economic activity reduced the number of economic functions which could be performed solely within the household, and created new occupational categories by encouraging occupational specialisation. Many of the new technologies of the time, such as the telephone, and the rise of bureaucratic procedures in business and government, can be seen as consequences of this same increase in the scale of human activity. At the same time these new technologies and bureaucratic forms presupposed a literate, numerate and essentially urban female population to provide a relatively cheap, but competent, workforce. The rural migrant woman of the mid-century would not have been able to perform the work of the Edwardian typist or clerk. Such work required a level of literacy and numeracy which she did not possess. Also, her ignorance of the recruitment channels of the urban labour market would have prevented a rural migrant from finding such a job, even supposing that she could have made her way to the town and supported herself whilst she looked for such employment. In short, the creation of new employment opportunities in late Victorian and Edwardian England presupposes a proportional reduction in the rural population, which was the mainstay of the domestic servant class. As such, the decline in the supply of domestics would not reflect the sudden availability of alternative employment, but a necessary precondition for such changes in the occupational structure of the British economy.

Whatever the precise manner in which this creation of new occupational groups took place, it is evident that the decline of domestic service was intimately connected with the decline of the rural population. According to John Burnett,

> In the middle of the (19th) century it is likely
> that two-thirds or more of all servants came from
> the countryside, but as numbers of agricultural
> labourers steadily diminished by migration and
> emigration (from 965,000 in England and Wales in

1851 to 643,000 in 1911) there were fewer
daughters to be recruited. Once settled in a
town and educated at a town elementary school
they were more likely to look to factory or shop
work than to what was increasingly considered a
low status occupation, fit only for country
bumpkins and orphan girls from the Poor Law
Institutions.[52]

As we have suggested above (Chapter 7), urban women
appear to have been far less willing to accept the discipline of the middle-class household. According to Durkheim,
however, this very decline in the potential supply of
domestic servants would tend to create new occupational
opportunities outside the middle-class home. In fact it
might be suggested that the decline in the relative number
of domestic servants recorded in the census statistics
merely represents the removal of certain functions from the
middle-class household. With the maturation of urban
society in the late nineteenth century, urban working women
would no longer perform servant functions within the homes
of their employers. The rising wages of servants forced
households to abandon the employment of resident servants
and to have these functions performed by women outside the
household. In this manner the decline of the rural population, the decline of the servant population and the rise of
alternative employment can be seen as one interacting
social process. This can be substantiated by examining the
relative decline of the rural population, and its effect on
the servant population, and then considering some of the
changes in employment patterns which may have ensued.

Some contemporaries certainly realised that rural de-
population was the root cause of the decline of the servant
population. According to the 1916 inquiry into domestic

service by the Women's Industrial Council,

> Rural depopulation has tapped the source from
> which the great majority of servants came, but
> the demand for them has risen. Hence come the
> circulars sent round to some villages by London
> registry offices and the facilities offered by
> the 'domestic' advertisements of many news-
> papers.[53]

This decline of the rural population can be followed in
some detail in Table 97 which shows the decennial decline
in the percentage of the occupied population active in
agriculture. The largest declines in agricultural work
appear to have been in the years between 1811 and 1831, and
then, after a comparative lull, in the years between 1851
and 1871. After 1871 the comparative decline in the number
of persons employed in agriculture slowed.[54] According to
Hobsbawm and Rude, the period between 1751 and 1831 actually saw a decline in the percentage of the natural increase
of the population of the agricultural counties which was
migrating elsewhere.[55] The relative decline in agricultural employment, coupled with a decline in migration from
the agricultural counties, suggests that in this period
there was increasing unemployment in the agricultural
counties, but that the population was kept on the land.
Hobsbawm and Rude suggest that this was the effect of the
Old Poor Law,[56] and that this agricultural crisis came to a
head in the Swing Riots of the early 1830's.[57]

It has been suggested that the key decades in the relative decline of the rural population in the nineteenth
century may have been the years between 1811 and 1831 and
also between 1851 and 1871. Deane and Cole certainly
believed that these latter decades were amongst the years

which saw the peak of the movement from the countryside to the town,

> For the first 80 years of the nineteenth century the movement from the countryside to the towns was strong and steady. The influx into the towns reached its peak in the forties when it was inflated by the Irish exodus. It was high throughout the middle four decades of the century. In the last two decades of the century, however, a change in the pattern of internal migration was evident in the population records. It seems as though the urbanisation which was particularly associated with the process of industrialisation had been completed. From then on, although there was still plenty of movement from one area to another, it could no longer be described in terms of the traditional drift to the towns but was explained by changes in the relative prosperity or depression of particular areas. The shifts between industrial areas or between home and overseas became more important factors in the situation than the movement between town and country. Women were still moving off the land in the latter decades of the nineteenth century, as agricultural employment continued to decline. However, the rate of decline in the last decades of the nineteenth century was lower than in previous years, and many of those who were leaving were not migrating into the towns of England and Wales, as they had done in previous decades.[58]

If the majority of domestic servants were rural women, and the potential supply of such women in the nineteenth century was at its highest in the middle decades of the century, then this might explain why the wages paid to servants were not increasing, in relative terms, between the 1840's and the late 1860's. In what virtually amounted to a perfectly competitive labour market, one would expect an increase in supply to depress wage rates, whilst a contraction in relative supply in the latter decades of the nineteenth century would lead to a relative increase in wage rates. This would explain the observed course of domestic wages. (Table 91) As we have seen (Chapter 9, Section VI), there appears to have been such a 'crisis' in the servant labour market in Rochdale at the end of the 1860's, and this appears in turn to have been related to a decline in the number of persons migrating into the Rochdale district. There is thus some evidence on which to base the proposition that the relative decline in the number of servants in the late nineteenth century was associated with the relative decline of the number of rural women migrating to the town.

The results of this shortage of suitable servants, and the changing economic and social structure of society consequent upon the urbanisation of the population, which appear to have been part of the same process, can easily be seen within the range of economic functions performed within the home. Urban women appear to have been unwilling to perform economic tasks within the homes of the middle classes, but do not seem to have objected to performing such work outside the home. As occupational differentiation spread, under the impact of urbanisation, activities once associated with the rural migrant servant working in the middle-class home, came to be performed outside the home by specialised urban female workers. The very

processes of specialisation of labour necessitated production on a scale larger than the household, and the products
so produced would have been cheaper than those produced
within the home by increasingly expensive domestic
servants. According to V. M. Firth in The Psychology of
the Servant Problem, written in 1925,

> This system is with us to a greater extent
> already than we realise; we send our washing to
> the public laundry; our bread, and often our
> cakes as well, come from the public bakery; in
> our grandmothers' day every cook had to undertake
> the heavy work of kneading the dough, as in our
> mothers' day every household had to endure the
> steam and tempers of washing day; these burdens
> have been lifted, together with jam-making,
> brewing, and a hundred minor details.[59]

Functions which were once performed by domestic servants
were now carried out by women working for commercial
enterprises, or by 'gadgetry' introduced into the home.
This process was recognised as inevitable as early as 1849,
when an article, written under the pseudonym 'Helix',
appeared in the Westminster Review, stating that,

> the word service is in itself a gracious word, as
> it is a gracious thing to serve our fellows: but
> in our domestic servants' apprehension it has
> lost its original meaning, and has become
> distasteful servitude, or service rendered for
> hire. So surely as the years roll on, higher
> wages and lessening performance will mark
> domestic service....Meanwhile the only remedy for
> the middle-classes, loving their ease, will be to

235

increase their mechanical applicances and labour-
saving processes, to make themselves self-
dependent as fast as their servants become
independent.[60]

Innovations within the home were advocated on the
grounds that they would save labour. Thus, J. J. Stevenson
in his House Architecture of 1880, advocated the abandon-
ment of the wash house, since, 'When clothes can be sent
out the work may be done as a cheaply, if we reckon the
expense of buildings and fittings and the wages of the
laundrymaid....'.[61] Stevenson even advocated the 'extrava-
gant luxury' of plumbing, and a bath in every bedroom
suite, since 'arrangements of this kind save servants'
labour which yearly becomes scarcer'.[62] Jill Franklin in
her article on domestic employment has gone on to chronicle
other innovations in the middle-class home which date from
this period of servant decline, including the decline of
home brewing, the rise of dry-cleaning, the increase in the
production of ready-made clothing, piped hot water,
electrical lighting and internal telephones, all of which
replaced female labour in the home, or removed it into the
factory.[63]

Even within the domestic service sector itself there was
a movement out of the home, and into forms of non-private
service. According to Ebery and Preston, there was a
distinct change in the structure of the Domestic Service
Sector of the economy, as defined by Booth. In 1871 some
80.96 per cent of the females in this employment sector
were working as private domestic servants, the others being
employed in similar 'domestic' tasks in inns, hotels,
colleges, clubs, offices and laundries. By 1911, however,
the percentage of females in Booth's Domestic Service

Sector employed in private household service had declined to only 71.6 per cent. At the same time, the percentage of women in the sector employed in hotels, inns, boarding houses and institutions such as clubs, had risen from only 2.09 per cent in 1871 to 10.12 per cent in 1911.[64] Thus, even whilst proportionally fewer women were being employed in this occupational sector of the economy, the relative proportion of private household servants within the group was declining.

This can be linked to the changing life-style of upper middle-class men and women in late Victorian and Edwardian England. It could be suggested that as such households employed fewer servants so the middle classes were forced to meet in public places, such as restuarants and tea rooms, and to abandon the formal visiting and 'at homes' of the mid-Victorian period, for the pleasures of bridge at the club or dancing. Services were no longer available in the home but could be procured in specialised institutions. The labour involved may have been identical to some of the functions previously performed by domestic servants, but women employed in restuarants, clubs and dance halls had far more specialised duties, and performed them outside of the middle-class home.

According to Table 96, the employment sector of the economy which grew most strongly in the late nineteenth century (presumably at the expense of domestic service) was dealing. Indeed, there does not seem to have been a decade, in the period 1851 to 1911, when the relative proportion of women occupied in shop work was not increasing, although the increase appears to have been far greater in the period after 1871. This shift in female employment can also be seen as part of the process by which economic functions were differentiated out of the household. As was revealed in Chapter 6, Section VII, a very

important section of the servant population of the Rochdale
district was involved in the provision of retailing
services through the households of the shopkeeping class.
In the mid-Victorian period retailing was primarily a
family business, but from the 1870's onwards there was
relative increase in scale, as the chain store made its
appearance.   In 1871 Thomas Lipton set up his first shop in
Glasgow; the Home and Colonial Trading Association was
founded in 1885; and the first shop of the Maypole Dairy
Company properly speaking was opened in March 1887 in
Wolverhampton.[65]   In general there appears to have been a
decline in the relative importance of the household in
retailing, as the size and complexity of retailing concerns
increased.   In the words of J. B. Jeffreys, in the period
1850 to 1914,

> the combined shop and dwelling-house wherein
> lived the shop assistants, as well as the owner
> and his family came to be replaced by the 'lock-
> up' shop. Retailing was becoming an occupation
> with starting and finishing times permitting a
> separate existence for the retailer away from the
> shop, instead of a life's work that was never
> completed.   Finally with the growth of large-
> scale retailing, a new and impersonal 'race of
> managers' was appearing alongside the highly
> personal and individual shopkeepers.[66]

Such large-scale retailing enterprises were, of course,
products of the great concentration of population in the
cities, and depended for their staff on urban women who had
a degree of education and 'sophistication' which were not
possessed by their rural contemporaries.   At the same time,
the small family shopkeeper may have been unable to compete

because of the rising costs of domestic servants. As retailing functions came to be separated from the house-hold, and as shop work thus beacame a specialised occupation, there must have been a tendency for household domestics who helped in the family business, or who allowed the wife of the shopkeeper to do so, to be replaced by shop assistants who lived outside the household of their employers.

The rise in the number of women employed in shop work might not, therefore represent the development of new occupational opportunities but merely the differentiation of functions within retailing. The shop assistant was not a new phonomenon but a specialist, fulfilling some of the functions of household servants, as retailing came to be dissociated from household work. Such work cannot, therefore, be opposed to domestic service but was to some extent a sub-category of household work, which increasingly came to have a separate existence as retailing and the household came to be dissociated.

In this section an attempt has been made to give a conceptual framework within which the 'rise and fall' of nineteenth-century service can be discussed as a whole. The expansion and contraction of supply has been posited as the determinant factor in the size of the domestic service sector; changes in the relative level of demand being of secondary importance. In the perfectly competitive labour market for servants, an expansion of the number of women migrating from the countryside in the middle decades of the nineteenth century depressed wage rates, and so enabled middle-class households to hire more servants. The contraction of the rural supply of servants in the last decades of the nineteenth century led to a comparative rise in the wages paid to servants and a comparative diminution of the servant population. As the rural population moved into the towns it no longer produced women who could be disciplined within the middle-class household. At the same time the processes of the differentiation of labour, and the expansion in the scale of commercial enterprises, ensured that the functions of domestic servants could now be carried on outside the home.

In this manner the decline of the domestic servant in the late nineteenth century was merely a change of nomenclature, the work originally being done by such women being sub-divided into different components, and performed by comparative specialists working as shop assistants, waitresses in restuarants, and in the industrial manufacture of confectionary, food, clothing and do on. Just as in the eighteenth century the 'industrial' activities of most men had moved out of the household into the factory, so in the nineteenth century the labour of women developed in the same direction. This comparatively late emergence from the authority of the household may partly explain why the development of the political power of women has lagged so far behind that of men.

APPENDIX A

Coding conventions used in the transformation of sample schedules into numerical data.

1) NEW HOUSEHOLDS: first individual or first servant recorded in household. If positive coding equals 1, otherwise 0.

2) CASE NUMBER: coding 001-999, all individuals with similar codes are from the same household.

3) MARITAL STATUS OF HEAD OF HOUSEHOLD: single, married, married but spouse absent, status unknown.

4) SEX OF HEAD OF HOUSEHOLD: male, female, unknown.

5) OCCUPATION OF HEAD OF HOUSEHOLD: coding 001-999, derived from a listing of occupations of household heads in the household samples.

6) AGE OF HEAD: the age of the household head in years.

7) SOCIAL-ECONOMIC GROUPING: this classification was based on that outlined by W. A. Armstrong in 'The Use of Information About Occupations, Part 1', in his contribution to E.A.Wrigley (ed.), The Study of Nineteenth Century Society (London, 1972). His social classification is based upon the occupational groupings given in the 1950 Classification of Occupations, published by the H.M.S.O. in 1951, with suitable revisions to bring it more in line with

241

nineteenth century conditions. This social classification based upon occupations has been attacked on numerous grounds. See for example H. J. Dyos (ed.) The Study of Urban History (London, 1968), Second Discussion, pp. 146-49. Changes in the definitions of occupational categories since the 19th century may well make impossible any atttempt to link social status and occupation. Also in this system it is necessary to know the number of hands which manufacturers and shopkeepers employed to place them in the correct social grouping.

It is to be hoped that these shortcomings have been mitigated here by coding for occupations, as well as for social class, so that these social-economic groupings can be broken down into their constituent parts. Also comparatively few servant employers came from the lowest social classes, whilst the more easily enumerated higher classes were over-represented. Thus there will be less confusion over the social position of a doctor, a clergyman, or a farmer, than over such obscure manual occupations as a 'cotton lapper' or 'tripe dresser'.

The general conventions for the coding were as follows:-

SOCIAL-ECONOMIC
GROUPING

1   PROFESSIONAL: all members of the professions; all proprietors; all manufacturers employing more than 25 hands.

2   INTERMEDIATE: all farmers; manufacturers employing between 2 and 24

	hands; retailers employing more than one assistant.
3	SKILLED MANUAL/SHOPKEEPER: all retailers employing less than 2 assistants; skilled industrial workers; clerks.
4	PARTLY SKILLED WORKERS: all servants; partly skilled industrial workers.
5	UNSKILLED WORKERS: labourers.
6	UNKNOWN: occupation cannot be traced. or unknown.
7	INDETERMINANT: occupation cannot be defined, eg 'a lady'.

8) NUMBER OF SERVANTS: number of 'true' servants in household.

9) TOTAL SIZE OF HOUSEHOLD: total number of persons in the household excluding 'true' servants.

10) TOTAL NUMBER AT WORK IN HOUSEHOLD: the number of persons in the household with stated occupations, excluding the head of the household and all servants.

11) DEPENDANTS OVER THE AGE OF 10 YEARS: number of persons in the household, aged over 10 years, with no stated occupation, excluding wives and servants.

12) DEPENDANTS TEN YEARS OLD OR UNDER: the number of persons in the household under the age of 11 years, excluding the kin of lodgers and 'true' servants.

13) DEPENDANTS TWO YEARS OLD OR UNDER: the number of persons in the household under the age of three years,

excluding the kin of lodgers and 'true' servants.

14) LODGERS OR BOARDERS IN HOUSEHOLD: the number of persons in the household whose relationship to the head of the household was either lodger or boarder, excluding those in servant occupations.

15) WIFE PRESENT IN THE HOUSEHOLD: head single or widowed, or wife with stated occupation; wife present in household as a 'housewife', coding equals 1, otherwise 0.

16) THE DISTANCE OF THE HEAD'S BIRTHPLACE FROM THE DISTRICT OF ROCHDALE: distance, in miles, of the head's birthplace from the district of Rochdale. If only the county of birth was given then a maximum and minimum possible distance was calculated for that county and a random number table was used to produce a hypothetical distance within the given range. Birthplaces within the registration district of Rochdale counted as 000 miles.

17) COUNTY WHERE THE HOUSEHOLD HEAD WAS BORN: the county where the household head was born. All statistics relating to 'Rochdale' refer to the Rochdale Registration District. No attempt has been made to differentiate between the urban centre of the Metropolitan Borough of Rochdale and the surrounding townships and hamlets. This has meant that it has not been possible to follow population movements within the district as a whole. This has been necessary since many census schedules do not give any definite information as to where the members of the family were born in relation to the registration district. Many persons were

simply enumerated as having been born in 'Rochdale', without recording whether this referred to the registration district, the parish, or the metropolitan borough. Since urban Rochdale was a composite settlement, including the townships of Spotland, Hundersfield, and Castleton, there was confusion as to whether certain birthplaces were part of urban Rochdale or were situated in one of the much larger sub-districts, such as Spotland, which contained a considerable area outside the urban centre of Rochdale.

18) TYPE OF SETTLEMENT WHERE THE HOUSEHOLD HEAD WAS BORN: the population of the settlement where heads of households were born. Using information contained in the census reports the settlements of birth were classified into whether they contained more than 5,000 inhabitants, between 5,000 and 2,000, or under 2,000. The figures were always from the previous census. Thus if a household head in the 1851 sample was born in settlement A, then the population of that settlement was calculated from the 1841 census returns. This was done to discover the settlement's size when the head migrated from it, rather than at the date at which he appeared in the Rochdale sample. No account could be taken of whether placenames in the schedules or in the census returns referred to the same type of settlement. Thus a person may have been born in a small hamlet but the figures contained in the census returns might have referred to a large parish of the same name.

All persons from within the Rochdale Registration District were considered as being resident in a settlement of over 5,000 inhabitants since many persons were simply recored as coming from 'Rochdale' without adding if this meant the town, the registration district, or the parish.

19) DISTANCE OF WIFE'S BIRTHPLACE FROM THE DISTRICT OF ROCHDALE: as for head of household (see Note 16).

20) COUNTY WHERE THE HOUSEHOLD HEAD'S WIFE WAS BORN: as for head of household (See Note 17).

21) TYPE OF SETTLEMENT WHERE WIFE OF HOUSEHOLD HEAD WAS BORN: as for head of household (See Note 18).

22) AGE OF WIFE: age of wife in years.

23) LENGTH OF RESIDENCE OF FAMILY IN THE ROCHDALE DISTRICT: if the heads was not born in the Rochdale District, than the age of the first child in the family who was born in the district.

24) LIFE CYCLE STAGE OF FAMILY: this coding was based upon that devised by Michael Anderson in his work on Preston in the 19th century and documented in Family Structure in Nineteenth Century Lancashire (London, 1972) p.200, note 46. Each household was designated as falling into one of seven categories and given appropriate numerical codes:-
   0) No wife present in household.
   1) Wife present and under the age of 45 years, no children at home.
   2) Wife present and under the age of 45 years, one child one year old or under at home.
   3) Wife present and children at home, but none in employment.

4) Wife present and children at home, and some but under half in employment.

5) Wife present and children at home, and half, or over half, in employment.

6) Wife present and 45 years old or over, no children at home, or only one aged over 20 years.

Persons employed excludes servants as kin.

25) SIMILARITY BETWEEN THE SERVANT'S NAME AND THAT OF THE EMPLOYER'S FAMILY: name similarity between family members and the servant, if kin relationship not stated. Excludes head.

26) SIMILARITY BETWEEN THE SERVANT'S NAME AND THAT OF THE HOUSEHOLD HEAD: as Note 25 but for the household head only.

27) RELATIONSHIP OF THE SERVANT'S KIN TO THE HOUSEHOLD HEAD: relationship to the household head of eldest person in the household with the same surname as the servant, i.e. employee, lodger, lodger's child (dependants under the age of 10 years), or servant.

28) SETTLEMENT TYPE OF RESIDENCE AREA: this classification was based upon the Ordnance Survey maps (6" to one mile) for the Rochdale area published in 1851 and 1892.

Occupied settlements shown on these maps were grouped according to their population (the number of households recorded in the census schedules) and their degree of physical dispersal. Settlements as particular entities were defined as all those occupied dwellings within 100 yards of each other. Thus a single household living in a dwelling more than 100 yards from any other household was defined as living in an isolated dwelling. Five households living in dwellings within 100 yards of each other were defined as living in a hamlet (a settlement containing between 2 and 10 households). All settlements with over 10 households were classified according to their degree of physical dispersion. If a settlement had more than 49 per cent of its households in a contiguous pattern it was classified as a nucleatead settlement; if under 50 per cent, it was classified as a dispersed settlement. The following settlement classification for the Rochdale district in 1851 was thus produced:-

a) The outer periphery of urban Rochdale-dwellings forming part of the urban mass of Rochdale within 100 yards of the country-side (non-settled land bounded on less than four sides by urban development).

b) The outer periphery of urban Rochdale-dwellings forming part of the urban mass of Rochdale between 100 and 200 yards from the country-side.

c) The centre of urban Rochdale-all of urban Rochdale not classified under a) or b).

d) Large nucleated settlements-nucleated settlements with more than 100 households.

e) Small nucleated settlements-nucleated settlements with between 11 and 100 households.

f) Large dispersed settlements-dispersed settlements with over 100 households.

g) Small dispersed settlements-dispersed settlements with between 11 and 100 households.

h) Hamlets-settlements with between 2 and 10 households.

i) Isolated dwellings.

j) The urban area of Bacup.

For this classification in 1871 three extra settlement types were added:-

k) The new constructed urban periphery-dwellings now part of urban Rochdale which had not been built in 1851.

l) The new incorporated urban periphery-dwellings now part of urban Rochdale which had been separate entities in 1851 but which by 1871 were incorporated in the urban mass of Rochdale by newly constructed dwellings.

m) The urban area of Heywood.

29) TRUE SERVANT HOUSEHOLDS IN GRID SQUARE: in the grid square where the household is resident, the number of households therein with true servants as a percentage of all the households in the grid square.

30) HOUSEHOLDS WITH NON-TRUE SERVANTS IN GRID SQUARE: in the grid square where the household is resident, the number of households with non-true servants as a percentage of all households in the grid square.

31) NUMBER OF TRUE SERVANTS PER HOUSEHOLD IN GRID SQUARE: in the grid square where the household is resident, the average number of true servants per household.

All the previous variables referred to the household as a unit, the following 17 variables refer to individual members of the household, in the case of the control sample households, and to individual servants in the other households.

32) RELATIONSHIP TO HEAD: relationship of person to head -numerical coding for differing relationships, eg, wife, mother, lodger, servant, etc.

33) MARITAL STATUS: marital status of individual-as for head (Note 3).

34) SEX: sex of individual-as for head (Note 4).

35) AGE: age of individual in years.

36) OCCUPATION: coding 001 to 999, derived from listing of occupations from samples.

37) DISTANCE OF BIRTHPLACE FROM DISTRICT OF ROCHDALE: coding as for head (Note 16).

38) COUNTY OF BIRTH: coding as for head (Note 17).

39) TYPE OF SETTLEMENT WHERE INDIVIDUAL BORN: coding as for head (Note 18).

40) TRUE SERVANT BORN IN THE SAME TOWN AS HEAD: town where head and true servant born the same-servants from Lancashire excluded.

41) TRUE SERVANT BORN IN SAME COUNTY AS HEAD: county where head and true servant born the same-servants from

Lancashire excluded.

42) TRUE SERVANT BORN IN SAME TOWN AS HEAD'S WIFE: town where the head's wife and the true servant were born the same-excluding servants from Lancashire.

43) TRUE SERVANT BORN IN THE SAME COUNTY AS HEAD'S WIFE: county where the head's wife and the true servant were born the same-excluding servants from Lancashire.

44) TRUE SERVANT BORN IN SAME TOWN AS OTHER RELATIONS OF HEAD: town of birth of other relations of head identical to that of the true servant-excluding servants from Lancashire.

45) TRUE SERVANT BORN IN SAME COUNTY AS OTHER RELATIONS OF HEAD: county of birth of other relations of head identical to that of the true servant-excluding servants from Lancashire.

In coding variables 40 to 45 a positive relationship between towns of birth took precedence over relationships between counties of birth. Similarly, positive relationships between the head's birthplace and that of the servant took precedence over all other relationships; that between a servant's birthplace and that of the head's wife took precedence over that between servants and other relations. It was thus possible to produce only one positive relationship for each family, and each servant. A positive relationship was coded 1, a lack of a relationship with a 0.

46) SERVANTS FROM THE SAME TOWN OF BIRTH: number of
    servants in the household born in the same town-
    excluding servants from Lancashire.

47) SERVANTS FROM THE SAME COUNTY OF BIRTH: number of
    servants in the household born in the same county-
    excluding servants from Lancashire.

In coding variables 46 and 47 relationships between towns
of birth took precedence over relationships between
counties of birth-excluding servants from Lancashire. Such
relationships were only recorded for the first servant
enumerated in a household.

BIBLIOGRAPHY

Books, articles, and theses

ANDERSON, M., Family Structure in Nineteenth-Century Lancashire, (Cambridge, 1971).

ANDERSON, M., 'Standard tabulation procedures', in WRIGLEY,
E. A. (ed.), The Study of Nineteenth-Century Society,
(London, 1972).

ANONYMOUS, Common Sense for Housemaids, (London, 1850).

ARMSTRONG, W. A., 'The use of information about
occupation', in WRIGLEY, E. A. (ed.), The Study of
Nineteenth-Century Society, (London, 1972).

ARMSTRONG, W. A., Stability and Change in an English
County Town: A Social Study of York, 1801-1851, (London,
1974).

ARNOLD, R. A., The History of the Cotton Famine, (London,
1864).

BANKS, J.A., Prosperity and Parenthood, (London, 1954).

BEETON, I., Mrs Beeton's Book of Household Management,
(London, 1863).

BEETON, I., Mrs Beeton's Book of Household Management,
(London, 1906).

BOOTH, C., Life and Labour of the People in London, Vol. 8,
(London, 1903).

BRANCA, P., Silent Sisterhood, (London, 1975).

BRIERLEY, H., The Rochdale Reminiscences, (Rochdale, 1923).

BROOM, L. and SMITH, J. H., 'Bridging occupations',
British Journal of Sociology, Vol. 14 (1963), 321-34.

BULLEY, A. Amy, 'Domestic service: a social study',
Westminster Review, Vol. 135 (1891), 177-86.

BURNETT, J. (ed.), Useful Toil, (London, 1974).

BUTLER, C. V., Domestic Service. An Enquiry by the Women's Industrial Council, (London, 1916).

CHAPLIN, D., 'The employment of domestic servants as a class indicator: a methodological discussion', a paper presented at the Social History Association meeting, Philadelphia, USA, October, 1976.

COOKE TAYLOR, W., A Tour of the Manufacturing Districts of Lancashire, (London, 1968).

CORNHILL MAGAZINE, 'Maids-of-all-work and Blue Books', Vol. XXX, 281-96.

DAVIDOFF, L., The Best Circles. Society, Etiquette and the Season, (London, 1973).

DEANE, P. and COLE, W. A., British Economic Growth, 1688-1959, (Cambridge, 1962).

DURKHEIM, E., The Division of Labour in Society, (Glencoe, Illinois, 1960).

DYOS, H. J. and BAKER, A. B. H., 'The possibilties of computerising census data', in DYOS, H. J. (ed.), The Study of Urban History, (London, 1968).

EBERY, M. and PRESTON, B., Domestic Service in late Victorian and Edwardian England, 1871-1914, (Reading, 1976). Reading University Geographical Papers, No. 42.

ECONOMY FOR THE SINGLE AND MARRIED, (London, 1845).

FIRTH, V. M., The Psychology of the Servant Problem, (London, 1925).

FISHWICK, H., The History of the Parish of Rochdale in the County of Lancashire, (Rochdale, 1889).

FOSTER, J., Class Struggle and the Industrial Revolution, (London, 1974).

FRANKLIN, J., 'Troops of servants: labour and planning in the country house, 1840-1914', Victorian Studies, Vol. XIX, (Dec. 1975), 211-39.

GASKELL, P., The Manufacturing Population of England,

(London, 1833).

GATHORNE-HARDY, J., The Rise and Fall of the British Nanny, (London, 1972).

GEORGE, M. Dorothy, 'The early history of registry offices', Economic History, Vol. IV, 570-90.

HARRISON, B., 'For Church, Queen and Family: the Girls' Friendly Society, 1874-1920', Past and Present, Vol. 61 (1973), 107-39.

HARRISON, J. F. C., The Early Victorians, 1832-1851, (London, 1971).

'HELIX', 'Human progress', Westminster Review, Vol. 52 (1849), 1-39.

HEWITT, M., Wives and Mothers in Victorian Industry, (London, 1958).

HOBSBAWM, E. J., Labouring Men, (London, 1964).

HOBSBAWM, E. J. and RUDE, G., Captain Swing, (London, 1969).

HOBSBAWM, E. J., The Age of Capital, (London, 1975).

HORN, P., The Rise and Fall of the Victorian Servant, (Dublin, 1975).

INNES, J. W., Class Fertility Trends in England and Wales, 1876-1934, (Princeton, 1938).

JEFFREYS, J. B., Retail Trading in Britain, 1850-1950, (Cambridge, 1954).

JONES, F. M., 'The aesthetic of the nineteenth-century industrial town', in DYOS, H. J. (ed.), The Study of Urban History, (London, 1968).

JONES, G. Steadman, Outcast London, (Oxford, 1971).

'JUSTICE', The Solution of the Domestic Servant Problem, (North Shields, 1910).

LASLETT, T. P. R., The World We Have Lost, (London, 1965).

LASLETT, T. P. R., Family life and Illicit Love in Earlier Generations, (Cambridge, 1977).

LAYARD, G. S., 'The doom of the domestic cook', Nineteenth

Century, Vol. XXXIII (1893), 309-19.

LAYTON, W. T., 'Changes in the wages of domestic servants during 50 years', Journal of the Royal Statistical Society, Vol. 71 (1908), 515-24.

LEWIS, E. A., 'A reformation of domestic service', Nineteenth Century, Vol. XXXIII, 127-38.

MCBRIDE, T., The Domestic Revolution, (London, 1976).

MCLEOD, M., Class and Religion in the Late Victorian City, (London, 1974).

MARCUS, S., The Other Victorians, (London, 1967).

MARSHALL, J. D., 'Colonisation as a factor in the planting of towns in north-west England', DYOS, H. J. (ed.), The Study of Urban History, (London, 1968).

MARX, K., Grundrisse. Introduction to the Critique of Political Economy, (London, 1973).

MATHIAS, P., The Retailing Revolution, (London, 1967).

MILNE, J., Rochdale As It Was, (Lancashire, 1973).

MITCHELL, B. R., and DEANE, P., Abstract of British Historical Statistics, (Cambridge, 1962).

NIE, N. H., HULL, C. Hadlai, JENKINS, J. G., STEINBRENNER, K., BENT, D. H., Statistical Package for the Social Sciences, (New York, 1975).

OBELKEVITCH, J., Religion and Rural Society: South Lindsey, 1825-1875, (Oxford, 1976).

PERKIN, H. J., The Origins of Modern English Society, 1780-1880, (London, 1969).

PINCHBECK, I., Women Workers and the Industrial Revolution, (London, 1930).

POWELL, M., Below Stairs, (London, 1968).

'A PRACTICAL MISTRESS OF A HOUSEHOLD', Domestic Servants as They Are and As They Ought to Be, (Brighton, 1859).

PRESTON, B., Occupations of Father and Son in Mid-Victorian England, (Reading, 1977). Reading University

Geographical Papers, No. 56.

REDFORD, A., Labour Migration in England, 1800-50, (Manchester, 1926).

SAGARRA, E., A Social History of Germany, 1648-1914, (London, 1977).

SMITH, C. M., The Law of Master and Servant, (London, 1852, 1860, 1870).

SMITH, M. L., 'Institutionalised servitude: the female domestic servant in Lima, Peru', Unpublished PhD Dissertation, 1971 (British Library Reference: 72-10007).

STEVENSON, J. J., House Architecture, 2 vols, (London, 1880).

SUNDAY TIMES MAGAZINE, 'Au pairs in Britain', (15 February, 1976).

TAYLOR, R. P., Rochdale Retrospective: A Centenary History of Rochdale, (Rochdale, 1956).

THIRSK, J. and COOPER, J. P., Seventeenth-Century Economic Documents, (Oxford, 1972).

THOMPSON, F., Lark Rise to Candleford, (London, 1973).

TILLOT, P. M., 'Sources of inaccuracy in the 1851 and 1861 censuses', in WRIGLEY, E. A. (ed.), The Study of Nineteenth-Century Society, (London, 1972).

VINCENT, J. R., 'The electoral sociology of Rochdale', Economic History Review, 2nd Series, Vol. XVI, 76-90.

WARREN, MRS E., How I Managed My House on Two Hundred Pounds a Year, (London, 1864).

WEBSTER, T. and PARKES, MRS, An Encyclopedia of Domestic Economy, (London, 1861).

WOOD, G. H., 'The course of women's wages during the nineteenth century', in HUTCHINS, B. L. and HARRISON, A., A History of Factory Legislation, Appendix A, 257-316, (London, 1903).

WRIGLEY, E. A. (ed.), The Study of Nineteenth-Century Society, (London, 1972).

Manuscript sources

LRO = Lancashire Record Office
MCL = Manchester Central Library
PRO = Public Record Office
RPL = Rochdale Public Library

LRO, DDCL/1184/18. Correspondence of John Cunliffe of
Myerscough Hall to Thomas Clifton of Lytham Hall, 1837.

LRO, DDX/664/13/11. The diary of 'Mrs Bird' (Mary Bird
Stopford) of Upholland near Wigan.

LRO, DP/393. Miss Lizabeth Appleton: correspondence, 1805.

LRO, PDD BL/53/57-59. Papers of the Blundells of Little
Crosby: the diaries of Agnes Blundell.

LRO, PUR 7. Rochdale Board of Guardians: Workhouse
Committee Minute Books, 1852-1871.

LRO, QAM/1/34. County Asylum, Lancaster: wages paid to
attendants, 1877-1883.

LRO, QAM/6/21. County Lunatic Asylum, Prestwich: servants'
wages, 1861-1864.

LRO, QAM/6/20. County Lunatic Asylum, Prestwich: list of
officers with their respective salaries, 1851-1875.

LRO, QAM/6/22. County Lunatic Asylum, Prestwich:
attendants' wage book, 1876-1890.

MCL, MFPR 242-259. Parish records of the Parish Church of
St John the Evangelist, Preston, 1851-1856.

MCL, 06/2/2/1-5. Correspondence of Mrs Munro of London to
Mrs Cartwright of Wem, Shropshire.

PRO, B3. Court of Bankruptcy files.

PRO, HO 107. Census Papers-Population Returns, 1851:
Enumerators Schedules.

PRO, RG 9. Census Papers-Population Returns, 1861:

Enumerators Schedules.

PRO, RG 10. Census Papers-Population Returns, 1871:
    Enumerators Schedules.
PRO, RG 29/9-16. General Register Office Letter Books: Out
    Letters relating to the 1891 Census.
RPL, DB 154. List of guardians and paid officers of the
    Rochdale Poor Law Union, 1853-1910.
RPL, Newspaper Collection.

Maps

Ordnance Survey of Gt Britain, 6 inches to 1 mile:
    Lancashire Sheets. (1st ed., Southampton, 1851).
Ordnance Survey of Gt Britain, 6 inches to 1 mile:
    Lancashire Sheets. (2nd ed., Southampton, 1892).

Parliamentary debates

Hansard, 1844, Vol. LXXXIII, cols 1,093-4.

Parliamentary papers

PP 1833, XXI. Second Report of the .....Commissioners....
    (on)......the Employment of Children in Factories......
    with Minutes of Evidence.
PP 1834, XXX. Report from His Majesty's Commissioners for
    Inquiring into the Administration and Practical Operation

of the Poor Laws. Appendix B(i): Answers to Rural Queries, Pt 1.

PP 1843, XII. Reports of the Special Poor Law Commissioners on the Employment of Women and Children in Agriculture.

PP 1843, XXII. Census of Gt Britain, 1841. Abstracts.

PP 1852-3, LXXXV. Census of Gt Britain, 1851. Population Tables I, Vol. I.

PP 1852-3, LXXXVI. Census of Gt Britain, 1851. Population Tables I, Vol. II.

PP 1852-3, LXXXVIII, Pts I and II. Census of Gt Britain, 1851. Population Tables II.

PP 1862, L. Census of England and Wales, 1861. Population Tables.

PP 1863, LIII, Pts I and II. Census of England and Wales, 1861.

PP 1872, LXVI. Census of England and Wales, 1871. Population Tables.

PP 1873, LXXI, Pts I and II. Census of England and Wales, 1871. Population Abstracts.

PP 1894, LXXXI, Pt II. Report (Miss Collet's) on the Statistics of Employment of Women and Girls.

PP 1899, XCII. Report (Miss Collet's) of the Labour Department of the Board of Trade on Money Wages of Indoor Domestic Servants.

PP 1904, XXXII, Appendix V. Evidence to the Inter-Departmental Committee on Physical Deterioration.

PP 1904, CVIII. Census of England and Wales. General Report.

PP 1919, XXIX. Ministry of Reconstruction. Report of the Domestic Service Sub-Committee IV.

Chapter 1.   Domestic Service in the Nineteenth Century

1. MITCHELL, B. R., and DEANE, P., Abstract of British
    Historical Statistics, (Cambridge, 1962), 60.

2. MCBRIDE, T., The Domestic Revolution, (London, 1976),
    13-14.

3. LASLETT, T. P. R., Family life and Illicit Love in
    Earlier Generations, (Cambridge, 1977), 31.

4. SMITH, M. L., 'Institutionalised servitude: the female
    domestic servant in Lima, Peru', Unpublished PhD
    Dissertation, 1971 (British Library Reference: 72-
    10007), 61.

5. BROOM, L. and SMITH, J. H., 'Bridging occupations',
    British Journal of Sociology, Vol. 14 (1963), 321-34.

6. MARX, K., Grundrisse. Introduction to the Critique of
    Political Economy, (London, 1973), 401.

7. BEETON, I., Mrs Beeton's Book of Household Management,
    (London, 1863), 8.

8. BANKS, J.A., Prosperity and Parenthood, (London,
    1954), 74.

9. JONES, F. M., 'The aesthetic of the nineteenth-century
    industrial town', in DYOS, H. J. (ed.), The Study of
    Urban History, (London, 1968), 173.

10. HORN, P., The Rise and Fall of the Victorian Servant,
    (Dublin, 1975); MCBRIDE, T., The Domestic Revolution,
    (London, 1976); EBERY, M. and PRESTON, B., Domestic
    Service in late Victorian and Edwardian England, 1871-
    1914, (Reading, 1976). Reading University
    Geographical Papers, No. 42.

11. EBERY, M. and PRESTON, B., Domestic Service in late

Victorian and Edwardian England, 1871-1914, (Reading, 1976). Reading University Geographical Papers, No. 42.

12. HORN, P., _The Rise and Fall of the Victorian Servant_, (Dublin, 1975).

Chapter 2. Methodological approach

1. PRO, HO 107. Census Papers-Population Returns, 1851: Enumerators Schedules; PRO, RG 9. Census Papers-Population Returns, 1861: Enumerators Schedules; PRO, RG 10. Census Papers-Population Returns, 1871: Enumerators Schedules.

2. ANDERSON, M., _Family Structure in Nineteenth-Century Lancashire_, (Cambridge, 1971); WRIGLEY, E. A. (ed.), _The Study of Nineteenth-Century Society_, (London, 1972); ARMSTRONG, W. A., _Stability and Change in an English County Town: A Social Study of York, 1801-1851_, (London, 1974).

3. _PP_ 1852-3, LXXXV. Census of Gt Britain,1851. Population Tables I, Vol. I, xiii; _PP_ 1863, LIII, Pt I. Census of England and Wales, 1861, 2; _PP_ 1873, LXXI, Pt II. Census of England and Wales, 1871. Population Abstracts, 169.

4. DEANE, P. and COLE, W. A., _British Economic Growth, 1688-1959_, (Cambridge, 1962), 171.

5. _PP_ 1852-3, LXXXV. Census of Gt Britain,1851. Population Tables I, Vol. I, cxlv-cxlvii; _PP_ 1873, LXXI, Pt II. Census of England and Wales, 1871. Population Abstracts, 169.

6. SMITH, C. M., _The Law of Master and Servant_, (London, 1852, 1860, 1870).

7.   DYOS, H. J. and BAKER, A. B. H., 'The possibilties of
     computerising census data', in DYOS, H. J. (ed.),
     The Study of Urban History, (London, 1968), 102;
     ANDERSON, M., Family Structure in Nineteenth-Century
     Lancashire, (Cambridge, 1971), 140-4.
8.   ANDERSON, M., Family Structure in Nineteenth-Century
     Lancashire, (Cambridge, 1971); ARMSTRONG, W. A.,
     Stability and Change in an English County Town: A
     Social Study of York, 1801-1851, (London, 1974).

Chapter 3.   Rochdale in the Nineteenth Century

1.   TAYLOR, R. P., Rochdale Retrospective: A Centenary
     History of Rochdale, (Rochdale, 1956).
2.   Ordnance Survey of Gt Britain, 6 inches to 1 mile:
     Lancashire Sheets. (1st ed., Southampton, 1851).
3.   REDFORD, A., Labour Migration in England, 1800-50,
     (Manchester, 1926).
4.   TAYLOR, R. P., Rochdale Retrospective: A Centenary
     History of Rochdale, (Rochdale, 1956).
5.   FISHWICK, H., The History of the Parish of Rochdale in
     the County of Lancashire, (Rochdale, 1889).
6.   FISHWICK, H., The History of the Parish of Rochdale in
     the County of Lancashire, (Rochdale, 1889).
7.   TAYLOR, R. P., Rochdale Retrospective: A Centenary
     History of Rochdale, (Rochdale, 1956).
8.   RPL. Newspaper Collection.
9.   PP 1852-3, LXXXVI. Census of Gt Britain, 1851.
     Population Tables I, Vol. II, Div. VIII, 44; PP
     1862, L. Census of England and Wales, 1861.
     Population Tables, 575; PP 1872, LXVI. Census of

England and Wales, 1871. Population Tables. Pt II,
403-4.

10. PP 1863, LIII, Pt II. Census of England and Wales,
     1861, 635-41.

11. PP 1863, LIII, Pt II. Census of England and Wales,
     1861, 635-41.

12. VINCENT, J. R., 'The electoral sociology of Rochdale',
     Economic History Review, 2nd Series, Vol. XVI, 85.

13. VINCENT, J. R., 'The electoral sociology of Rochdale',
     Economic History Review, 2nd Series, Vol. XVI, 76-90.

**Chapter 4.   The Social Position of the 'Servant' in the
mid-Nineteenth Century Census**

1.   Cited in EBERY, M. and PRESTON, B., Domestic Service
     in late Victorian and Edwardian England, 1871-1914,
     (Reading, 1976), 11.

2.   TILLOT, P. M., 'Sources of inaccuracy in the 1851 and
     1861   censuses', in WRIGLEY, E. A. (ed.), The
     Study of Nineteenth-Century Society, (London, 1972),
     124.

3.   PRO, HO 107. Census Papers-Population Returns, 1851:
     Enumerators Schedules; PRO, RG 9. Census Papers-
     Population Returns, 1861:   Enumerators Schedules;
     PRO, RG 10. Census Papers-Population Returns, 1871:
     Enumerators Schedules.

4.   PP 1873, LXXI, Pt II. Census of England and Wales,
     1871. Population Abstracts, 168.

5.   PRO, RG 9. Census Papers-Population Returns, 1861:
     Enumerators Schedules.

6.   PRO, RG 29/9-16. General Register Office Letter
     Books: Out   Letters relating to the 1891 Census. 25

March 1891.

7. PRO, RG 29/9-16. General Register Office Letter
    Books: Out Letters relating to the 1891 Census. 16
    March 1891.

8. PRO, RG 29/9-16. General Register Office Letter
    Books: Out Letters relating to the 1891 Census. 17
    March 1891.

9. PP 1852-3, LXXXVIII, Pts I and II. Census of Gt
    Britain, 1851. Population Tables II; PP 1863, LIII,
    Pts I and II. Census of England and Wales, 1861.

10. PP 1852-3, LXXXVIII, Pts I and II. Census of Gt
    Britain, 1851. Population Tables II; PP 1863, LIII,
    Pts I and II. Census of England and Wales, 1861.

11. PP 1852-3, LXXXVIII, Pts I and II. Census of Gt
    Britain, 1851. Population Tables II; PP 1863, LIII,
    Pts I and II. 'Census of England and Wales, 1861.

12. PP 1852-3, LXXXVIII, Pts I and II. Census of Gt
    Britain, 1851. Population Tables II; PP 1863, LIII,
    Pts I and II. Census of England and Wales, 1861.
    PP 1873, LXXI, Pts I and II. Census of England and
    Wales, 1871. Population Abstracts.

13. BRIERLEY, H., The Rochdale Reminiscences, (Rochdale,
    1923), 5-7.

14. LASLETT, T. P. R., Family life and Illicit Love in
    Earlier Generations, (Cambridge, 1977), 204-5;
    ANDERSON, M., Family Structure in Nineteenth-Century
    Lancashire, (Cambridge, 1971), 140.

15. ANDERSON, M., Family Structure in Nineteenth-Century
    Lancashire, (Cambridge, 1971), 170-9.

16. Difference in 1851 statistically significant at the
    80% level.

17. Difference in 1851 statistically significant at the
    90% level.

18. Difference in 1851 statistically significant at the

80% level. Difference in 1861 not statistically significant at the 80% level.

19. PP 1852-3, LXXXVIII, Pts I and II. Census of Gt Britain, 1851. Population Tables II. Difference statistically significant at the 90% level.

20. PP 1863, LIII, Pts I and II. Census of England and Wales, 1861. Difference not statistically significant at the 80% level.

21. Difference statistically significant at the 90% level.

22. PP 1904, XXXII, Appendix V. Evidence to the Inter-Departmental Committee on Physical Deterioration, 128.

23. HEWITT, M., Wives and Mothers in Victorian Industry, (London, 1958), 14.

24. BUTLER, C. V., Domestic Service. An Enquiry by the Women's Industrial Council, (London, 1916), 66.

25. Difference statistically significant at the 90% level.

26. Difference with respect to single persons statistically significant in 1861 at the 80% level.

27. Difference statistically significant at the 90% level.

28. Difference with respect to age groups 10-30 years in 1861 statistically significant at the 90% level. Difference with respect to age groups 50 years plus in 1851 statistically significant at the 80% level.

29. Differences in 1851 and 1871 statistically significant at the 80% level.

30. Difference statistically significant at the 90% level.

31. Difference not statistically significant at the 80% level.

32. Difference in 1861 statistically significant at the 90% level. Difference in 1871 statistically significant at the 80% level.

33. PRO, RG 29/9-16. General Register Office Letter Books: Out Letters relating to the 1891 Census. 16

March 1891.

Chapter 5. The 'True' Servant Population of Rochdale, 1851-1871.

1. TILLOT, P. M., 'Sources of inaccuracy in the 1851 and 1861 censuses', in WRIGLEY, E. A. (ed.), The Study of Nineteenth-Century Society, (London, 1972), 125.
2. BEETON, I., Mrs Beeton's Book of Household Management, (London, 1863), 8.
3. BEETON, I., Mrs Beeton's Book of Household Management, (London, 1863), 961-1024.
4. CORNHILL MAGAZINE, 'Maids-of-all-work and Blue Books', Vol. XXX, 285.
5. EBERY, M. and PRESTON, B., Domestic Service in late Victorian and Edwardian England, 1871-1914, (Reading, 1976), 70.
6. EBERY, M. and PRESTON, B., Domestic Service in late Victorian and Edwardian England, 1871-1914, (Reading, 1976), 38.
7. MCBRIDE, T., The Domestic Revolution, (London, 1976), 20.
8. EBERY, M. and PRESTON, B., Domestic Service in late Victorian and Edwardian England, 1871-1914, (Reading, 1976), 73.
9. Difference statistically significant at the 80% level.
10. LASLETT, T. P. R., Family life and Illicit Love in Earlier Generations, (Cambridge, 1977), 31.
11. EBERY, M. and PRESTON, B., Domestic Service in late Victorian and Edwardian England, 1871-1914, (Reading, 1976), 76.
12. EBERY, M. and PRESTON, B., Domestic Service in late

Victorian and Edwardian England, 1871-1914, (Reading, 1976), 76.

13. EBERY, M. and PRESTON, B., _Domestic Service in late Victorian and Edwardian England, 1871-1914_, (Reading, 1976), 34.

14. Difference statistically significant at the 90% level.

15. Difference not statistically significant at the 80% level.

16. REDFORD, A., _Labour Migration in England, 1800-50_, (Manchester, 1926).

17. Difference not statistically significant at the 80% level.

18. Difference statistically significant at the 90% level.

19. PP 1852-3, LXXXVIII, Pts I and II. Census of Gt Britain, 1851. Population Tables II; PP 1873, LXXI, Pts I and II. Census of England and Wales, 1871. Population Abstracts.

20. MCL, MFPR 242-259. Parish records of the Parish Church of St John the Evangelist, Preston, 1851-1856.

21. EBERY, M. and PRESTON, B., _Domestic Service in late Victorian and Edwardian England, 1871-1914_, (Reading, 1976), 77.

22. LAYTON, W. T., 'Changes in the wages of domestic servants during 50 years', _Journal of the Royal Statistical Society_, Vol. 71 (1908), 518-19.

23. HORN, P., _The Rise and Fall of the Victorian Servant_, (Dublin, 1975), 184-7.

24. Cited in HORN, P., _The Rise and Fall of the Victorian Servant_, (Dublin, 1975), 130.

25. WOOD, G. H., 'The course of women's wages during the nineteenth century', in HUTCHINS, B. L. and HARRISON, A., _A History of Factory Legislation_, (London, 1903), 279.

26. PP 1899, XCII. Report (Miss Collet's) of the Labour Department of the Board of Trade on Money Wages of Indoor Domestic Servants, 11.

27. LRO, QAM/6/21. County Lunatic Asylum, Prestwich: servants' wages, 1861-1864; LRO, QAM/6/20. County Lunatic Asylum, Prestwich: list of officers with their respective salaries, 1851-1875; LRO, QAM/6/22. County Lunatic Asylum, Prestwich: attendants' wage book, 1876-1890.

28. LRO, QAM/1/34. County Asylum, Lancaster: wages paid to attendants, 1877-1883.

29. RPL, DB 154. List of guardians and paid officers of the Rochdale Poor Law Union, 1853-1910.

30. RPL, Newspaper Collection.

31. LRO, PDD BL/53/57-59. Papers of the Blundells of Little Crosby: the diaries of Agnes Blundell.

32. ANDERSON, M., Family Structure in Nineteenth-Century Lancashire, (Cambridge, 1971), 128.

33. BANKS, J.A., Prosperity and Parenthood, (London, 1954), 71-2.

34. BURNETT, J. (ed.), Useful Toil, (London, 1974), 159.

35. Cited in HORN, P., The Rise and Fall of the Victorian Servant, (Dublin, 1975), 117.

36. Cited in HORN, P., The Rise and Fall of the Victorian Servant, (Dublin, 1975), 100-01.

37. BUTLER, C. V., Domestic Service. An Enquiry by the Women's Industrial Council, (London, 1916), 17.

38. Cited in MCBRIDE, T., The Domestic Revolution, (London, 1976), 62-3.

39. SMITH, M. L., 'Institutionalised servitude: the female domestic servant in Lima, Peru', Unpublished PhD Dissertation, 1971 (British Library Reference: 72-10007), 197.

40. Cited in HORN, P., The Rise and Fall of the Victorian Servant, (Dublin, 1975), 50.

41. BUTLER, C. V., Domestic Service. An Enquiry by the Women's Industrial Council, (London, 1916), 49.

42. BUTLER, C. V., Domestic Service. An Enquiry by the Women's Industrial Council, (London, 1916), 53.

43. BEETON, I., Mrs Beeton's Book of Household Management, (London, 1863), 1001.

44. LRO, DDX/664/13/11. The diary of 'Mrs Bird' (Mary Bird Stopford) of Upholland near Wigan.

45. BOOTH, C., Life and Labour of the People in London, Vol. 8, (London, 1903), 219.

46. POWELL, M., Below Stairs, (London, 1968), 45.

47. HORN, P., The Rise and Fall of the Victorian Servant, (Dublin, 1975), 96.

48. BUTLER, C. V., Domestic Service. An Enquiry by the Women's Industrial Council, (London, 1916), 44.

49. MARCUS, S., The Other Victorians, (London, 1967), 77-196.

50. RPL. Newspaper Collection.

51. RPL. Newspaper Collection.

52. MCBRIDE, T., The Domestic Revolution, (London, 1976), 88.

53. MCBRIDE, T., The Domestic Revolution, (London, 1976), 84.

54. MCBRIDE, T., The Domestic Revolution, (London, 1976), 91.

55. MCL, MFPR 242-259. Parish records of the Parish Church of St John the Evangelist, Preston, 1851-1856.

56. POWELL, M., Below Stairs, (London, 1968), 159-60.

Chapter 6. Servant Employers in Rochdale and the Factors Affecting their Employment of Servants.

1. MARX, K., Grundrisse. Introduction to the Critique of Political Economy, (London, 1973), 401.

2. HORN, P., The Rise and Fall of the Victorian Servant, (Dublin, 1975), 50.

3. BEETON, I., Mrs Beeton's Book of Household Management, (London, 1863).

4. EBERY, M. and PRESTON, B., Domestic Service in late Victorian and Edwardian England, 1871-1914, (Reading, 1976), 63.

5. HOBSBAWM, E. J., Labouring Men, (London, 1964), 280.

6. ECONOMY FOR THE SINGLE AND MARRIED, (London, 1845), 25.

7. Difference statistically significant at the 80% level.

8. Difference with respect to servants aged under 20 years in 1861 statistically significant at the 90% level.

9. HORN, P., The Rise and Fall of the Victorian Servant, (Dublin, 1975), 18.

10. BANKS, J.A., Prosperity and Parenthood, (London, 1954), 74.

11. PRO, B3. Court of Bankruptcy files.

12. Difference, 1851-1871, in the percentage of households in Social-Economic Group 2 with more than one servant not statistically significant at the 80% level.

13. Difference, 1851-1871, in the percentage of households in Social-Economic Group 3 with more than one servant not statistically significant at the 80% level.

14. Difference not statistically significant at the 80% level.

15. MCLEOD, M., Class and Religion in the Late Victorian City, (London, 1974), 15.

16. EBERY, M. and PRESTON, B., Domestic Service in late

Victorian and Edwardian England, 1871-1914, (Reading, 1976), 64.

17. Difference statistically significant at the 80% level.

18. Differences statistically significant at the 80% level.

19. BANKS, J.A., Prosperity and Parenthood, (London, 1954), 129-69.

20. Difference between Rochdale households and servant-employing households in Social-Economic Group 5 statistically significant at the 90% level.

21. Differences between Rochdale households and servant-employing households in Social-Economic Groups 4 and 5 not statistically significant at the 80% level.

22. EBERY, M. and PRESTON, B., Domestic Service in late Victorian and Edwardian England, 1871-1914, (Reading, 1976), 68.

23. Difference not statistically significant at the 80% level.

24. NIE, N. H., HULL, C. Hadlai, JENKINS, J. G., STEINBRENNER, K., BENT, D. H., Statistical Package for the Social Sciences, (New York, 1975), 320-67.

25. SMITH, M. L., 'Institutionalised servitude: the female domestic servant in Lima, Peru', Unpublished PhD Dissertation, 1971 (British Library Reference: 72-10007), 105.

26. Cross-census search of samples of servant-employing households in the Rochdale Registration District, 1851-1871.

27. PP 1852-3, LXXXVIII, Pt I. Census of Gt Britain, 1851, lxxxviii.

28. ANDERSON, M., Family Structure in Nineteenth-Century Lancashire, (Cambridge, 1971), 71.

29. LRO, PUR 7. Rochdale Board of Guardians: Workhouse Committee Minute Books, 1852-1871.

30. MCBRIDE, T., The Domestic Revolution, (London, 1976),

115; EBERY, M. and PRESTON, B., <u>Domestic Service in late Victorian and Edwardian England, 1871-1914</u>, (Reading, 1976), 21.

Chapter 7. Domestic Service and the Rural Woman

1. Difference in 1861 statistically significant at the 90% level.
2. Samples of servant-employing households, Rochdale Registration District, 1851-1871.
3. RPL. Newspaper Collection.
4. HORN, P., <u>The Rise and Fall of the Victorian Servant</u>, (Dublin, 1975), 28.
5. JONES, G. Steadman, <u>Outcast London</u>, (Oxford, 1971), 138-9.
6. MCBRIDE, T., <u>The Domestic Revolution</u>, (London, 1976), 94.
7. Cited in HEWITT, M., <u>Wives and Mothers in Victorian Industry</u>, (London, 1958), 49.
8. GASKELL, P., <u>The Manufacturing Population of England</u>, (London, 1833), 147.
9. <u>Hansard</u>, 1844, Vol. LXXXIII, cols 1,093-4.
10. HEWITT, M., <u>Wives and Mothers in Victorian Industry</u>, (London, 1958).
11. HEWITT, M., <u>Wives and Mothers in Victorian Industry</u>, (London, 1958), 51-2.
12. LASLETT, T. P. R., <u>The World We Have Lost</u>, (London, 1965), 150-1.
13. <u>PP</u> 1833, XXI. Second Report of the .....Commissioners....(on)......the Employment of Children in Factories......with Minutes of Evidence;

D3, 4.

14. PINCHBECK, I., Women Workers and the Industrial Revolution, (London, 1930), 310.

15. BEETON, I., Mrs Beeton's Book of Household Management, (London, 1906), 15.

16. LRO, PUR 7. Rochdale Board of Guardians: Workhouse Committee Minute Books, 1852-1871.

17. RPL. Newspaper Collection

18. FIRTH, V. M., The Psychology of the Servant Problem, (London, 1925), 48.

19. Cited in HORN, P., The Rise and Fall of the Victorian Servant, (Dublin, 1975), 32.

20. BUTLER, C. V., Domestic Service. An Enquiry by the Women's Industrial Council, (London, 1916), 16.

21. PP 1834, XXX. Report from His Majesty's Commissioners for Inquiring into the Administration and Practical Operation of the Poor Laws. Appendix B(i): Answers to Rural Queries, Pt 1, 604 (a).

22. PP 1834, XXX. Report from His Majesty's Commissioners for Inquiring into the Administration and Practical Operation of the Poor Laws. Appendix B(i): Answers to Rural Queries, Pt 1, 74 (a).

23. PP 1834, XXX. Report from His Majesty's Commissioners for Inquiring into the Administration and Practical Operation of the Poor Laws. Appendix B(i): Answers to Rural Queries, Pt 1, 643 (a).

24. PP 1834, XXX. Report from His Majesty's Commissioners for Inquiring into the Administration and Practical Operation of the Poor Laws. Appendix B(i): Answers to Rural Queries, Pt 1, 641 (a).

25. PP 1843, XII. Reports of the Special Poor Law Commissioners on the Employment of Women and Children in Agriculture, 358.

26. THOMPSON, F., Lark Rise to Candleford, (London, 1973),

155.

27. Personal correspondence with Mr E. Gittins.

28. BUTLER, C. V., Domestic Service. An Enquiry by the Women's Industrial Council, (London, 1916), 38.

29. THOMPSON, F., Lark Rise to Candleford, (London, 1973), 109.

30. ANDERSON, M., Family Structure in Nineteenth-Century Lancashire, (Cambridge, 1971), 157.

31. ANDERSON, M., Family Structure in Nineteenth-Century Lancashire, (Cambridge, 1971), 118.

32. ANDERSON, M., Family Structure in Nineteenth-Century Lancashire, (Cambridge, 1971), 119.

33. PRESTON, B., Occupations of Father and Son in Mid-Victorian England, (Reading, 1977), 31.

34. Difference between the percentages of Rochdale-born women employed in the provision of dress and 'urban' migrants so employed statistically significant at the 90% level.

35. SMITH, M. L., 'Institutionalised servitude: the female domestic servant in Lima, Peru', Unpublished PhD Dissertation, 1971 (British Library Reference: 72-10007), 95-6.

36. BUTLER, C. V., Domestic Service. An Enquiry by the Women's Industrial Council, (London, 1916), 119-20.

37. Personal correspondence with Mr E. Gittins.

38. HARRISON, B., 'For Church, Queen and Family: the Girls' Friendly Society, 1874-1920', Past and Present, Vol. 61 (1973), 107-39.

39. Cited HARRISON, B., 'For Church, Queen and Family: the Girls' Friendly Society, 1874-1920', Past and Present, Vol. 61 (1973), 119.

40. Cited HARRISON, B., 'For Church, Queen and Family: the Girls' Friendly Society, 1874-1920', Past and Present, Vol. 61 (1973), 117.

41. HARRISON, B., 'For Church, Queen and Family: the Girls' Friendly Society, 1874-1920', Past and Present, Vol. 61 (1973), 120.

42. SAGARRA, E., A Social History of Germany, 1648-1914, (London, 1977), 383.

43. SMITH, M. L., 'Institutionalised servitude: the female domestic servant in Lima, Peru', Unpublished PhD Dissertation, 1971 (British Library Reference: 72-10007), 166.

44. MCL, 06/2/2/1-5. Correspondence of Mrs Munro of London to Mrs Cartwright of Wem, Shropshire. 4 February, 1803.

45. MCL, 06/2/2/1-5. Correspondence of Mrs Munro of London to Mrs Cartwright of Wem, Shropshire. 8 March, 1803.

46. MCL, 06/2/2/1-5. Correspondence of Mrs Munro of London to Mrs Cartwright of Wem, Shropshire. June 1803.

47. OBELKEVITCH, J., Religion and Rural Society: South Lindsey, 1825-1875, (Oxford, 1976), 318.

48. HOBSBAWM, E. J. and RUDE, G., Captain Swing, (London, 1969), 99, 154-6, 249.

49. ANDERSON, M., Family Structure in Nineteenth-Century Lancashire, (Cambridge, 1971), Chapters 7-9.

50. ARNOLD, R. A., The History of the Cotton Famine, (London, 1864), 62.

51. BUTLER, C. V., Domestic Service. An Enquiry by the Women's Industrial Council, (London, 1916), 39-40.

52. BULLEY, A. Amy, 'Domestic service: a social study', Westminster Review, Vol. 135 (1891), 177-8.

53. THOMPSON, F., Lark Rise to Candleford, (London, 1973), 155.

54. BUTLER, C. V., Domestic Service. An Enquiry by the Women's Industrial Council, (London, 1916), 89.

55. COOKE TAYLOR, W., A Tour of the Manufacturing Districts of Lancashire, (London, 1968), 149.

56. BUTLER, C. V., <u>Domestic Service. An Enquiry by the Women's Industrial Council</u>, (London, 1916), 11.

57. <u>PP</u> 1919, XXIX. Ministry of Reconstruction. Report of the Domestic Service Sub-Committee IV, 22.

58. <u>PP</u> 1919, XXIX. Ministry of Reconstruction. Report of the Domestic Service Sub-Committee IV, 22.

Chapter 8. The Effect of Location on Servant Employment

1. FOSTER, J., <u>Class Struggle and the Industrial Revolution</u>, (London, 1974), 177-9.

2. FOSTER, J., <u>Class Struggle and the Industrial Revolution</u>, (London, 1974), 177-9.

3. Difference between the percentage of textile manufacturers resident in large nucleated settlements employing more than one servant and the average for all textile manufacturers is statistically significant at the 90% level.

4. MARSHALL, J. D., 'Colonisation as a factor in the planting of towns in north-west England', DYOS, H. J. (ed.), <u>The Study of Urban History</u>, (London, 1968), 225-9.

5. MILNE, J., <u>Rochdale As It Was</u>, (Lancashire, 1973), 33.

Chapter 9. The Recruitment of Servants in Rochdale, 1851-1871

1. <u>PP</u> 1899, XCII. Report (Miss Collet's) of the Labour Department of the Board of Trade on Money Wages of Indoor Domestic Servants, 25-6.

2. EBERY, M. and PRESTON, B., <u>Domestic Service in late Victorian and Edwardian England, 1871-1914</u>, (Reading, 1976), 100.

3. <u>PP</u> 1862, L. Census of England and Wales, 1861. Population Tables, 575; <u>PP</u> 1872, LXVI. Census of England and Wales, 1871. Population Tables. Pt II, 403-4.

4. <u>PP</u> 1862, L. Census of England and Wales, 1861. Population Tables, 575; <u>PP</u> 1872, LXVI. Census of England and Wales, 1871. Population Tables. Pt II, 403-4.

5. <u>PP</u> 1862, L. Census of England and Wales, 1861. Population Tables, 575; <u>PP</u> 1872, LXVI. Census of England and Wales, 1871. Population Tables. Pt II, 403-4.

6. LASLETT, T. P. R., <u>Family life and Illicit Love in Earlier Generations</u>, (Cambridge, 1977), 73.

7. RPL. Newspaper Collection

8. LRO, PUR 7. Rochdale Board of Guardians: Workhouse Committee Minute Books, 1851-1871.

9. SMITH, M. L., 'Institutionalised servitude: the female domestic servant in Lima, Peru', Unpublished PhD Dissertation, 1971 (British Library Reference: 72-10007), 361.

10. BEETON, I., <u>Mrs Beeton's Book of Household Management</u>, (London, 1906), 14

11. BEETON, I., <u>Mrs Beeton's Book of Household Management</u>, (London, 1863), 6-7.

12. WEBSTER, T. and PARKES, MRS, <u>An Encyclopedia of Domestic Economy</u>, (London, 1861), 330.

13. BEETON, I., <u>Mrs Beeton's Book of Household Management</u>, (London, 1906), 14

14. LRO, DP/393. Miss Lizabeth Appleton: correspondence,

1805.

15. LRO, DDCL/1184/18. Correspondence of John Cunliffe of Myerscough Hall with Thomas Clifton of Lytham Hall, 1837.

16. Difference statistically significant at the 90% level.

17. Difference statistically significant at the 90% level.

18. Difference statistically significant at the 80% level.

19. Difference statistically significant at the 80% level.

20. Difference not statistically significant at the 80% level.

21. Differences between the percentages of servant-employing household heads in Social-Economic Group 3 who were born in the district of Rochdale and the percentages of control sample heads so born not statistically significant at the 80% level in 1851, 1861 and 1871.

22. Differences between the percentages of servant-employing household heads in Social-Economic Group 1 who were born in the district of Rochdale and the percentages of control sample heads so born statistically significant at the 80% level in 1861.

23. Differences between the percentages of servant-employing household heads in all Social-Economic Groups who were born in the district of Rochdale and the percentages of control sample heads so born not statistically significant at the 80% level in 1871.

24. Difference statistically significant at the 90% level.

25. Difference statistically significant at the 90% level.

26. Difference statistically significant at the 90% level.

27. LRO, PUR 7. Rochdale Board of Guardians: Workhouse Committee Minute Books, 1851-1871. 25 February, 1853.

28. LRO, PUR 7. Rochdale Board of Guardians: Workhouse Committee Minute Books, 1851-1871. 20 January, 1865.

29. LRO, PUR 7. Rochdale Board of Guardians: Workhouse

Committee Minute Books, 1851-1871. 3 March, 1865.

30. LRO, PUR 7. Rochdale Board of Guardians: Workhouse
Committee Minute Books, 1851-1871. 13 April, 1855.

31. LRO, PUR 7. Rochdale Board of Guardians: Workhouse
Committee Minute Books, 1851-1871. 23 May, 1855.

32. LRO, PUR 7. Rochdale Board of Guardians: Workhouse
Committee Minute Books, 1851-1871. 29 June, 1855.

33. LRO, PUR 7. Rochdale Board of Guardians: Workhouse
Committee Minute Books, 1851-1871. 8 February, 1856.

34. LRO, PUR 7. Rochdale Board of Guardians: Workhouse
Committee Minute Books, 1851-1871. 8 August, 1856.

35. LRO, PUR 7. Rochdale Board of Guardians: Workhouse
Committee Minute Books, 1851-1871. 3 October, 1856.

36. LRO, PUR 7. Rochdale Board of Guardians: Workhouse
Committee Minute Books, 1851-1871. 29 May, 1857.

37. HORN, P., The Rise and Fall of the Victorian Servant,
(Dublin, 1975), 120.

38. LRO, PUR 7. Rochdale Board of Guardians: Workhouse
Committee Minute Books, 1851-1871. 6 June, 1851.

39. LRO, PUR 7. Rochdale Board of Guardians: Workhouse
Committee Minute Books, 1851-1871. 27 November, 1863.

40. LRO, PUR 7. Rochdale Board of Guardians: Workhouse
Committee Minute Books, 1851-1871. 19 February, 1864.

41. LRO, PUR 7. Rochdale Board of Guardians: Workhouse
Committee Minute Books, 1851-1871.

42. LRO, PUR 7. Rochdale Board of Guardians: Workhouse
Committee Minute Books, 1851-1871. 13 April, 1866.

43. LRO, PUR 7. Rochdale Board of Guardians: Workhouse
Committee Minute Books, 1851-1871.

44. LRO, PUR 7. Rochdale Board of Guardians: Workhouse
Committee Minute Books, 1851-1871.

45. LRO, PUR 7. Rochdale Board of Guardians: Workhouse
Committee Minute Books, 1851-1871.

46. GEORGE, M. Dorothy, 'The early history of registry

offices', <u>Economic History</u>, Vol. IV, 570-90.

47. HORN, P., <u>The Rise and Fall of the Victorian Servant</u>, (Dublin, 1975), 39.

48. RPL. Newspaper Collection.

49. RPL. Newspaper Collection. <u>Rochdale Observer</u>, 2 June, 1860.

50. RPL. Newspaper Collection. <u>Rochdale Observer</u>, 23 November, 1867.

51. RPL. Newspaper Collection. <u>Rochdale Observer</u>, 8 May, 1869.

52. RPL. Newspaper Collection. <u>Rochdale Observer</u>, 3 September, 1869.

53. RPL. Newspaper Collection. <u>Rochdale Observer</u>, 1856-1871.

54. RPL. Newspaper Collection. <u>Rochdale Observer</u>, 30 November, 1861.

55. RPL. Newspaper Collection. <u>Rochdale Observer</u>, 7 January, 1871.

56. RPL. Newspaper Collection. <u>Rochdale Observer</u>, 19 August, 1871.

57. RPL. Newspaper Collection. <u>Rochdale Observer</u>, 24 December, 1869.

58. RPL. Newspaper Collection. <u>Rochdale Observer</u>, 8 October, 1870.

59. RPL. Newspaper Collection. <u>Rochdale Observer</u>, 26 March, 1864.

60. LRO, PUR 7. Rochdale Board of Guardians: Workhouse Committee Minute Books, 1851-1871. 13 April, 1866.

61. RPL, DB 154. List of guardians and paid officers of the Rochdale Poor Law Union, 1859-1866.

62. LRO, PUR 7. Rochdale Board of Guardians: Workhouse Committee Minute Books, 1851-1871. 31 August, 1866.

63. RPL, DB 154. List of guardians and paid officers of

the Rochdale Poor Law Union, 1873.

64. RPL, DB 154. List of guardians and paid officers of the Rochdale Poor Law Union, 1879.

65. LRO, QAM/6/21. County Lunatic Asylum, Prestwich: servants' wages, 1861-1864; LRO, QAM/6/20. County Lunatic Asylum, Prestwich: list of officers with their respective salaries, 1851-1875; LRO, QAM/6/22. County Lunatic Asylum, Prestwich: attendants' wage book, 1876-1890.

66. LRO, QAM/6/21. County Lunatic Asylum, Prestwich: servants' wages, 1861-1864; LRO, QAM/6/20. County Lunatic Asylum, Prestwich: list of officers with their respective salaries, 1851-1875; LRO, QAM/6/22. County Lunatic Asylum, Prestwich: attendants' wage book, 1876-1890.

67. LRO, QAM/6/21. County Lunatic Asylum, Prestwich: servants' wages, 1861-1864; LRO, QAM/6/20. County Lunatic Asylum, Prestwich: list of officers with their respective salaries, 1851-1875; LRO, QAM/6/22. County Lunatic Asylum, Prestwich: attendants' wage book, 1876-1890.

68. ARMSTRONG, W. A., 'The use of information about occupation', in WRIGLEY, E. A. (ed.), The Study of Nineteenth-Century Society, (London, 1972), 255-81.

69. Information supplied by Mrs E. Higgs of Lancaster.

Chapter 10.   Domestic Service in Nineteenth-Century
              Rochdale: Some Implications for Contemporary
              Historical Research

1. MCBRIDE, T., The Domestic Revolution, (London, 1976).

2. HORN, P., The Rise and Fall of the Victorian Servant,

(Dublin, 1975).

3. PERKIN, H. J., The Origins of Modern English Society, 1780-1880, (London, 1969), 143.

4. EBERY, M. and PRESTON, B., Domestic Service in late Victorian and Edwardian England, 1871-1914, (Reading, 1976). Reading University Geographical Papers, No. 42.

5. HORN, P., The Rise and Fall of the Victorian Servant, (Dublin, 1975).

6. BURNETT, J. (ed.), Useful Toil, (London, 1974).

7. CHAPLIN, D., 'The employment of domestic servants as a class indicator: a methodological discussion', a paper presented at the Social History Association meeting, Philadelphia, USA, October, 1976. Table 1.

8. CHAPLIN, D., 'The employment of domestic servants as a class indicator: a methodological discussion', a paper presented at the Social History Association meeting, Philadelphia, USA, October, 1976. Table 1.

9. BRANCA, P., Silent Sisterhood, (London, 1975).

10. Cited in BRANCA, P., Silent Sisterhood, (London, 1975), 41-2.

11. Cited in BRANCA, P., Silent Sisterhood, (London, 1975), 43-4.

12. BRANCA, P., Silent Sisterhood, (London, 1975), 54.

13. WARREN, MRS E., How I Managed My House on Two Hundred Pounds a Year, (London, 1864).

14. HORN, P., The Rise and Fall of the Victorian Servant, (Dublin, 1975).

15. THIRSK, J. and COOPER, J. P., Seventeenth-Century Economic Documents, (Oxford, 1972), 773.

16. DEANE, P. and COLE, W. A., British Economic Growth, 1688-1959, (Cambridge, 1962), 143.

17. MCBRIDE, T., The Domestic Revolution, (London, 1976), 14.

18. ARMSTRONG, W. A., 'The use of information about occupation', in WRIGLEY, E. A. (ed.), The Study of Nineteenth-Century Society, (London, 1972), 245.

19. ARMSTRONG, W. A., 'The use of information about occupation', in WRIGLEY, E. A. (ed.), The Study of Nineteenth-Century Society, (London, 1972), 226-311.

20. EBERY, M. and PRESTON, B., Domestic Service in late Victorian and Edwardian England, 1871-1914, (Reading, 1976), 19.

21. ARMSTRONG, W. A., 'The use of information about occupation', in WRIGLEY, E. A. (ed.), The Study of Nineteenth-Century Society, (London, 1972), 255-81.

22. FRANKLIN, J., 'Troops of servants: labour and planning in the country house, 1840-1914', Victorian Studies, Vol. XIX, (Dec. 1975), 211.

23. FRANKLIN, J., 'Troops of servants: labour and planning in the country house, 1840-1914', Victorian Studies, Vol. XIX, (Dec. 1975), 239.

24. PP 1852-3, LXXXVIII, Pt I. Census of Gt Britain, 1851, ccxxii-ccxxvii; PP 1863, LIII, Pt I. Census of England and Wales, 1861, xlii-lxv; PP 1873, LXXI. Census of England and Wales, 1871, xxxvii-xlviii.

25. PP 1904, CVIII. Census of England and Wales. General Report, 95.

26. PERKIN, H. J., The Origins of Modern English Society, 1780-1880, (London, 1969), 143.

27. MCLEOD, M., Class and Religion in the Late Victorian City, (London, 1974), 26.

28. ARMSTRONG, W. A., 'The use of information about occupation', in WRIGLEY, E. A. (ed.), The Study of Nineteenth-Century Society, (London, 1972), 193.

29. PP 1852-3, LXXXVIII, Pt II. Census of Gt Britain, 1851; PP 1873, LXXI, Pt I. Census of England and Wales, 1871.

30. HARRISON, J. F. C., The Early Victorians, 1832-1851, (London, 1971), 110.

31. FOSTER, J., Class Struggle and the Industrial Revolution, (London, 1974), 179.

32. 1871 census sample of servant-employing households.

33. 1871 census sample of servant-employing households.

34. 1861 census sample of servant-employing households.

35. FIRTH, V. M., The Psychology of the Servant Problem, (London, 1925); LAYARD, G. S., 'The doom of the domestic cook', Nineteenth Century, Vol. XXXIII (1893), 309-19; 'JUSTICE', The Solution of the Domestic Servant Problem, (North Shields, 1910); LEWIS, E. A., 'A reformation of domestic service', Nineteenth Century, Vol. XXXIII, 127-38; BUTLER, C. V., Domestic Service. An Enquiry by the Women's Industrial Council, (London, 1916); PP 1919, XXIX. Ministry of Reconstruction. Report of the Domestic Service Sub-Committee IV.

36. MCBRIDE, T., The Domestic Revolution, (London, 1976), 67.

37. BANKS, J.A., Prosperity and Parenthood, (London, 1954), 132.

38. BANKS, J.A., Prosperity and Parenthood, (London, 1954), 168.

39. BANKS, J.A., Prosperity and Parenthood, (London, 1954), 205.

40. INNES, J. W., Class Fertility Trends in England and Wales, 1876-1934, (Princeton, 1938), 43.

41. HEWITT, M., Wives and Mothers in Victorian Industry, (London, 1958), 98.

42. INNES, J. W., Class Fertility Trends in England and Wales, 1876-1934, (Princeton, 1938), 65-6.

43. FRANKLIN, J., 'Troops of servants: labour and planning

in the country house, 1840-1914', <u>Victorian Studies</u>, Vol. XIX, (Dec. 1975), 221.

44. MCBRIDE, T., <u>The Domestic Revolution</u>, (London, 1976), 67.

45. DAVIDOFF, L., <u>The Best Circles. Society, Etiquette and the Season</u>, (London, 1973), 87-9.

46. GATHORNE-HARDY, J., <u>The Rise and Fall of the British Nanny</u>, (London, 1972), 181.

47. GATHORNE-HARDY, J., <u>The Rise and Fall of the British Nanny</u>, (London, 1972), 181.

48. EBERY, M. and PRESTON, B., <u>Domestic Service in late Victorian and Edwardian England, 1871-1914</u>, (Reading, 1976), 34.

49. EBERY, M. and PRESTON, B., <u>Domestic Service in late Victorian and Edwardian England, 1871-1914</u>, (Reading, 1976), 20.

50. EBERY, M. and PRESTON, B., <u>Domestic Service in late Victorian and Edwardian England, 1871-1914</u>, (Reading, 1976), 21.

51. DURKHEIM, E., <u>The Division of Labour in Society</u>, (Glencoe, Illinois, 1960), Vol. 2, Chapter 2.

52. BURNETT, J. (ed.), <u>Useful Toil</u>, (London, 1974), 139-40.

53. BUTLER, C. V., <u>Domestic Service. An Enquiry by the Women's Industrial Council</u>, (London, 1916), 73.

54. DEANE, P. and COLE, W. A., <u>British Economic Growth, 1688-1959</u>, (Cambridge, 1962), 142.

55. HOBSBAWM, E. J. and RUDE, G., <u>Captain Swing</u>, (London, 1969), 43.

56. HOBSBAWM, E. J. and RUDE, G., <u>Captain Swing</u>, (London, 1969), 50-1.

57. HOBSBAWM, E. J. and RUDE, G., <u>Captain Swing</u>, (London, 1969), 73-91.

58. DEANE, P. and COLE, W. A., <u>British Economic Growth,</u>

1688-1959, (Cambridge, 1962), 10-11.

59. FIRTH, V. M., The Psychology of the Servant Problem, (London, 1925), 77.

60. 'HELIX', 'Human progress', Westminster Review, Vol. 52 (1849), 21.

61. STEVENSON, J. J., House Architecture, (London, 1880), Vol. II, 98.

62. STEVENSON, J. J., House Architecture, (London, 1880), Vol. II, 75.

63. FRANKLIN, J., 'Troops of servants: labour and planning in the country house, 1840-1914', Victorian Studies, Vol. XIX, (Dec. 1975), 226-31.

64. EBERY, M. and PRESTON, B., Domestic Service in late Victorian and Edwardian England, 1871-1914, (Reading, 1976), 24.

65. MATHIAS, P., The Retailing Revolution, (London, 1967), 40-1, 126, 166.

66. JEFFREYS, J. B., Retail Trading in Britain, 1850-1950, (Cambridge, 1954), 36.

TABLES

The following tables contain statistics derived from the computer analysis of Rochdale's servant-employing households. In the majority of tables the figures relate to percentages of defined populations having certain common characteristics. In all cases the statistics have been rounded up or down, usually to the first decimal place.

The information given was not complete for all households; the age, sex or other characteristics of some servants and household heads being unknown. Unless otherwise stated the cases included in all tables are only those where the necessary information existed.

TABLE 1

THE DISTRIBUTION OF HOUSEHOLDS IN THE ROCHDALE DISTRICT
ACCORDING TO SETTLEMENT TYPE, 1851 AND 1871
(SEE APPENDIX A, NOTE 28, FOR SETTLEMENT CLASSIFICATION)

SETTLEMENT TYPE	HOUSEHOLDS AS % OF DISTRICT		% INCREASE NO. OF HOUSEHOLDS
	1851	1871	
URBAN CENTRE OF ROCHDALE	3.68	2.81	23.78
INNER URBAN PERIPHERY	9.54	6.93	17.83
OUTER URBAN PERIPHERY	29.63	15.33	-16.04
NEW PERIPHERY -INCORPORATED	0.00	5.50	
NEW PERIPHERY -CONSTRUCTED	0.00	20.25	
LARGE NUCLEATED SETTLEMENTS	15.64	25.81	167.78
SMALL NUCLEATED SETTLEMENTS	21.49	11.21	-15.36
LARGE DISPERSED SETTLEMENTS	2.55	0.46	-70.99

TABLE 1 (CONT.)

THE DISTRIBUTION OF HOUSEHOLDS IN THE ROCHDALE DISTRICT
ACCORDING TO SETTLEMENT TYPE, 1851 AND 1871
(SEE APPENDIX A, NOTE 28, FOR SETTLEMENT CLASSIFICATION)

SETTLEMENT TYPE	HOUSEHOLDS AS % OF DISTRICT		% INCREASE NO. OF HOUSEHOLDS
	1851	1871	
SMALL DISPERSED SETTLEMENTS	4.37	1.36	-49.43
SETTLEMENTS 2 TO 10 HOUSEHOLDS	9.61	4.69	-20.91
ISOLATED DWELLINGS	1.39	0.81	-5.15
URBAN AREA OF BACUP	2.10	3.78	191.81
URBAN AREA OF HEYWOOD	0.00	1.09	
ROCHDALE HOUSEHOLDS	13,934	22,604	62.22

TABLE 2

POPULATION OF THE DISTRICT OF ROCHDALE, 1801-1901
(SOURCE: CENSUSES OF ENGLAND AND WALES, 1801-1901)

YEAR	1801	1811	1821	1831	1841
POPULATION	26,577	33,577	42,124	52,387	60,578
% INCREASE	-----	26.34	25.45	24.36	15.64

YEAR	1851	1861	1871	1881	1891
POPULATION	72,515	91,754	109,858	118,334	123,853
% INCREASE	19.71	26.53	19.73	7.72	4.66

YEAR	1891*	1901
POPULATION	112,758	120,433
% INCREASE	-----	6.81

* CHANGE IN BOUNDARIES OF ROCHDALE REGISTRATION DISTRICT

TABLE 3

PERCENTAGE OF OCCUPATIONAL GROUPS RESIDENT IN DIFFERING
SETTLEMENT TYPES, 1851

OCCUPATIONAL GROUPING	URBAN BACUP	URBAN CENTRE	INNER PERIPH.	OUTER PERIPH.	LARGE NUC.
AGRICULTURE	0.00	0.00	0.00	4.76	0.00
TEXTILES	1.96	1.63	10.46	15.69	23.86
METALS	0.00	0.00	14.29	28.57	42.86
COAL	0.00	0.00	0.00	16.67	0.00
BUILDING	0.00	0.00	35.71	14.29	7.14
WOODWORK	0.00	0.00	9.09	36.36	27.27
DRESS	3.57	17.86	14.29	21.43	14.29
TRANSPORT	0.00	0.00	0.00	37.50	12.50
LABOURERS	15.79	5.26	10.53	5.26	5.26
PROFESSIONS	0.00	0.00	0.00	0.00	100.00
COMMERCE	0.00	0.00	0.00	12.50	12.50
RETAILERS	3.23	3.23	16.13	48.39	19.35
SERVANTS	0.00	4.35	13.04	43.49	13.04
ALL HOUSEHOLDS	2.10	3.68	9.54	29.63	15.64

OCCUPATIONAL GROUPINGS INCLUDE WORKERS PROVIDING PRODUCTS
OR SERVICES IN THESE INDUSTRIES, OR RAW MATERIALS FOR THESE
INDUSTRIES.

FOR SETTLEMENT TYPES SEE APPENDIX A, NOTE 28.

TABLE 3 (CONT.)

PERCENTAGE OF OCCUPATIONAL GROUPS RESIDENT IN DIFFERING
SETTLEMENT TYPES, 1851

OCCUPATIONAL GROUPING	SMALL NUC.	LARGE DISP.	SMALL DISP.	2-10 HOUSEHOLDS
AGRICULTURE	28.57	0.00	0.00	19.05
TEXTILES	27.78	5.56	4.25	6.54
METALS	14.29	0.00	0.00	0.00
COAL	33.33	8.30	0.00	41.67
BUILDING	35.71	0.00	7.14	0.00
WOODWORK	27.27	0.00	0.00	0.00
DRESS	14.29	0.00	3.57	10.72
TRANSPORT	25.00	0.00	0.00	12.50
LABOURERS	26.32	10.53	10.53	10.53
PROFESSIONS	0.00	0.00	0.00	0.00
COMMERCE	50.00	0.00	0.00	25.00
RETAILERS	6.45	0.00	0.00	3.23
SERVANTS	8.70	4.35	0.00	4.35
ALL HOUSEHOLDS	21.49	2.55	4.37	9.61

OCCUPATIONAL GROUPINGS INCLUDE WORKERS PROVIDING PRODUCTS
OR SERVICES IN THESE INDUSTRIES, OR RAW MATERIALS FOR THESE
INDUSTRIES.

FOR SETTLEMENT TYPES SEE APPENDIX A, NOTE 28.

TABLE 3 (CONT.)

PERCENTAGE OF OCCUPATIONAL GROUPS RESIDENT IN DIFFERING
SETTLEMENT TYPES, 1851

OCCUPATIONAL GROUPING	ISOLATED HOUSES	CASES
AGRICULTURE	47.62	21
TEXTILES	2.29	306
METALS	0.00	7
COAL	0.00	12
BUILDING	0.00	14
WOODWORK	0.00	11
DRESS	0.00	28
TRANSPORT	12.50	8
LABOURERS	0.00	19
PROFESSIONS	0.00	3
COMMERCE	0.00	8
RETAILERS	0.00	31
SERVANTS	8.70	23
ALL HOUSEHOLDS	1.39	13.934

OCCUPATIONAL GROUPINGS INCLUDE WORKERS PROVIDING PRODUCTS
OR SERVICES IN THESE INDUSTRIES, OR RAW MATERIALS FOR THESE
INDUSTRIES.

FOR SETTLEMENT TYPES SEE APPENDIX A, NOTE 28.

TABLE 4

OCCUPATIONS OF EMPLOYED PERSONS AGED 20 YEARS AND OVER IN
THE REGISTRATION DISTRICT OF ROCHDALE AND IN ENGLAND AND
WALES, 1861

GROUP	MEN %	
	ROCHDALE	ENGLAND AND WALES
GOVERNMENT	0.38	1.68
MILITARY	0.19	2.37
PROFESSIONS	0.14	3.09
INN/BOARDING	1.42	1.80
DOMESTIC SERVICE/ATTENDANCE	0.33	2.07
COMMERCIAL/DEALING	4.65	2.75
TECHNICAL/ENGINEERING	5.60	6.89
BUILDING	7.12	8.63
TRANSPORT	4.56	7.11
AGRICULTURE	6.79	25.50
TEXTILES	40.65	7.22
DRESS	4.31	7.02
WOOD/SKINS	2.67	3.05
MINING/METALS	14.24	15.33
LABOURERS	4.27	5.45
TOTAL NO. OF EMPLOYED PERSONS	24,122	4,752,410

SOURCE: PP 1863 LIII, PT. II, 635-47.

TABLE 4 (CONT.)

OCCUPATIONS OF EMPLOYED PERSONS AGED 20 YEARS AND OVER IN THE REGISTRATION DISTRICT OF ROCHDALE AND IN ENGLAND AND WALES, 1861

GROUP	WOMEN %	
	ROCHDALE	ENGLAND AND WALES
GOVERNMENT	0.02	0.16
MILITARY	0.00	0.00
PROFESSIONS	0.93	3.32
INN/BOARDING	2.59	7.33
DOMESTIC SERVICE/ATTENDANCE	13.29	26.39
COMMERCIAL/DEALING	3.43	1.20
TECHNICAL/ENGINEERING	0.41	1.04
BUILDING	0.00	1.11
TRANSPORT	0.05	0.27
AGRICULTURE	4.47	13.89
TEXTILES	62.78	14.10
DRESS	10.96	29.10
WOOD/SKINS	0.16	0.73
MINING/METALS	0.12	1.36
LABOURERS	0.00	0.00
TOTAL NO. OF EMPLOYED PERSONS	13,419	2,292,084

SOURCE: PP 1863 LIII, PT. II, 635-47.

TABLE 5

NUMBER OF HANDS RECORDED AS EMPLOYED BY CAPITALISTS

INDUSTRY	NO. OF EMPLOYERS	TOTAL HANDS	AVERAGE
WOOLLEN TEXTILES	14	1,130	80.7
COTTON TEXTILES	26	6,792	261.2
FLANNEL TEXTILES	8	1,062	132.8
SILK TEXTILES	1	141	141.0
IRON FOUNDARIES	3	569	189.7
MACHINERY	3	756	252.0
BOILERMAKING	1	70	70.0

POOLED FROM HOUSEHOLD SAMPLES 1851, 1861, AND 1871.

TABLE 6

SERVANTS AGED 20 YEARS AND OVER IN THE ROCHDALE SAMPLE,1851

SERVANT TYPES	TOTAL SAMPLE	OUT SERVS	POSSIBLE SERVS	WRONG SERVS	TRUE SERVS	CENSUS TOTAL/4
GENERAL(F)	217	10	49	0	158	244.75
BUTLER	1	0	0	0	1	0.00
GENERAL(M)	21	9	3	0	9	17.75
COACHMAN	3	2	0	0	1	0.25
GROOM	4	4	0	0	0	0.25
GARDENER	16	14	0	0	2	0.00
HOUSEKEEPER	66	2	0	54	10	65.50
COOK	5	0	0	0	5	8.75
HOUSEMAID	18	0	9	0	9	13.25
NURSE	9	3	0	0	6	5.75
GOVERNESS	3	0	0	1	2	0.00
LADIES MAID	2	0	0	0	2	0.00
LAUNDRYMAID	1	0	0	0	1	0.00
KITCHENMAID	1	0	0	0	1	0.00
FOOTMAN	0	0	0	0	0	0.00
COMPANION	0	0	0	0	0	0.00
TOTAL	367	44	61	55	207	356.25

SOURCE: HOUSEHOLD SAMPLE AND PP 1852-53, LXXXVIII, PT II.

TABLE 7

SERVANTS AGED 20 YEARS AND OVER IN THE ROCHDALE SAMPLE,1861

SERVANT TYPES	TOTAL SAMPLE	OUT SERVS	POSSIBLE SERVS	WRONG SERVS	TRUE SERVS	CENSUS TOTAL $\frac{}{4}$
GENERAL(F)	258	20	61	3	174	244.75
BUTLER	1	1	0	0	0	0.00
GENERAL(M)	7	4	1	0	2	7.75
COACHMAN	18	17	0	0	1	3.75
GROOM	8	8	0	0	0	0.75
GARDENER	19	19	0	0	0	2.50
HOUSEKEEPER	242	1	0	224	17	63.25
COOK	22	2	1	0	19	24.25
HOUSEMAID	31	0	8	0	23	25.50
NURSE	15	5	4	0	6	10.75
GOVERNESS	2	0	0	0	2	0.00
LADIES MAID	1	0	0	0	1	0.00
LAUNDRYMAID	2	0	0	0	2	0.00
KITCHENMAID	1	0	0	0	1	0.00
FOOTMAN	1	1	0	0	0	0.00
COMPANION	0	0	0	0	0	0.00
TOTAL	628	78	75	227	248	383.25

SOURCE: HOUSEHOLD SAMPLE AND PP 1863, LIII, PT II.

TABLE 7A

SERVANTS AGED 20 YEARS AND OVER IN THE ROCHDALE SAMPLE,1871

SERVANT TYPES	TOTAL SAMPLE	OUT SERVS	POSSIBLE SERVS	WRONG SERVS	TRUE SERVS	CENSUS TOTAL 4
GENERAL(F)	260	26	50	0	184	
BUTLER	2	2	0	0	0	
GENERAL(M)	8	2	0	0	6	
COACHMAN	33	32	0	0	1	
GROOM	12	11	0	0	1	
GARDENER	35	34	0	0	1	
HOUSEKEEPER	396	1	0	377	18	
COOK	29	1	1	0	27	
HOUSEMAID	24	0	3	0	21	
NURSE	23	6	2	0	15	
GOVERNESS	6	0	0	1	5	
LADIES MAID	1	0	0	0	1	
LAUNDRYMAID	1	0	0	0	1	
KITCHENMAID	2	0	0	0	2	
FOOTMAN	1	1	0	0	0	
COMPANION	1	0	0	0	1	
TOTAL	834	116	56	378	284	573*

SOURCE: HOUSEHOLD SAMPLE AND PP 1873, LXXI, PT I.
*APPROXIMATE FIGURE CALCULATED FROM CENSUS CLASS II/ORDER 5

TABLE 8

COMPARISON OF SIZE OF THE SERVANT POPULATION DERIVED FROM
DIFFERING SOURCES

SOURCE	SERVANTS	TOTAL NUMBER OF- 'TRUE' SERVANTS	SERVANTS OVER 19 YEARS
1851			
ALL HOUSEHOLDS	2065	1113	----
HOUSEHOLD SAMPLE	2120	----	1468
OFFICIAL CENSUS	----	----	1425
1861			
ALL HOUSEHOLDS	2955	1321	----
HOUSEHOLD SAMPLE	2904	----	2512
OFFICIAL CENSUS	----	----	1533
1871			
ALL HOUSEHOLDS	3962	1591	----
HOUSEHOLD SAMPLE	4084	----	3336
OFFICIAL CENSUS	----	----	2292*

CENSUS SOURCES: <u>PP</u> 1852-3, LXXXVIII, PT II; <u>PP</u> 1863, LIII,
PT II; <u>PP</u> 1873, LXXI, PT I.

* APPROXIMATE CALCULATION FROM CENSUS CLASS II/ORDER 5.

TABLE 9

PERCENTAGE OF SERVANTS UNDER THE AGE OF 20 YEARS IN SELECTED BOROUGHS

	BOLTON	PRESTON	OLDHAM	YORK	CHESTER	LANCASTER
DATE						
1851	26.29	32.28	31.03	37.92	37.34	30.56
1861	30.35	25.95	31.88	43.35	39.08	35.90

CENSUS SOURCES: PP 1851-3, LXXXVIII, PT II; PP 1863, LIII, PT II.

TABLE 10

FLUCTUATIONS IN THE NUMBER OF HOUSEKEEPERS IN SELECTED BOROUGHS

	BOLTON	PRESTON	BLACKBURN	OLDHAM	LANCASTER
DATE					
1851	369	213	733	48	166
1861	138	114	51	146	32
% CHANGE	-62.6	-46.5	-93.0	+204.2	-80.7
% CHANGE ALL SERVANTS EXCLUDING HOUSKEEPERS	+31.8	+0.7	+6.1	+74.2	-23.5

CENSUS SOURCES: PP 1851-3, LXXXVIII, PT II; PP 1863, LIII, PT II.

TABLE 11

SERVANT CATEGORIES AS PROPORTION OF THE TOTAL SAMPLE

	1851	1861	1871
% 'TRUE SERVANTS'	56.4	39.5	34.1
% 'WRONG SERVANTS'	15.0	36.2	45.3
% 'OUT SERVANTS'	12.0	12.4	13.9
% 'POSSIBLE SERVANTS'	16.6	11.9	6.7
SAMPLE TOTAL	367	628	834
CENSUS TOTAL AS % OF SAMPLE	97.1	61.0	68.7

TABLE 12

BIRTHPLACES OF 'WRONGLY ENUMERATED' SERVANTS
DISTANCE IN MILES FROM THE ROCHDALE ENUMERATION DISTRICT

	'WRONG' SERVANTS	ROCHDALE WOMEN 20 YEARS AND OVER
1851		
% BORN WITHIN:		
ROCHDALE	54.7	66.3
1-19 MILES	30.8	19.5
20-49 MILES	6.0	4.5
OVER 49 MILES	8.5	9.7
(CASES)	(64)	(267)
1861		
% BORN WITHIN:		
ROCHDALE	55.4	57.7
1-19 MILES	17.8	19.0
20-49 MILES	6.1	6.2
OVER 49 MILES	20.7	17.2
(CASES)	(231)	(248)
1871		
% BORN WITHIN:		
ROCHDALE	50.6	57.0
1-19 MILES	25.9	15.1
20-49 MILES	7.2	10.0
OVER 49 MILES	16.3	18.0
(CASES)	(391)	(271)

TABLE 13

BIRTHPLACE OF HEADS OF HOUSEHOLDS DEFINED AS 'WRONGLY'
ENUMERATED SERVANTS

1851	'WRONG' SERVANTS	ROCHDALE HEADS
% BORN IN:		
ROCHDALE	33.3	64.7
REST OF LANCS.	23.8	17.4
YORKS.	23.8	9.5
IRELAND	14.3	2.0
REST OF U.K.	4.8	6.4
CASES	21	201

1861	'WRONG' SERVANTS	ROCHDALE HEADS
% BORN IN:		
ROCHDALE	48.9	61.0
REST OF LANCS.	13.8	20.0
YORKS.	11.7	8.5
IRELAND	16.0	5.0
REST OF U.K.	3.3	5.5
CASES	94	197

TABLE 13 (CONT.)

BIRTHPLACE OF HEADS OF HOUSEHOLDS DEFINED AS 'WRONGLY'
ENUMERATED SERVANTS

1871	'WRONG' SERVANTS	ROCHDALE HEADS
% BORN IN:		
ROCHDALE	48.5	59.0
REST OF LANCS.	16.9	17.0
YORKS.	11.0	9.5
IRELAND	13.9	6.0
REST OF U.K.	9.6	8.5
CASES	136	200

TABLE 14

RESIDENCE PATTERNS OF WIDOWED PERSONS AGED 65 AND OVER

LIVING WITH:	UNMARRIED CHILDREN	MARRIED CHILDREN	ALONE OR IN INSTITUTIONS
PRE-INDUSTRIAL SAMPLE			
% MALES	23.0	14.0	62.0
% FEMALES	20.0	28.0	53.0
PRESTON-1851			
% MALES	27.0	50.0	23.0
% FEMALES	34.0	41.0	24.0
BRITAIN-1960's			
% MALES	18.0	23.0	59.0
% FEMALES	20.0	17.0	63.0

SOURCES: LASLETT (1977), 204-5; ANDERSON (1971), 140.

TABLE 15

SOCIAL-ECONOMIC GROUP OF HEADS OF HOUSEHOLDS WHOSE WIVES
WERE DEFINED AS 'WRONGLY ENUMERATED' SERVANTS

1851	HEADS-WIFE AS 'WRONG' SERVANT	ROCHDALE HEADS
SOCIAL-ECONOMIC GROUP*		
1	0.0	3.5
2	0.0	10.9
3	42.9	58.2
4	28.6	12.9
5	28.6	9.5
6	0.0	0.0
7	0.0	5.0
CASES	14	201

1861	HEADS-WIFE AS 'WRONG' SERVANT	ROCHDALE HEADS
SOCIAL-ECONOMIC GROUP*		
1	0.0	1.0
2	4.7	6.6
3	53.5	63.5
4	19.8	20.3
5	20.9	5.6
6	0.0	0.0
7	1.2	3.0
CASES	86	197

TABLE 15 (CONT.)

SOCIAL-ECONOMIC GROUP OF HEADS OF HOUSEHOLDS WHOSE WIVES
WERE DEFINED AS 'WRONGLY ENUMERATED' SERVANTS

1871	HEADS-WIFE AS 'WRONG' SERVANT	ROCHDALE HEADS
SOCIAL-ECONOMIC GROUP*		
1	1.3	2.5
2	3.8	5.0
3	55.8	60.0
4	25.0	18.0
5	13.5	12.0
6	0.6	0.0
7	0.0	2.5
CASES	156	200

*SEE APPENDIX A, NOTE 7 FOR DEFINTION OF SOCIAL-ECONOMIC
GROUPINGS.

TABLE 16

RELATIONSHIP OF 'WRONGLY ENUMERATED' SERVANTS TO HEAD OF
HOUSEHOLD

RELATIONSHIP TO HEAD*	% IN DIFFERING CATEGORIES		
	1851	1861	1871
HEAD	35.9	40.7	37.3
WIFE	23.4	37.7	40.4
NUCLEAR FAMILY	15.6	7.4	10.2
ELDERS	3.1	3.5	3.6
JUNIORS	6.3	0.0	1.5
PEERS	9.4	4.8	4.1
OTHERS	6.3	6.0	2.8
CASES	64	231	391

*CATEGORIES:

HEAD = HEAD
WIFE = WIFE
NUCLEAR FAMILY = SON, DAUGHTER
ELDERS = MOTHER, MOTHER-IN-LAW, AUNT
JUNIORS = STEP-DAUGHTER, NEICE, GRAND-CHILDREN
PEERS = SISTER, SISTER-IN-LAW, COUSIN
OTHERS = LODGER, 'RELATIVE', FRIEND

TABLE 17

THE SEX AND MARITAL STATUS OF HEADS OF HOUSEHOLDS
CONTAINING 'WRONGLY ENUMERATED' SERVANTS

% MARITAL STATUS	'WRONG' SERVANT HOUSEHOLDS		ROCHDALE HEADS	
1851	MALE	FEMALE	MALE	FEMALE
UNKNOWN	0.0	3.8	0.0	0.0
UNMARRIED	10.8	11.5	5.2	11.1
MARRIED	56.8	0.0	84.9	0.0
WIDOWED	29.7	76.9	7.0	88.9
SPOUSE ABSENT	2.7	7.7	2.9	0.0
% SEX	58.7	41.3	86.4	13.6
CASES	37	26	172	27

% MARITAL STATUS	'WRONG' SERVANT HOUSEHOLDS		ROCHDALE HEADS	
1861	MALE	FEMALE	MALE	FEMALE
UNKNOWN	0.0	0.0	0.0	0.0
UNMARRIED	8.8	6.5	0.6	23.5
MARRIED	74.3	1.1	88.9	0.0
WIDOWED	15.4	85.9	7.8	58.8
SPOUSE ABSENT	1.5	6.5	2.8	17.6
% SEX	59.8	40.2	91.4	8.6
CASES	137	92	180	17

TABLE 17 (CONT.)

THE SEX AND MARITAL STATUS OF HEADS OF HOUSEHOLDS
CONTAINING 'WRONGLY ENUMERATED' SERVANTS

% MARITAL STATUS	'WRONG' SERVANT HOUSEHOLDS		ROCHDALE HEADS	
1871	MALE	FEMALE	MALE	FEMALE
UNKNOWN	0.4	0.0	0.0	0.0
UNMARRIED	4.9	9.9	1.8	16.7
MARRIED	78.3	0.0	90.0	0.0
WIDOWED	15.6	80.9	7.0	80.0
SPOUSE ABSENT	0.8	9.2	1.2	3.3
% SEX	63.6	36.4	85.0	15.0
CASES	246	141	170	30

TABLE READS AS FOLLOWS: OF THE 63 HOUSEHOLD HEADS WHOSE
HOUSEHOLDS CONTAINED 'WRONGLY ENUMERATED' SERVANTS IN 1851,
37 OR 58.7% WERE MALES. OF THESE 37 HOUSEHOLD HEADS, 10.8%
WERE UNMARRIED, 2.7% WERE MARRIED BUT THEIR WIVES WERE
ABSENT FROM THE HOUSEHOLD, ETC.

TABLE 18

HOUSEHOLDS CONTAINING KIN AS 'NURSES'- ECONOMIC SECTOR IN
WHICH HEAD EMPLOYED AS PERCENT OF ALL OCCUPATIONS

| | % EMPLOYED IN SECTOR | |
SECTOR	HEADS OF 'NURSE' HOUSEHOLDS	ROCHDALE MALES (20+)
1851		
AGRICULTURE	5.6	7.3
TEXTILES	55.6	41.6
SERVICE	2.8	0.4
TRANSPORT	2.8	4.2
METALS/MINING	14.0	11.9
BUILDING	2.8	5.3
LABOURING	8.4	5.8
RETAILING	2.8	6.2
CORN/WOOD	2.8	2.2
CASES	38	

TABLE 18 (CONT.)

HOUSEHOLDS CONTAINING KIN AS 'NURSES'- ECONOMIC SECTOR IN
WHICH HEAD EMPLOYED AS PERCENT OF ALL OCCUPATIONS

	% EMPLOYED IN SECTOR	
SECTOR	HEADS OF 'NURSE' HOUSEHOLDS	ROCHDALE MALES (20+)
1861		
AGRICULTURE	4.5	6.8
TEXTILES	50.0	40.7
SERVICE	9.0	0.3
TRANSPORT	4.5	4.6
METALS/MINING	4.5	14.2
BUILDING	0.0	7.1
LABOURING	0.0	4.3
RETAILING	4.5	6.1
CORN/WOOD	4.5	2.1
CASES	22	

CENSUS SOURCES: <u>PP</u> 1852-3 LXXXVIII, PT II, DIV. VIII, 636-
47; <u>PP</u> 1863 LIII, PT II, DIV. VIII, 634-47.

TABLE 19

MARITAL STATUS OF KIN/SERVANTS (EXCLUDING 'NURSES')

MARITAL STATUS (%)	KIN/SERVANTS	ROCHDALE WOMEN
1851		
UNKNOWN	0.0	0.0
UNMARRIED	78.4	60.0
MARRIED	6.8	33.9
WIDOWED	14.8	6.1
SPOUSE ABSENT	0.0	0.0
CASES	88	478
1861		
UNKNOWN	0.0	0.0
UNMARRIED	67.7	58.7
MARRIED	6.1	36.0
WIDOWED	22.2	4.1
SPOUSE ABSENT	4.0	1.3
CASES	99	467
1871		
UNKNOWN	1.2	0.2
UNMARRIED	68.7	57.8
MARRIED	12.0	33.7
WIDOWED	15.7	6.8
SPOUSE ABSENT	2.4	1.5
CASES	83	457

TABLE 20

AGES OF KIN/SERVANTS (EXCLUDING 'NURSES') DESCRIBED AS
GENERAL SERVANTS

AGE GROUP (%)	KIN/SERVANTS	ROCHDALE WOMEN
1851		
1 - 9	0.0	24.3
10 - 29	55.7	41.3
30 - 49	27.1	22.6
50 AND OVER	17.1	11.9
CASES	70	478
1861		
1 - 9	0.0	22.0
10 - 29	56.2	45.5
30 - 49	23.0	22.8
50 AND OVER	20.6	9.9
CASES	87	467
1871		
1 - 9	1.4	22.7
10 - 29	51.4	40.9
30 - 49	23.7	24.2
50 AND OVER	23.6	12.4
CASES	72	457

TABLE 21

RELATIONSHIP TO HOUSEHOLD HEAD OF KIN/SERVANTS
(EXCLUDING 'NURSES')

RELATIONSHIP TO HEAD (%)*	KIN/SERVANTS	ROCHDALE WOMEN
1851		
HEAD	4.5	5.4
WIFE	2.3	30.8
NUCLEAR FAMILY	46.6	48.7
ELDERS	8.0	1.2
JUNIORS	24.9	3.3
PEERS	10.2	2.5
OTHERS	3.3	7.9
CASES	88	478
1861		
HEAD	9.1	3.4
WIFE	4.0	34.3
NUCLEAR FAMILY	42.4	50.7
ELDERS	11.1	0.6
JUNIORS	11.1	2.4
PEERS	19.2	2.1
OTHERS	3.0	6.2
CASES	99	467

TABLE 21 (CONT.)

RELATIONSHIP TO HOUSEHOLD HEAD OF KIN/SERVANTS
(EXCLUDING 'NURSES')

RELATIONSHIP TO HEAD (%)*	KIN/SERVANTS	ROCHDALE WOMEN
1871		
HEAD	6.0	6.8
WIFE	7.2	32.8
NUCLEAR FAMILY	39.8	45.1
ELDERS	8.4	1.0
JUNIORS	20.3	2.3
PEERS	18.0	2.0
OTHERS	0.0	9.9
CASES	83	457

* SEE TABLE 16 FOR DEFINITION OF CATEGORIES

TABLE 22

MARITAL STATUS OF HEADS OF HOUSEHOLDS CONTAINING
KIN/SERVANTS (EXCLUDING 'NURSES')

MARITAL STATUS (%)	KIN/SERVANT HOUSEHOLDS	ROCHDALE HOUSEHOLDS
1851		
UNKNOWN	1.3	0.5
UNMARRIED	8.9	6.0
MARRIED	48.1	72.6
WIDOWED	39.2	17.9
SPOUSE ABSENT	2.5	3.0
CASES	79	201
1861		
UNKNOWN	0.0	0.0
UNMARRIED	6.4	2.5
MARRIED	60.6	81.2
WIDOWED	30.9	12.2
SPOUSE ABSENT	2.1	4.1
CASES	94	197
1871		
UNKNOWN	0.0	0.0
UNMARRIED	3.7	6.0
MARRIED	63.7	76.5
WIDOWED	25.0	16.0
SPOUSE ABSENT	7.5	1.5
CASES	80	200

TABLE 23

SOCIAL-ECONOMIC GROUP OF HEADS OF HOUSEHOLDS CONTAINING
KIN/SERVANTS (EXCLUDING 'NURSES')*

SOCIAL-ECONOMIC GROUP (%)	KIN/SERVANT HOUSEHOLDS	ROCHDALE HOUSEHOLDS
1851		
1	2.5	3.5
2	21.5	10.9
3	43.0	58.2
4	17.7	12.9
5	6.3	9.5
6	6.3	0.0
7	2.5	5.0
CASES	79	201
1861		
1	4.3	1.0
2	14.9	6.6
3	52.1	63.5
4	22.3	20.3
5	2.1	5.6
6	0.0	0.0
7	4.3	3.0
CASES	94	197

320

TABLE 23 (CONT.)

SOCIAL-ECONOMIC GROUP OF HEADS OF HOUSEHOLDS CONTAINING
KIN/SERVANTS (EXCLUDING 'NURSES')*

SOCIAL-ECONOMIC GROUP (%)	KIN/SERVANT HOUSEHOLDS	ROCHDALE HOUSEHOLDS
1851		
1	1.2	2.5
2	17.5	5.0
3	55.0	60.0
4	15.0	18.0
5	7.5	12.0
6	3.7	0.0
7	0.0	2.5
CASES	80	200

* SEE APPENDIX A, NOTE 7 FOR DEFINITIONS OF SOCIAL-ECONOMIC
GROUPINGS.

TABLE 24

OCCUPATIONAL GROUP OF HEADS OF HOUSEHOLDS CONTAINING
KIN/SERVANTS (EXCLUDING 'NURSES')

OCCUPATIONAL GROUP (%)	KIN/SERVANT HOUSEHOLDS	ROCHDALE HOUSEHOLDS
1851		
PROFESSIONS	0.0	0.5
TEXTILE MANUFACTURERS	1.3	2.0
OTHER LARGE MANUFACTURERS	0.0	0.5
FARMERS	11.4	4.5
RETAILERS	22.9	12.0
SMALL MANUFACTURERS	0.0	2.0
COMMERCIAL SERVICES	0.0	2.0
ANNUITANTS/PROPRIETORS	0.0	1.0
ARTISANS/MANUAL WORKERS	58.1	70.1
OTHERS	6.3	5.5
CASES	79	201
1861		
PROFESSIONS	0.0	0.5
TEXTILE MANUFACTURERS	4.3	1.0
OTHER LARGE MANUFACTURERS	0.0	0.0
FARMERS	5.3	3.0
RETAILERS	25.5	8.0
SMALL MANUFACTURERS	1.1	1.0
COMMERCIAL SERVICES	5.3	1.5
ANNUITANTS/PROPRIETORS	0.0	0.0
ARTISANS/MANUAL WORKERS	55.3	82.2
OTHERS	3.2	3.2
CASES	94	197

TABLE 24 (CONT.)

OCCUPATIONAL GROUP OF HEADS OF HOUSEHOLDS CONTAINING
KIN/SERVANTS (EXCLUDING 'NURSES')

OCCUPATIONAL GROUP (%)	KIN/SERVANT HOUSEHOLDS	ROCHDALE HOUSEHOLDS
1871		
PROFESSIONS	1.2	0.5
TEXTILE MANUFACTURERS	0.0	1.0
OTHER LARGE MANUFACTURERS	0.0	0.0
FARMERS	5.0	3.0
RETAILERS	27.5	13.5
SMALL MANUFACTURERS	0.0	1.0
COMMERCIAL SERVICES	7.5	2.5
ANNUITANTS/PROPRIETORS	0.0	0.5
ARTISANS/MANUAL WORKERS	55.1	77.0
OTHERS	3.7	1.0
CASES	80	200

TABLE 25

BIRTHPLACES OF KIN/SERVANTS (EXCLUDING 'NURSES')
DISTANCE IN MILES FROM THE ROCHDALE ENUMERATION DISTRICT

	KIN/SERVANTS	ROCHDALE WOMEN 20 YEARS AND OVER
1851		
% BORN WITHIN:		
ROCHDALE	72.7	69.9
1-19 MILES	20.4	17.1
20-49 MILES	3.4	3.3
OVER 49 MILES	3.4	9.7
(CASES)	(88)	(362)
1861		
% BORN WITHIN:		
ROCHDALE	71.7	61.5
1-19 MILES	12.1	16.4
20-49 MILES	3.0	4.9
OVER 49 MILES	13.1	17.2
(CASES)	(99)	(366)
1871		
% BORN WITHIN:		
ROCHDALE	66.3	58.4
1-19 MILES	13.2	15.3
20-49 MILES	7.2	9.3
OVER 49 MILES	13.2	17.3
(CASES)	(83)	(353)

TABLE 26

NUMBER OF SERVANTS EMPLOYED PER HOUSEHOLD, 1871

DISTRICT	% OF HOUSEHOLDS EMPLOYING		
	1 SERVANT	2 SERVANTS	3 SERVANTS PLUS
HASTINGS	56.6	25.8	17.7
LINCOLN	77.8	15.6	6.6
READING	69.0	21.6	9.4
COVENTRY	73.3	15.6	11.1
BOLTON	79.2	15.0	5.8
FARNWORTH	70.7	19.5	9.8
HALLIWELL	58.8	5.9	35.3
HULTON	68.2	14.7	17.1
TURTON	73.2	13.4	13.4
WINDSOR	59.4	17.2	23.4
COOKHAM	47.8	26.1	26.1
EASTHAMPSTEAD	45.5	18.2	36.3
WOKINGHAM	54.1	27.0	18.9
BRADFIELD	38.7	25.8	35.5
WALLINGFORD	69.7	21.2	9.1
ABINGDON	64.0	18.0	18.0
NEWBURY	66.2	20.0	13.8
WANTAGE	72.5	17.5	10.0
HUNGERFORD	73.1	19.2	7.7
FARINGDON	51.9	33.3	14.8
ROCHDALE	75.5	14.2	10.3

SOURCE: EBERY AND PRESTON (1976), 70.

TABLE 27

TYPES OF SERVANTS EMPLOYED PER HOUSEHOLD, 1871

| DISTRICT | % OF SERVANTS EMPLOYED | | | |
	MAID-OF-ALL-WORK	HOUSE MANAGEMENT/ PERSONAL (M & F)	HOUSE SERVANT (F)	HOUSE SERVANT (M)
HASTINGS	35.3	14.6	18.8	4.7
LINCOLN	57.7	8.1	11.3	4.0
READING	49.4	12.8	12.8	4.1
COVENTRY	61.9	2.2	13.4	2.9
BOLTON	71.2	7.0	6.3	0.6
FARNWORTH	62.6	5.5	9.9	1.1
HALLIWELL	45.5	3.0	24.2	3.0
HULTON	73.5	5.8	11.7	---
TURTON	48.5	12.1	12.2	3.0
WINDSOR	26.7	13.0	19.8	5.2
COOKHAM	43.3	11.4	15.5	5.2
EASTHAMPSTEAD	54.0	11.2	7.9	5.4
WOKINGHAM	55.1	2.8	13.0	2.9
BRADFIELD	56.0	8.8	6.6	5.5
WALLINGFORD	49.1	11.4	9.4	5.7
ABINGDON	51.3	11.4	15.0	2.5
NEWBURY	59.4	11.6	16.0	---
WANTAGE	56.1	3.0	12.1	1.5
HUNGERFORD	60.6	6.0	12.1	6.0
FARINGDON	67.3	1.8	9.1	1.8
ROCHDALE	67.7	3.0	8.9	1.7

TABLE 27 (CONT.)

TYPES OF SERVANTS EMPLOYED PER HOUSEHOLD, 1871

	% OF SERVANTS EMPLOYED			
DISTRICT	NURSERY	KITCHEN	OUTDOOR	CASES
HASTINGS	9.8	15.4	1.4	357
LINCOLN	4.9	11.4	1.6	123
READING	4.7	13.4	2.9	172
COVENTRY	7.5	10.4	1.4	134
BOLTON	6.4	6.4	1.8	156
FARNWORTH	13.2	7.7	---	91
HALLIWELL	---	24.2	---	33
HULTON	5.9	2.9	---	34
TURTON	9.1	12.1	3.0	33
WINDSOR	11.2	19.0	5.2	116
COOKHAM	4.1	17.5	3.1	97
EASTHAMPSTEAD	3.2	11.1	6.4	63
WOKINGHAM	11.6	14.4	---	69
BRADFIELD	13.2	7.7	2.2	91
WALLINGFORD	9.4	13.2	1.9	53
ABINGDON	6.3	6.8	5.0	80
NEWBURY	4.3	10.1	---	69
WANTAGE	10.6	10.6	6.1	66
HUNGERFORD	6.1	6.1	3.0	33
FARINGDON	3.6	9.1	7.2	55
ROCHDALE	10.0	7.5	0.2	398

SOURCE: EBERY AND PRESTON (1976), 73.

TABLE 28

PERCENT OF SERVANTS IN OCCUPATIONAL GROUPS

SERVANT TYPES	1851	1861	1871
GENERAL(F)	78.4	71.7	67.7
BUTLER	0.3	0.0	0.0
GENERAL(M)	4.7	1.3	1.5
COACHMAN	0.3	0.3	0.2
GROOM	0.0	0.0	0.0
GARDENER	0.7	0.3	0.0
HOUSEKEEPER	4.7	5.1	3.0
COOK	1.4	5.7	7.0
HOUSEMAID	2.7	7.9	8.2
NURSE	3.7	4.1	8.5
GOVERNESS	0.7	0.6	1.5
LADIES MAID	0.7	0.3	0.5
KITCHENMAID	0.3	0.3	0.5
LAUNDRYMAID	0.3	0.6	0.0
FOOTMAN	0.0	0.0	0.2
COMPANION	0.0	0.0	0.2
TOTAL	296	315	402

TABLE 29

PRIVATE FEMALE INDOOR SERVANTS AS A PERCENTAGE OF ALL WOMEN
IN DIFFERING AGE GROUPS, ENGLAND AND WALES, 1871

AGE GROUPS (%)					
UNDER 15	15-19	20-24	25-44	45-64	65 PLUS
2.72	33.31	25.95	9.85	6.33	6.04

SOURCE: EBERY AND PRESTON (1976), 34.

TABLE 30

% OF AGE GROUPS IN SERVICE IN SIX PRE-INDUSTRIAL ENGLISH
SETTLEMENTS (MEDIANS)

AGE	MALES %	FEMALES %
0-9	1	1
10-14	5	4
15-19	35	27
20-24	30	40
25-29	15	15
30-34	7	10
35-39	4	5
40-44	2	2
OVER 45	2	2

SOURCE: P. LASLETT (1977), 34.

TABLE 31

AGE DISTRIBUTION OF PRIVATELY EMPLOYED INDOOR AND OUTDOOR
SERVANTS, 1871

DISTRICT	UNDER 20	AGE GROUP (%) 20-29	30 PLUS
HASTINGS	28.6	47.7	24.5
LINCOLN	51.9	36.7	11.2
READING	39.0	29.1	32.4
COVENTRY	44.1	38.8	16.8
BOLTON	32.7	39.6	26.9
FARNWORTH	34.1	37.4	28.6
HALLIWELL	21.1	54.6	24.1
HULTON	23.4	49.9	26.1
TURTON	36.4	27.2	36.2
WINDSOR	35.2	42.1	22.8
COOKHAM	33.0	42.4	24.7
EASTHAMPSTEAD	27.1	47.7	25.6
WOKINGHAM	50.5	24.3	24.3
BRADFIELD	49.5	28.6	22.0
WALLINGFORD	50.9	30.4	19.0
ABINGDON	40.1	41.4	19.2
NEWBURY	14.3	50.4	44.2
WANTAGE	59.2	27.0	10.9
HUNGERFORD	48.6	39.3	12.1
FARINGDON	52.7	27.2	19.9
AVERAGE	38.6	38.0	23.3
ROCHDALE	30.1	40.8	29.1

SOURCE: EBERY AND PRESTON (1976), 76.

TABLE 32

AGE OF FEMALE SERVANTS, 1851-1911

CENSUS	AGE GROUP (%)		
	UNDER 20	20-34	35 PLUS
1851	35.61	45.88	18.51
1861	39.14	42.38	18.48
1871	39.57	40.30	20.13
1881	42.94	---NOT AVAILABLE---	
1891	------------NOT COMPARABLE----------		
1901	34.97	47.15	17.88
1911	31.44	47.70	20.86

SOURCE: CENSUSES OF ENGLAND AND WALES 1851-1911.

TABLE 33

AGE OF SERVANTS IN ROCHDALE, 1851-1871

CENSUS	0-19	% OF SERVANTS IN AGE GROUPS			CASES
		20-39	40-59	60 PLUS	
1851	29.9	58.5	8.5	3.0	296
1861	21.6	65.1	10.5	3.2	315
1871	30.1	55.5	12.0	2.5	402

TABLE 34

AGE OF SERVANTS ACCORDING TO THEIR PLACE OF BIRTH

REGION OF BIRTH*	0-19	% OF SERVANTS IN AGE GROUPS 20-39	40-59	60 PLUS	CASES
1851					
ROCHDALE	34.5	49.1	10.9	5.4	110
LANCS.	27.3	61.4	6.8	4.6	43
YORKS	28.0	66.0	6.0	0.0	50
S. ENG.	23.1	64.1	10.3	2.6	39
N. ENG.	10.0	90.0	0.0	0.0	10
WALES	22.2	77.8	0.0	0.0	18
SCOTLAND	0.0	99.9	0.0	0.0	2
IRELAND	60.0	33.3	6.7	0.0	15
ABROAD	0.0	99.9	0.0	0.0	2
1861					
ROCHDALE	24.3	57.2	11.5	7.1	70
LANCS.	25.9	57.4	13.0	3.7	54
YORKS	18.1	66.7	13.9	1.4	72
S. ENG.	21.7	69.6	8.7	0.0	46
N. ENG.	0.0	75.0	25.0	0.0	4
WALES	23.3	73.3	3.3	0.0	30
SCOTLAND	10.0	90.0	0.0	0.0	10
IRELAND	13.6	68.2	9.1	9.1	22
ABROAD	50.0	50.0	0.0	0.0	2

TABLE 34 (CONT.)

AGE OF SERVANTS ACCORDING TO THEIR PLACE OF BIRTH

REGION OF BIRTH*	0-19	% OF SERVANTS IN AGE GROUPS 20-39	40-59	60 PLUS	CASES
1871					
ROCHDALE	22.6	48.8	23.8	4.8	84
LANCS.	41.4	32.8	22.4	3.4	58
YORKS	22.9	68.8	8.3	0.0	48
S. ENG.	33.0	62.5	4.5	0.0	112
N. ENG.	16.7	66.7	0.0	16.7	6
WALES	34.5	62.1	3.4	0.0	58
SCOTLAND	25.0	66.7	8.3	0.0	12
IRELAND	13.3	46.7	26.7	13.3	15
ABROAD	0.0	99.9	0.0	0.0	1

* KEY:

LANCS.   = LANCASHIRE EXCLUDING THE ROCHDALE DISTRICT

S. ENG. = ENGLISH COUNTIES TO THE SOUTH OF LANCASHIRE AND
                YORKSHIRE

N. ENG. = ENGLISH COUNTIES TO THE NORTH OF LANCASHIRE AND
                YORKSHIRE

SERVANTS BORN IN 'LANCASHIRE' EXCLUDED

TABLE 35

MARITAL STATUS OF SERVANTS AGED OVER 40 YEARS BY
OCCUPATIONAL GROUP

MARITAL STATUS	GENERAL SERVANTS	SPECIALISED SERVANTS	ROCHDALE WOMEN 40 YEARS PLUS
1851			
SINGLE	52.9	9.0	11.1
MARRIED	17.7	45.5	63.6
WIDOWED	29.4	45.5	25.3
SPOUSE ABSENT	0.0	0.0	0.0
CASES	17	11	99
1861			
SINGLE	57.6	63.6	5.3
MARRIED	3.0	0.0	76.6
WIDOWED	30.3	36.4	14.9
SPOUSE ABSENT	9.1	0.0	3.2
CASES	33	11	94
1871			
SINGLE	50.0	63.6	9.7
MARRIED	2.8	4.6	59.2
WIDOWED	30.6	31.8	28.2
SPOUSE ABSENT	16.7	0.0	2.9
CASES	36	22	103

TABLE 36

AGE OF SERVANTS ACCORDING TO THEIR OCCUPATIONS

| OCCUPATION | % OF SERVANTS IN AGE GROUPS | | | | CASES |
	0-19	20-39	40-59	60 PLUS	
GENERAL FEMALE SERVANTS					
1851	32.8	58.3	6.6	2.1	235
1861	22.6	62.4	11.5	3.5	226
1871	30.4	54.8	11.1	3.7	270
MALE SERVANTS					
1851	29.4	47.1	17.6	5.9	17
1861	50.0	50.0	0.0	0.0	6
1871	25.0	62.5	12.5	0.0	8
OTHER FEMALE SERVANTS					
1851	11.4	61.4	25.0	2.3	44
1861	14.5	73.5	8.4	3.6	83
1871	23.6	60.1	13.0	3.3	123

TABLE 37

AGES OF GENERAL SERVANTS IN ROCHDALE, 1851-1871

1851	0-	5-	10-	15-	20-	25-	30-	35-
GENERAL SERVANTS	0.0	0.4	8.5	23.8	30.6	15.3	7.7	4.7
ROCHDALE WOMEN	12.8	11.5	10.8	10.7	10.4	9.4	7.3	5.9

1851	40-	45-	50-	55-	60-	65-	70+	CASES
GENERAL SERVANTS	1.7	2.6	1.3	1.0	0.4	0.4	1.3	235
ROCHDALE WOMEN	5.1	4.3	3.5	2.7	2.3	1.6	1.8	467

1861	0-	5-	10-	15-	20-	25-	30-	35-
GENERAL SERVANTS	0.0	0.0	6.2	16.4	26.5	19.0	8.8	8.0
ROCHDALE WOMEN	11.3	10.7	12.4	12.4	12.6	8.1	8.6	3.9

1861	40-	45-	50-	55-	60-	65-	70+	CASES
GENERAL SERVANTS	2.2	4.4	2.2	2.7	0.9	1.3	1.3	226
ROCHDALE WOMEN	6.0	4.3	4.1	2.4	1.7	1.3	0.4	467

TABLE 37 (CONT.)

AGES OF GENERAL SERVANTS IN ROCHDALE, 1851–1871

1871	0–	5–	10–	15–	20–	25–	30–	35–
GENERAL SERVANTS	0.0	0.0	3.3	27.0	26.3	16.3	7.4	4.8
ROCHDALE WOMEN	12.0	10.7	8.3	10.5	11.6	10.5	8.5	6.1

1851	40–	45–	50–	55–	60–	65–	70+	CASES
GENERAL SERVANTS	5.6	1.9	3.0	0.7	1.1	0.7	1.9	270
ROCHDALE WOMEN	4.8	4.8	4.2	2.8	2.6	1.5	1.3	457

TABLE 38

AGE AND SEX RATIOS OF SERVANTS IN ENGLAND AND WALES
1851–1911

	1851	1861	1871	1881
PRIVATE DOMESTICS AS % OF TOTAL POPULATION	5.10	5.35	5.85	5.52
% OF ALL SERVANTS WHO WERE FEMALE	88.14	89.75	90.64	85.78
% OF FEMALE SERVANTS UNDER 20 YEARS OF AGE	35.61	39.14	39.57	42.94

	1891*	1901	1911
PRIVATE DOMESTICS AS % OF TOTAL POPULATION	----	4.60	4.27
% OF ALL SERVANTS WHO WERE FEMALE	----	85.89	83.51
% OF FEMALE SERVANTS UNDER 20 YEARS OF AGE	----	34.97	31.44

* FIGURES FOR 1891 NOT COMPARABLE.

TABLE 39

DISTANCE FROM THE ROCHDALE DISTRICT OF THE BIRTHPLACES OF
DOMESTIC SERVANTS, 1851-1871

DISTANCE IN MILES (%)	SERVANTS	ROCHDALE WOMEN (10-30 YEARS)
1851		
ROCHDALE	38.2	70.4
1-29	24.5	19.4
30-99	25.5	5.6
OVER 100	12.6	4.6
CASES	296	196
1861		
ROCHDALE	22.2	69.8
1-29	29.5	16.0
30-99	28.6	5.2
OVER 100	19.7	9.0
CASES	315	212
1871		
ROCHDALE	20.9	60.7
1-29	19.0	16.9
30-99	37.3	13.7
OVER 100	22.8	8.8
CASES	402	183

TABLE 40

REGIONS IN WHICH SERVANTS WERE BORN, 1851-1871

REGION* OF BIRTH (%)	SERVANTS	ROCHDALE WOMEN (10-30 YEARS)
1851		
ROCHDALE	38.2	70.4
LANCS.	15.2	13.3
YORKS	16.6	11.2
SOUTH ENGLAND	14.6	1.4
NORTH ENGLAND	3.4	0.0
WALES	6.1	0.0
SCOTLAND	0.3	0.2
IRELAND	5.0	2.7
ABROAD	0.6	0.0
CASES	296	196
1861		
ROCHDALE	22.2	69.8
LANCS.	17.2	13.2
YORKS	24.1	5.7
SOUTH ENGLAND	16.2	2.8
NORTH ENGLAND	1.2	0.8
WALES	8.5	0.5
SCOTLAND	3.1	0.0
IRELAND	6.9	8.0
ABROAD	0.6	0.0
CASES	315	212

TABLE 40 (CONT.)

REGIONS IN WHICH SERVANTS WERE BORN, 1851-1871

REGION* OF BIRTH (%)	SERVANTS	ROCHDALE WOMEN (10-30 YEARS)
1871		
ROCHDALE	20.9	60.7
LANCS.	14.4	15.8
YORKS	11.9	7.7
SOUTH ENGLAND	29.6	6.8
NORTH ENGLAND	1.4	1.1
WALES	14.7	2.5
SCOTLAND	3.0	1.6
IRELAND	4.1	3.8
ABROAD	0.0	0.0
CASES	402	183

* SEE TABLE 34 FOR KEY.

TABLE 41

SIZE OF SETTLEMENTS WHERE SERVANTS BORN, 1851

REGION (A) OF BIRTH (%)	POPULATION OF SERVANTS' BIRTHPLACES			
	UNKOWN	OVER 5000	UNDER 5000	CASES
ROCHDALE	0.0	100.0	0.0	110
LANCS	31.8	56.8	11.4	44
YORKS	20.0	48.0	32.0	50
SOUTH ENGLAND	34.2	31.7	34.2	41
NORTH ENGLAND	22.2	11.1	66.7	9
WALES	94.4	0.0	5.6	18
SCOTLAND	100.0	0.0	0.0	2
IRELAND	71.4	28.6	0.0	7
ABROAD	0.0	100.0	0.0	2
ALL SERVANTS	23.8	59.9	16.3	296
ROCHDALE WOMEN	10.3	84.1	5.7	478
FEMALE MIGRANTS (b)	37.4	42.0	20.6	131

(a) SEE TABLE 34 FOR KEY.

(b) WOMEN IN THE ROCHDALE CONTROL SAMPLE BORN OUTSIDE THE ROCHDALE DISTRICT.

TABLE 42

SIZE OF SETTLEMENTS WHERE SERVANTS BORN, 1861

REGION (a) OF BIRTH (%)	POPULATION OF SERVANTS' BIRTHPLACES			
	UNKOWN	OVER 5000	UNDER 5000	CASES
ROCHDALE	0.0	100.0	0.0	70
LANCS	13.1	79.6	7.4	54
YORKS	18.6	58.5	22.9	72
SOUTH ENGLAND	37.5	29.2	33.3	48
NORTH ENGLAND	0.0	66.7	33.3	3
WALES	56.7	16.7	26.7	30
SCOTLAND	100.0	0.0	0.0	9
IRELAND	91.7	4.2	4.2	24
ABROAD	100.0	0.0	0.0	2
ALL SERVANTS	27.6	57.5	14.9	315
ROCHDALE WOMEN	12.8	83.3	3.8	467
FEMALE MIGRANTS (b)	40.0	48.0	12.0	150

(a) SEE TABLE 34 FOR KEY.

(b) WOMEN IN THE ROCHDALE CONTROL SAMPLE BORN OUTSIDE THE ROCHDALE DISTRICT.

TABLE 43

SIZE OF SETTLEMENTS WHERE SERVANTS BORN, 1871

REGION (a) OF BIRTH (%)	POPULATION OF SERVANTS' BIRTHPLACES UNKOWN	OVER 5000	UNDER 5000	CASES
ROCHDALE	0.0	100.0	0.0	84
LANCS	15.5	82.8	1.7	58
YORKS	16.7	45.8	37.5	48
SOUTH ENGLAND	25.4	35.5	39.1	110
NORTH ENGLAND	40.0	20.0	40.0	5
WALES	62.7	23.7	13.6	59
SCOTLAND	73.3	20.0	6.7	15
IRELAND	88.3	11.8	0.0	17
ABROAD	100.0	0.0	0.0	1
ALL SERVANTS	28.9	53.2	17.9	402
ROCHDALE WOMEN	12.0	82.7	5.3	457
FEMALE MIGRANTS (b)	33.5	51.8	14.6	164

(a) SEE TABLE 34 FOR KEY.

(b) WOMEN IN THE ROCHDALE CONTROL SAMPLE BORN OUTSIDE THE ROCHDALE DISTRICT.

TABLE 44

SIZE OF SETTLEMENTS WHERE SERVANTS BORN
RESULTS OF ALL SAMPLES POOLED

	POPULATION OF SERVANTS' BIRTHPLACES			
COUNTY (%)	UNKOWN	OVER 5000	UNDER 5000	CASES
CHESHIRE	25.6	41.9	32.6	43
DERBYSHIRE	46.2	23.1	30.8	13
LINCOLNSHIRE	15.4	0.0	84.6	13
SHROPSHIRE	32.4	29.7	37.8	37
STAFFORDSHIRE	30.0	40.0	30.0	20

SOURCES: PP 1843, XXII; PP 1852-3, LXXXV & LXXXVI;
PP 1862, L.

TABLE 45

PERCENTAGE INCREASE IN SIZE OF FEMALE AGE GROUPS, 1851-1871

	UNDER 5	5-14	15-24	25-34
CAERNARVONSHIRE	16.3	23.8	13.6	19.4
FLINTSHIRE	13.9	-1.5	-1.3	10.3
DENBIGHSHIRE	16.4	13.3	0.9	6.4
MONTGOMERYSHIRE	10.6	1.2	-7.4	2.5
CHESHIRE	33.7	27.3	19.0	23.6
SHROPSHIRE	15.3	12.4	1.2	6.1
STAFFORDSHIRE	46.2	43.3	33.5	33.0
DERBYSHIRE	35.3	24.9	14.9	19.9
NOTTINGHAMSHIRE	25.9	23.1	14.4	20.3
LINCOLNSHIRE	8.2	6.9	1.4	0.8
ENGLAND AND WALES	31.0	28.5	22.4	22.5
	35-44	45-54	55-64	65 PLUS
CAERNARVONSHIRE	21.2	31.5	33.0	25.4
FLINTSHIRE	8.9	9.4	4.2	32.7
DENBIGHSHIRE	7.9	19.8	12.3	8.8
MONTGOMERYSHIRE	-0.7	0.2	1.0	-0.1
CHESHIRE	32.7	39.1	40.7	36.0
SHROPSHIRE	5.9	11.2	18.0	12.3
STAFFORDSHIRE	43.8	51.2	43.2	49.2
DERBYSHIRE	24.6	26.9	30.3	27.2
NOTTINGHAMSHIRE	20.5	22.0	29.3	31.0
LINCOLNSHIRE	6.9	16.7	25.2	35.3
ENGLAND AND WALES	27.6	34.6	33.3	30.8

SOURCES: PP 1852-3 LXXXVIII, PT I-II; PP 1873 LXXI, PT I-II

TABLE 46

OCCUPATIONS OF THE FATHERS OF BRIDES IN THE MARRIAGE REGISTERS OF THE PARISH CHURCH OF ST JOHN THE EVANGELIST, PRESTON (DECEMBER 1851-MAY 1856)

SOCIAL-ECONOMIC GROUP	OCCUPATIONAL GROUP	% FATHERS OF SERVANTS	% FATHERS OF OTHER WOMEN
PROFESSIONAL	PROFESSIONS	0.4	0.5
	PROPRIETORS	0.0	0.1
	MANUFACTURERS	0.0	0.2
INTERMEDIATE	FARMER	19.4	5.2
	COMMERCIAL	0.8	2.6
SKILLED MANUAL/ RETAIL	DRESS	8.4	5.8
	BUILDING	7.6	4.4
	TEXTILES	2.1	26.3
	METALS	3.4	3.5
	RETAIL	4.2	6.4
	WOOD	6.8	5.0
	OTHERS	5.5	7.5
PARTLY SKILLED	SERVICE	4.6	2.0
	TRANSPORT	2.1	1.4
	BUILDING	0.8	1.3
	OTHERS	1.7	3.4
UNSKILLED	TEXTILES	0.0	0.8
	PENSIONER	0.0	0.6
	LABOURER	27.4	15.5
	OTHERS	0.8	1.1
CASES		237	1,486

SOURCE: MANCHESTER CENTRAL LIBRARY-PARISH REGISTERS
       (REF. MFPR 242-259)

TABLE 47

PERCENTAGE OF DOMESTICS BORN IN VARIOUS BIRTHPLACE
CATEGORIES

TOWN OF EMPLOYMENT	BORN IN TOWN OF EMPLOYMENT	BORN WITHIN:	
		5 MILES	5-20 MILES
HASTINGS	14.2	7.1	32.5
LINCOLN	18.2	7.4	47.7
READING	25.7	12.6	35.3
COVENTRY	28.1	17.8	37.0
BOLTON	16.3	5.8	22.1
BATH	20.8	11.5	34.3

TOWN OF EMPLOYMENT	BORN IN:		% MIGRANT SERVANTS OF RURAL BIRTH
	REST OF ENGLAND AND WALES	SCOTLAND IRELAND, ETC,	
HASTINGS	46.1	2.9	53.0
LINCOLN	26.5	1.6	77.8
READING	26.3	---	79.8
COVENTRY	14.8	2.2	81.9
BOLTON	44.4	11.1	50.0
BATH	28.5	5.0	76.0

SOURCE: EBERY AND PRESTON (1976), 77.

TABLE 48

AVERAGE WAGES (£ PER ANNUM) OF WOMEN IN ENGLAND, 1823-1907

DATE	GENERAL SERVANTS	COOKS
1823-27	7.7 (19.7)	12.5 (24.5)
28-32	9.2 (21.2)	12.5 (24.5)
33-37	9.5 (21.5)	12.3 (24.3)
38-42	10.4 (22.4)	13.5 (25.5)
43-47	12.5 (24.5)	14.5 (26.5)
48-52	11.4 (23.4)	14.9 (26.9)
53-57	12.6 (24.6)	15.0 (27.0)
58-62	11.7 (23.7)	16.3 (28.3)
63-67	12.8 (24.8)	20.4 (32.4)
68-72	13.3 (25.3)	18.7 (30.7)
73-77	13.2 (25.2)	29.8 (41.8)
78-82	14.4 (26.4)	22.0 (34.0)
83-87	14.0 (26.0)	29.7 (41.7)
88-92	16.1 (28.1)	29.1 (41.1)
93-97	18.8 (30.8)	24.0 (36.0)
1904	16.7 (28.7)	23.4 (35.4)
07	18.0 (30.0)	29.1 (41.1)

TABLE 48 (CONT.)

AVERAGE WAGES (£ PER ANNUM) OF WOMEN IN ENGLAND, 1823-1907

DATE	FEMALE WORKERS IN:		GENERAL INDUSTRIAL AVERAGE
	WOOL	COTTON	
1823-27	----	22.9	19.3
28-32	----	----	18.6
33-37	20.6	20.8	19.1
38-42	19.1	18.8	19.1
43-47	19.1	20.6	19.1
48-52	20.2	20.6	19.6
53-57	----	20.8	20.8
58-62	25.8	22.1	22.9
63-67	28.8	24.9	24.9
68-72	29.9	25.2	27.2
73-77	32.0	32.7	30.6
78-82	34.0	28.4	31.0
83-87	31.9	34.7	29.2
88-92	30.3	35.7	33.8
93-97	30.3	37.1	31.2
1904	----	----	----
07	----	----	----

TABLE 49

WAGES (£ PER ANNUM) PAID TO HOUSEMAIDS AND GENERAL SERVANTS
IN LANCASHIRE

DATES	PRESTWICH ASYLUM/ HOUSEMAIDS	LANCASTER ASYLUM/ HOUSEMAIDS	ROCHDALE WORKHOUSE /SERVANTS	ROCHDALE OBSERVER/ SERVANTS
1838-42	----	----	----	----
43-47	----	----	----	----
48-52	10.5	----	----	----
53-57	7.0	----	----	10.0
58-62	10.3	----	7.8	----
63-67	10.0	----	7.8	12.0
68-72	14.0	----	9.9	15.0
73-77	17.0	16.0	11.2	----
78-82	17.5	15.5	18.0	----
83-87	20.0	----	22.5	----
88-92	18.5	----	----	----
93-97	----	----	----	----
1904	----	----	23.0	----
07	----	----	23.0	----

SOURCES: LANCASHIRE RECORD OFFICE. QAM/6/20-22.

LANCASHIRE RECORD OFFICE. QAM/1/34.

ROCHDALE PUBLIC LIBRARY. DB-154.

ROCHDALE PUBLIC LIBRARY. NEWSPAPER COLLECTION.

ALL WAGES QUOTED ARE AVERAGES FOR PERIOD.

TABLE 50

BIRTHPLACES OF SERVANTS ACCORDING TO SOCIAL-ECONOMIC GROUP
OF EMPLOYER, 1851-1871

SOCIAL-ECONOMIC GROUPING OF EMPLOYER*	% OF SERVANTS BORN IN		
	ROCHDALE	LANCASHIRE	YORKSHIRE
1851			
PROFESSIONAL	26.5	11.8	26.5
INTERMEDIATE	37.7	11.7	15.6
SKILLED MANUAL	47.3	20.5	8.6

SOCIAL-ECONOMIC GROUPING OF EMPLOYER*	% OF SERVANTS BORN ELSEWHERE	CASES
1851		
PROFESSIONAL	35.2	102
INTERMEDIATE	35.0	77
SKILLED MANUAL	23.6	93

TABLE 50 (CONT.)

BIRTHPLACES OF SERVANTS ACCORDING TO SOCIAL-ECONOMIC GROUP
OF EMPLOYER, 1851-1871

SOCIAL-ECONOMIC GROUPING OF EMPLOYER*	% OF SERVANTS BORN IN		
	ROCHDALE	LANCASHIRE	YORKSHIRE
1861			
PROFESSIONAL	16.4	12.3	26.2
INTERMEDIATE	19.3	15.7	25.3
SKILLED MANUAL	35.8	22.2	17.3

SOCIAL-ECONOMIC GROUPING OF EMPLOYER*	% OF SERVANTS BORN ELSEWHERE	CASES
1861		
PROFESSIONAL	45.1	122
INTERMEDIATE	39.7	83
SKILLED MANUAL	24.7	81

TABLE 50 (CONT.)

BIRTHPLACES OF SERVANTS ACCORDING TO SOCIAL-ECONOMIC GROUP
OF EMPLOYER, 1851-1871

SOCIAL-ECONOMIC GROUPING OF EMPLOYER*	% OF SERVANTS BORN IN		
	ROCHDALE	LANCASHIRE	YORKSHIRE
1871			
PROFESSIONAL	12.1	12.8	15.7
INTERMEDIATE	18.3	16.3	9.6
SKILLED MANUAL	31.9	15.6	11.2

SOCIAL-ECONOMIC GROUPING OF EMPLOYER*	% OF SERVANTS BORN ELSEWHERE	CASES
1871		
PROFESSIONAL	59.4	140
INTERMEDIATE	55.8	104
SKILLED MANUAL	41.3	116

TABLE 51

NUMBER OF INHABITANTS IN SETTLEMENTS WHERE SERVANTS BORN
ACCORDING TO SOCIAL-ECONOMIC GROUP OF EMPLOYERS, 1851-1871

SOCIAL-ECONOMIC GROUPING OF EMPLOYER*	% OF SERVANTS BORN IN SETTLEMENTS WITH FOLLOWING NUMBER OF INHABITANTS			
	UNKNOWN	OVER 5000	UNDER 5000	CASES
1851				
PROFESSIONAL	25.5	51.0	23.6	102
INTERMEDIATE	28.6	61.0	10.4	77
SKILLED MANUAL	22.6	68.8	8.6	93
1861				
PROFESSIONAL	28.7	51.6	19.7	122
INTERMEDIATE	30.1	55.4	14.4	83
SKILLED MANUAL	22.2	66.7	11.1	81
1871				
PROFESSIONAL	31.4	45.7	22.9	140
INTERMEDIATE	31.7	50.0	18.3	104
SKILLED MANUAL	21.6	66.4	12.0	116

* SEE APPENDIX A, NOTE 7.
  FOR SETTLEMENT TYPES SEE APPENDIX A, NOTE 18.

TABLE 52

AVERAGE AGE AT FIRST MARRIAGE OF SERVANTS AND OTHER WOMEN
FROM DIFFERENT SOCIAL-ECONOMIC GROUPS AT THE PARISH CHURCH
OF ST JOHN THE EVANGELIST, PRESTON, 1851-1856

| SOCIAL-ECONOMIC GROUP OF FATHER* | AVERAGE AGE AT FIRST MARRIAGE | | | |
	SERVANTS	CASES	OTHER WOMEN	CASES
1	20.0	1	25.9	11
2	26.1	48	24.1	115
3	25.4	90	23.4	876
4	25.8	22	23.5	119
5	24.7	67	24.2	267
6	24.7	8	24.3	89
7	32.0	1	23.4	9
ALL SERVANTS	25.3	237		

SOURCE: MANCHESTER CENTRAL LIBRARY.   MFPR 242-259.

* SEE APPENDIX A, NOTE 7.

TABLE 53

SOCIAL STATUS OF THE HUSBANDS OF SERVANTS AT FIRST
MARRIAGE, PRESTON, 1851-1856

SOCIAL-ECONOMIC GROUP* OF HUSBAND	SOCIAL-ECONOMIC GROUP* OF FATHER- % OF SERVANTS/OTHER WOMEN FROM DIFFERING BACKGROUNDS MARRYING HUSBANDS IN VARIOUS SOCIAL-ECONOMIC GROUPS				
SERVANTS	1	2	3	4	5
1) PROFESSIONAL	0.0	0.0	0.0	0.0	0.0
2) INTERMEDIATE	0.0	6.4	3.4	4.6	4.4
3) SKILLED MAN.	0.0	53.2	65.9	50.0	55.1
4) PARTLY SKILLED	0.0	21.3	13.7	18.2	8.7
5) UNSKILLED	0.0	19.2	17.1	27.3	31.9
6) UNKNOWN	0.0	0.0	0.0	0.0	0.0
7) INDETERMINANT	0.0	0.0	0.0	0.0	0.0
CASES	0	47	88	22	67
OTHER WOMEN	1	2	3	4	5
1) PROFESSIONAL	33.3	0.0	0.5	0.9	0.4
2) INTERMEDIATE	8.3	18.4	2.4	0.9	0.4
3) SKILLED MAN.	58.3	66.1	81.7	80.3	71.5
4) PARTLY SKILLED	0.0	6.4	5.9	10.3	7.5
5) UNSKILLED	0.0	9.2	9.5	7.7	20.2
6) UNKNOWN	0.0	0.0	0.0	0.0	0.0
7) INDETERMINANT	0.0	0.0	0.0	0.0	0.0
CASES	11	109	876	117	267

SOURCE: MANCHESTER PUBLIC LIBRARY. MFPR 242-259.
*SEE APPENDIX A, NOTE 7
TABLE READS AS FOLLOWS: OF THE 47 SERVANTS WHOSE FATHERS
WERE IN SEG 2, 6.4% MARRIED HUSBANDS FROM THE SAME SEG,
53.2% MARRIED HUSBANDS FROM SEG 3, AND SO ON.

TABLE 54

PERCENTAGE OF HOUSEHOLD HEADS IN SOCIAL-ECONOMIC GROUPS*

DISTRICTS WITH SERVANT POPULATIONS:	% OF HEADS IN SOCIAL-ECONOMIC GROUP				
	1	2	3	4	5
ABOVE THE MODE	5.9	15.2	30.5	35.1	13.2
BELOW THE MODE	3.0	12.2	44.3	30.3	10.2
BOLTON	1.7	8.7	62.4	16.2	10.9
ROCHDALE	2.5	5.0	60.0	18.0	12.0

* SOCIAL-ECONOMIC GROUPINGS AS IN APPENDIX A, NOTE 7.
SOURCE: EBERY AND PRESTON (1976), 63.

TABLE 55

SOCIAL-ECONOMIC GROUPING* OF SERVANT EMPLOYERS

HOUSEHOLD HEADS	% OF HEADS IN SOCIAL-ECONOMIC GROUPS				
	1	2	3	4	5
1851					
SERVANT EMPLOYERS	28.5	27.6	34.6	2.6	1.3
% SERVANTS EMPLOYED BY GROUP	34.1	25.0	31.1	2.0	1.4
CONTROL SAMPLE	3.5	10.9	58.2	12.9	9.5

HOUSEHOLD HEADS	% OF HEADS IN SOCIAL-ECONOMIC GROUPS		
	6	7	CASES
1851			
SERVANT EMPLOYERS	3.5	1.3	228
% SERVANTS EMPLOYED BY GROUP	4.1	2.3	296
CONTROL SAMPLE	0.0	5.0	201

TABLE 55 (CONT.)

SOCIAL-ECONOMIC GROUPING OF SERVANT EMPLOYERS

HOUSEHOLD HEADS	% OF HEADS IN SOCIAL-ECONOMIC GROUPS				
	1	2	3	4	5
1861					
SERVANT EMPLOYERS	29.6	28.8	32.6	2.1	0.4
% SERVANTS EMPLOYED BY GROUP	38.7	26.3	25.7	1.6	0.3
CONTROL SAMPLE	1.0	6.6	63.5	20.3	5.6

HOUSEHOLD HEADS	% OF HEADS IN SOCIAL-ECONOMIC GROUPS		
	6	7	CASES
1861			
SERVANT EMPLOYERS	0.4	6.0	233
% SERVANTS EMPLOYED BY GROUP	0.6	6.7	315
CONTROL SAMPLE	0.0	3.0	197

TABLE 55 (CONT.)

SOCIAL-ECONOMIC GROUPING OF SERVANT EMPLOYERS

HOUSEHOLD HEADS	% OF HEADS IN SOCIAL-ECONOMIC GROUPS				
	1	2	3	4	5
1871					
SERVANT EMPLOYERS	23.8	26.2	37.2	2.8	3.2
% SERVANTS EMPLOYED BY GROUP	34.8	25.9	28.9	2.0	2.2
CONTROL SAMPLE	2.5	5.0	60.0	18.0	12.0

HOUSEHOLD HEADS	% OF HEADS IN SOCIAL-ECONOMIC GROUPS		
	6	7	CASES
1861			
SERVANT EMPLOYERS	2.5	4.3	282
% SERVANTS EMPLOYED BY GROUP	1.7	4.5	402
CONTROL SAMPLE	0.0	2.5	200

* SEE APENDIX A, NOTE 7.

TABLE 56

AGE OF SERVANTS BY SOCIAL-ECONOMIC GROUP OF EMPLOYER

SOCIAL-ECONOMIC GROUP* OF EMPLOYERS	% OF SERVANTS IN AGE GROUPS (YEARS)			
	0-19	20-39	OVER 40	CASES
1851				
1. PROFESSIONAL	7.0	81.5	11.5	102
2. INTERMEDIATE	8.9	76.8	14.3	77
3. SKILLED MANUAL	20.7	59.9	19.4	93
1861				
1. PROFESSIONAL	16.3	77.3	6.4	122
2. INTERMEDIATE	25.2	60.0	14.8	83
3. SKILLED MANUAL	26.7	51.9	21.4	81
1871				
1. PROFESSIONAL	22.5	66.4	11.1	140
2. INTERMEDIATE	33.6	54.8	11.6	104
3. SKILLED MANUAL	33.6	42.8	23.6	116

* SEE APPENDIX A, NOTE 7.

TABLE 57

MARITAL STATUS OF SERVANTS ACCORDING TO THE SOCIAL-ECONOMIC
GROUP OF EMPLOYERS

SOCIAL-ECONOMIC GROUP* OF EMPLOYER	% MARITAL STATUS OF SERVANTS		
	NOT KNOWN	SINGLE	MARRIED
PROFESSIONAL			
1851	0.0	92.2	5.9
1861	3.3	85.2	0.8
1871	3.6	92.1	0.0

SOCIAL-ECONOMIC GROUP* OF EMPLOYER	% MARITAL STATUS OF SERVANTS		
	WIDOWED	SPOUSE ABSENT	CASES
PROFESSIONAL			
1851	2.0	0.0	102
1861	4.9	5.7	122
1871	1.4	2.9	140

TABLE 57 (CONT.)

MARITAL STATUS OF SERVANTS ACCORDING TO THE SOCIAL-ECONOMIC
GROUP OF EMPLOYERS

SOCIAL-ECONOMIC GROUP* OF EMPLOYER	% MARITAL STATUS OF SERVANTS NOT KNOWN	SINGLE	MARRIED
INTERMEDIATE			
1851	1.3	97.4	0.0
1861	0.0	91.6	0.0
1871	0.0	91.3	2.9

SOCIAL-ECONOMIC GROUP* OF EMPLOYER	% MARITAL STATUS OF SERVANTS WIDOWED	SPOUSE ABSENT	CASES
INTERMEDIATE			
1851	1.3	0.0	77
1861	7.2	1.2	83
1871	3.8	1.9	104

TABLE 57 (CONT.)

MARITAL STATUS OF SERVANTS ACCORDING TO THE SOCIAL-ECONOMIC
GROUP OF EMPLOYERS

SOCIAL-ECONOMIC GROUP* OF EMPLOYER	% MARITAL STATUS OF SERVANTS NOT KNOWN	SINGLE	MARRIED
SKILLED MANUAL			
1851	1.1	83.9	7.5
1861	2.5	84.0	0.0
1871	2.6	81.0	0.9

SOCIAL-ECONOMIC GROUP* OF EMPLOYER	% MARITAL STATUS OF SERVANTS WIDOWED	SPOUSE ABSENT	CASES
SKILLED MANUAL			
1851	7.5	0.0	93
1861	8.6	4.9	81
1871	11.2	4.3	116

* SEE APPENDIX A, NOTE 7.

TABLE 58

OCCUPATIONS OF SERVANT-EMPLOYING HEADS OF HOUSEHOLDS

| OCCUPATIONAL GROUPING* | % OF HEADS | | | |
| | 1851 | | 1861 | |
	SERV. HEADS	ROCH. HEADS	SERV. HEADS	ROCH. HEADS
PROFESSIONAL	8.5	0.5	8.4	0.0
PROPRIETOR	4.5	0.5	5.3	0.0
TEXTILE MANU.	13.0	2.0	13.8	1.0
OTHER LARGE MANU.	3.1	0.5	2.7	0.0
FARMER	5.4	4.5	2.7	3.0
RETAILERS	33.0	12.0	33.3	8.0
SMALL MANU.	6.7	2.0	8.4	1.0
INDUST/COMMERCIAL SERVICES	2.6	2.0	4.4	1.5
ANNUITANT	1.8	0.5	0.4	0.0
ARTISAN/MANUAL	17.0	70.1	13.3	82.2
UNIDENTIFIED	4.5	5.5	7.1	3.2
CASES	224	201	225	197

TABLE 58 (CONT.)

OCCUPATIONS OF SERVANT-EMPLOYING HEADS OF HOUSEHOLDS

OCCUPATIONAL GROUPING*	% OF HEADS 1871	
	SERV. HEADS	ROCH. HEADS
PROFESSIONAL	9.0	0.5
PROPRIETOR	2.9	0.0
TEXTILE MANU.	8.2	1.0
OTHER LARGE MANU.	2.2	0.0
FARMER	2.9	3.0
RETAILERS	33.7	13.5
SMALL MANU.	5.0	1.0
INDUST/COMMERCIAL SERVICES	8.2	2.5
ANNUITANT	5.0	0.5
ARTISAN/MANUAL	16.1	77.0
UNIDENTIFIED	6.8	1.0
CASES	279	200

* OCCUPATIONAL GROUPINGS:
PROFESSIONAL - DOCTORS, CLERGYMEN, SOLICITORS, ETC.
PROPRIETOR - OWNERS OF LAND AND HOUSES.
TEXTILE MANU. - MANUFACTURERS OF TEXTILES EMPLOYING
                MORE THAN 25 HANDS.
OTHER LARGE MANU. - MANUFACTURERS OTHER THAN TEXTILE
                MANUFACTURERS EMPLOYING MORE THAN 25
                HANDS.
FARMER - SO DESCRIBED.
RETAILERS - SELLERS OF FOOD, ALCOHOL, PROVISIONS, ETC.
SMALL MANU. - MANUFACTURERS EMPLOYING BETWEEN 2 AND 24
                HANDS.
INDUST./COMERCIAL SERVICES - MANAGERS, AUCTIONEERS,
                TEACHERS, ETC.
ANNUITANT - SO DESCRIBED.
ARTISAN/MANUAL - OTHER OCCUPATIONS.
UNIDENTIFIED - OCCUPATIONS CANNOT BE DEFINED.

TABLE 58 (CONT)

PERCENTAGE OF SERVANTS IN 'COMMERCIAL UNITS'

TYPE OF EMPLOYER	SERVANTS IN HOUSEHOLDS (% OF ALL SERVANTS)		
	1851	1861	1871
FARMERS	4.1	1.9	2.5
RETAILERS OF ALCOHOL	12.2	9.2	13.9
OTHER RETAILERS	19.4	17.1	19.4
EATINGHOUSE KEEPER	0.7	0.0	0.0
NUMBER OF ALL SERVANTS	296	315	402

TABLE 59

PERCENT OF HOUSEHOLDS IN DIFFERENT SOCIAL-ECONOMIC GROUPS
WITH RESIDENT SERVANTS

SOCIAL-ECONOMIC GROUP*	1	2	3	4	5
1851	53.3	16.6	3.9	1.3	1.2
1871	45.7	8.3	3.0	0.8	1.3

* SEE APPENDIX A, NOTE 7.

TABLE 60

PRECENT OF ANNUAL FAMILY INCOME SPENT ON SERVANTS
COURT OF BANKRUPTCY RECORDS, 1822-1833

INCOME (£)	AVERAGE % OF INCOME SPENT ON SERVANTS	HIGHEST%	LOWEST%	CASES
0-300	2.4	2.9	1.9	5
300-500	4.3	9.4	2.6	7
500-1000	4.2	15.5	1.1	7
1000 PLUS	6.0	19.2	0.4	7

SOURCE: PUBLIC RECORD OFFICE. B 3.

TABLE 61

PERCENT OF HOUSEHOLDS IN DIFFERING SOCIAL-ECONOMIC GROUPS
WITH ONLY ONE SERVANT

SOCIAL-ECONOMIC GROUP*	% HOUSEHOLDS EMPLOYING ONLY ONE SERVANT					
	1851	CASES	1861	CASES	1871	CASES
PROFESSIONAL	63.1	65	58.0	69	43.3	67
INTERMEDIATE	82.5	63	79.1	67	75.7	74
SKILLED MANUAL/ SMALL RETAILER	87.3	79	94.7	76	91.4	105

* SEE APPENDIX A, NOTE 7.

TABLE 62

NUMBER OF SERVANTS EMPLOYED BY DIFFERING SOCIAL-ECONOMIC
GROUPS

SOCIAL-ECONOMIC GROUP* OF HEAD	NUMBER OF SERVANTS IN HOUSEHOLDS (%)			
	1	2	3	4
PROFESSIONAL				
1851	63.1	30.8	3.1	0.0
1861	58.0	24.6	7.2	7.2
1871	43.3	25.4	16.4	9.0

SOCIAL-ECONOMIC GROUP* OF HEAD	NUMBER OF SERVANTS IN HOUSEHOLDS (%)		
	5	OVER 5	CASES
PROFESSIONAL			
1851	1.5	1.5	65
1861	1.4	1.4	69
1871	6.0	0.0	67

TABLE 62 (CONT.)

NUMBER OF SERVANTS EMPLOYED BY DIFFERING SOCIAL-ECONOMIC
GROUPS

SOCIAL-ECONOMIC GROUP* OF HEAD	NUMBER OF SERVANTS IN HOUSEHOLDS (%)			
	1	2	3	4
INTERMEDIATE				
1851	82.5	12.7	3.2	1.6
1861	79.1	17.9	3.0	0.0
1871	75.7	17.6	1.4	2.7

SOCIAL-ECONOMIC GROUP* OF HEAD	NUMBER OF SERVANTS IN HOUSEHOLDS (%)		
	5	OVER 5	CASES
INTERMEDIATE			
1851	0.0	0.0	63
1861	0.0	0.0	67
1871	1.4	1.4	74

TABLE 62 (CONT.)

NUMBER OF SERVANTS EMPLOYED BY DIFFERING SOCIAL-ECONOMIC
GROUPS

SOCIAL-ECONOMIC GROUP* OF HEAD	NUMBER OF SERVANTS IN HOUSEHOLDS (%)			
	1	2	3	4
SKILLED MANUAL/SMALL SHOPKEEPER				
1851	87.3	8.9	3.8	0.0
1861	94.7	3.9	1.3	0.0
1871	91.4	6.7	1.9	0.0

SOCIAL-ECONOMIC GROUP* OF HEAD	NUMBER OF SERVANTS IN HOUSEHOLDS (%)		
	5	OVER 5	CASES
SKILLED MANUAL/SMALL SHOPKEEPER			
1851	0.0	0.0	79
1861	0.0	0.0	76
1871	0.0	0.0	105

TABLE 63

NUMBER OF SERVANTS EMPLOYED BY OCCUPATIONAL GROUPS, 1851–71

| | 1851 | |
| | AVERAGE SERVANTS | |
OCCUPATIONAL GROUP*	EMPLOYED	CASES
SOCIAL-ECONOMIC GROUP 1		
PROFESSIONS	1.3	19
TEXTILE MANUFACTURERS	1.8	31
PROPRIETORS	1.3	9
OTHER MANUFACTURERS	2.0	5
SOCIAL-ECONOMIC GROUP 2		
FARMERS	1.0	12
SMALL MANUFACTURERS	2.1	11
LARGE RETAILERS	1.0	25
INDUSTRIAL SERVICE	2.2	5
SOCIAL-ECONOMIC GROUP 3		
SMALL RETAILERS	1.2	51
MANUAL/CLERK	1.1	29

TABLE 63 (CONT.)

NUMBER OF SERVANTS EMPLOYED BY OCCUPATIONAL GROUPS, 1851-71

OCCUPATIONAL GROUP*	1871 AVERAGE SERVANTS EMPLOYED	CASES	% INCREASE 1851-1871 IN SERVANTS EMPLOYED
SOCIAL-ECONOMIC GROUP 1			
PROFESSIONS	1.7	16	+30.8
TEXTILE MANUFACTURERS	2.9	23	+61.1
PROPRIETORS	2.0	21	+53.8
OTHER MANUFACTURERS	2.2	6	+10.0
SOCIAL-ECONOMIC GROUP 2			
FARMERS	1.3	8	+30.0
SMALL MANUFACTURERS	1.7	9	-19.0
LARGE RETAILERS	1.7	33	+70.0
INDUSTRIAL SERVICE	1.4	21	-36.4
SOCIAL-ECONOMIC GROUP 3			
SMALL RETAILERS	1.1	68	-9.1
MANUAL/CLERK	1.1	32	0.0

* SEE TABLE 58.

TABLE 64

TYPES OF SERVANTS EMPLOYED BY DIFFERING SOCIAL-ECONOMIC
GROUPS

SOCIAL-ECONOMIC GROUP* OF HEAD	SERVANT TYPES AS % OF ALL SERVANTS EMPLOYED					
	1851	CASES	1861	CASES	1871	CASES
PROFESSIONAL						
GENERAL FEMALE SERVANTS	73.3	74	65.3	77	46.1	59
MALE SERVANTS	4.0	4	2.5	3	2.3	3
SPECIALISED FEMALE SERVANTS	22.8	23	32.2	38	51.6	66
INTERMEDIATE						
GENERAL FEMALE SERVANTS	86.1	62	72.0	59	67.0	69
MALE SERVANTS	4.2	3	1.2	1	1.0	1
SPECIALISED FEMALE SERVANTS	9.7	7	26.8	22	32.0	33
OTHER EMPLOYERS WITH STATED OCCUPATIONS						
GENERAL FEMALE SERVANTS	81.4	83	80.0	68	80.9	106
MALE SERVANTS	6.7	7	2.4	2	3.8	5
SPECIALISED FEMALE SERVANTS	11.8	12	17.7	15	15.3	20

* SEE APPENDIX A, NOTE 7.

TABLE 65

AGE (IN YEARS) OF HEADS OF HOUSEHOLD EMPLOYING SERVANTS
PERCENT IN AGE GROUPS

	UNDER 30	30-49	50 PLUS	CASES
<u>1851</u>	%	%	%	
SERVANT HOUSEHOLDS	12.7	53.5	30.9	228
CONTROL HOUSEHOLDS	18.4	43.8	36.8	201
<u>1861</u>				
SERVANT HOUSEHOLDS	12.0	56.3	30.9	233
CONTROL HOUSEHOLDS	24.4	46.2	28.9	197
<u>1871</u>				
SERVANT HOUSEHOLDS	9.9	49.3	38.9	282
CONTROL HOUSEHOLDS	22.0	46.0	31.5	200

TABLE 66

AGE OF SERVANT EMPLOYERS BY SOCIAL-ECONOMIC GROUP

| SOCIAL-ECONOMIC GROUP* | % OF EMPLOYERS IN AGE GROUPS (YEARS) | | | | |
	UNDER 20	20-39	40-60	OVER 60	CASES
1851					
1. PROFESSIONAL	0.0	44.6	40.0	15.4	65
2. INTERMEDIATE	0.0	31.7	46.0	22.2	63
3. SKILLED MANUAL	0.0	32.9	53.2	13.9	79
1861					
1. PROFESSIONAL	0.0	34.7	46.4	18.8	69
2. INTERMEDIATE	0.0	47.7	38.8	13.5	67
3. SKILLED MANUAL	2.7	47.3	35.5	14.5	76
1871					
1. PROFESSIONAL	0.0	20.9	49.3	29.8	67
2. INTERMEDIATE	0.0	40.6	44.6	14.9	74
3. SKILLED MANUAL	2.0	36.2	50.5	11.4	105

* SEE APPENDIX A, NOTE 7.

TABLE 67

PERCENT OF SERVANT-EMPLOYING HOUSEHOLDS IN KNOWN LIFE-CYCLE
STAGES - RESULTS 1851-1871 POOLED

SOCIAL-ECONOMIC GROUP*	LIFE CYCLE STAGE** (%)			
	0	1	2	3
1. PROFESSIONAL	30.4	7.5	3.5	35.8
2. INTERMEDIATE	31.5	7.9	3.5	36.0
3. SKILLED MANUAL	31.8	6.1	1.5	40.2
4. PARLY SKILLED	57.9	5.3	0.0	21.1
5. UNSKILLED	46.2	7.7	0.0	23.0
6. UNKNOWN	93.8	0.0	0.0	0.0
7. INDETERMINATE	85.7	0.0	0.0	10.7
ROCHDALE HOUSEHOLDS	22.2	9.7	5.5	25.2

SOCIAL-ECONOMIC GROUP*	LIFE CYCLE STAGE** (%)			
	4	5	6	CASES
1. PROFESSIONAL	5.0	8.0	10.0	201
2. INTERMEDIATE	5.9	10.8	4.4	203
3. SKILLED MANUAL	5.8	9.6	5.0	261
4. PARLY SKILLED	0.0	5.3	10.5	19
5. UNSKILLED	0.0	23.0	0.0	13
6. UNKNOWN	0.0	0.0	6.3	16
7. INDETERMINATE	3.6	0.0	0.0	28
ROCHDALE HOUSEHOLDS	6.2	24.5	5.5	598

* SEE APPENDIX A, NOTE 7.

** SEE APPENDIX A, NOTE 24.

TABLE 68

MARITAL STATUS AND SEX OF SERVANT-EMPLOYING HEADS, 1851

MARITAL STATUS	% OF HEADS BY MARITAL STATUS AND SEX			
	SERVANT EMPLOYERS		CONTROL SAMPLE	
	MALE	FEMALE	MALE	FEMALE
UNKNOWN	1.1	3.2	0.0	0.0
SINGLE	7.9	32.3	5.2	11.1
MARRIED	82.6	3.2	84.9	0.0
WIDOWED	7.9	58.1	7.1	88.9
SPOUSE ABSENT	0.5	3.2	2.9	0.0
SEX (%)*	84.1	13.7	86.4	13.6
CASES	190	31	172	27

* EXCLUDES CASES WHERE SEX OF HEAD UNKNOWN

TABLE 69

MARITAL STATUS AND SEX OF SERVANT-EMPLOYING HEADS, 1861

MARITAL STATUS	% OF HEADS BY MARITAL STATUS AND SEX			
	SERVANT EMPLOYERS		CONTROL SAMPLE	
	MALE	FEMALE	MALE	FEMALE
UNKNOWN	0.0	0.0	0.0	0.0
SINGLE	12.2	29.0	0.6	23.5
MARRIED	72.6	0.0	88.9	0.0
WIDOWED	13.7	71.0	7.8	58.8
SPOUSE ABSENT	1.5	0.0	2.8	17.6
SEX (%)*	84.5	13.3	91.4	8.6
CASES	197	31	180	17

* EXCLUDES CASES WHERE SEX OF HEAD UNKNOWN

TABLE 70

MARITAL STATUS AND SEX OF SERVANT-EMPLOYING HEADS, 1871

| MARITAL STATUS | % OF HEADS BY MARITAL STATUS AND SEX | | | |
| | SERVANT EMPLOYERS | | CONTROL SAMPLE | |
	MALE	FEMALE	MALE	FEMALE
UNKNOWN	0.9	0.0	0.0	0.0
SINGLE	5.8	18.0	1.8	16.7
MARRIED	77.0	0.0	90.0	0.0
WIDOWED	13.7	74.0	7.0	80.0
SPOUSE ABSENT	2.7	8.0	1.2	3.3
SEX (%)*	80.0	17.7	85.0	15.0
CASES	226	50	170	30

* EXCLUDES CASES WHERE SEX OF HEAD UNKNOWN

TABLE 71

AVERAGE NUMBER OF SERVANTS EMPLOYED BY SOCIAL-ECONOMIC
GROUPS ACCORDING TO NUMBER OF PERSONS IN HOUSEHOLD**

SOCIAL-ECONOMIC GROUP*	AVERAGE NUMBER OF SERVANTS (CASES IN BRACKETS)				

1851	NUMBER OF PERSONS IN HOUSEHOLD				
	1	2	3	4	5
PROFESSIONAL	1.2(5)	1.4(15)	1.5(10)	2.0(15)	1.7(10)
INTERMEDIATE	1.0(2)	1.2(6)	1.1(12)	1.1(12)	1.3(7)
SKILLED MAN.	1.0(4)	1.2(10)	1.1(13)	1.2(19)	1.1(13)

1851	NUMBER OF PERSONS IN HOUSEHOLD			
	6	7	8	9
PROFESSIONAL	1.3(3)	1.3(3)	1.0(2)	1.0(1)
INTERMEDIATE	1.2(10)	1.5(4)	1.0(2)	1.9(7)
SKILLED MAN.	1.8(4)	1.3(4)	1.0(5)	1.0(8)

1861	NUMBER OF PERSONS IN HOUSEHOLD				
	1	2	3	4	5
PROFESSIONAL	1.1(7)	1.5(17)	1.5(11)	1.5(11)	2.2(6)
INTERMEDIATE	1.0(4)	1.1(14)	1.1(15)	1.4(11)	1.4(5)
SKILLED MAN.	1.0(6)	1.1(11)	1.1(18)	1.1(13)	1.2(9)

1861	NUMBER OF PERSONS IN HOUSEHOLD			
	6	7	8	9
PROFESSIONAL	1.6(5)	2.7(6)	3.3(3)	3.7(3)
INTERMEDIATE	1.7(3)	1.3(4)	1.4(5)	1.3(6)
SKILLED MAN.	1.0(8)	1.0(9)	1.0(2)	0.0(0)

TABLE 71 (CONT.)

AVERAGE NUMBER OF SERVANTS EMPLOYED BY SOCIAL-ECONOMIC
GROUPS ACCORDING TO NUMBER OF PERSONS IN HOUSEHOLD**

SOCIAL-ECONOMIC GROUP*	AVERAGE NUMBER OF SERVANTS (CASES IN BRACKETS)				
	NUMBER OF PERSONS IN HOUSEHOLD				
1871	1	2	3	4	5
PROFESSIONAL	1.2(6)	1.7(20)	2.1(10)	1.9(7)	2.8(10)
INTERMEDIATE	1.0(2)	1.1(10)	1.4(18)	1.2(14)	1.7(6)
SKILLED MAN.	1.1(9)	1.1(21)	1.0(12)	1.1(15)	1.1(18)

	NUMBER OF PERSONS IN HOUSEHOLD			
1871	6	7	8	9
PROFESSIONAL	2.2(5)	4.0(4)	5.0(1)	2.8(9)
INTERMEDIATE	1.6(13)	1.0(4)	1.0(1)	2.2(6)
SKILLED MAN.	1.1(15)	1.3(4)	1.0(4)	1.4(7)

TABLE 72

AVERAGE NUMBER OF SERVANTS EMPLOYED BY SOCIAL-ECONOMIC GROUPS ACCORDING TO NUMBER OF DEPENDANTS AGED TEN YEARS OR UNDER IN HOUSEHOLD**

SOCIAL-ECONOMIC GROUP*	AVERAGE NUMBER OF SERVANTS (CASES IN BRACKETS)				

1851	NUMBER OF DEPENDANTS UNDER 11 YEARS				
	0	1	2	3	4
PROFESSIONAL	1.5(37)	1.3(6)	1.9(13)	1.8(5)	1.0(3)
INTERMEDIATE	1.1(31)	1.2(13)	1.7(6)	1.3(8)	1.5(2)
SKILLED MAN.	1.1(35)	1.2(17)	1.3(12)	1.1(10)	1.0(2)

1851	NUMBER OF PERSONS IN HOUSEHOLD	
	5	6
PROFESSIONAL	1.0(1)	0.0(0)
INTERMEDIATE	1.5(2)	0.0(0)
SKILLED MAN.	1.3(4)	0.0(0)

1861	NUMBER OF DEPENDANTS UNDER 11 YEARS				
	0	1	2	3	4
PROFESSIONAL	1.4(35)	1.5(10)	1.7(11)	2.6(9)	4.3(3)
INTERMEDIATE	1.1(35)	1.3(10)	1.3(10)	1.3(4)	1.5(4)
SKILLED MAN.	1.1(35)	1.1(13)	1.0(13)	1.1(11)	1.0(4)

1861	NUMBER OF PERSONS IN HOUSEHOLD	
	5	6
PROFESSIONAL	3.0(1)	0.0(0)
INTERMEDIATE	1.3(3)	1.0(1)
SKILLED MAN.	0.0(0)	0.0(0)

TABLE 72 (CONT.)

AVERAGE NUMBER OF SERVANTS EMPLOYED BY SOCIAL-ECONOMIC
GROUPS ACCORDING TO NUMBER OF DEPENDANTS AGED TEN YEARS
OR UNDER IN HOUSEHOLD**

SOCIAL-ECONOMIC GROUP*	AVERAGE NUMBER OF SERVANTS (CASES IN BRACKETS)				
1871	NUMBER OF DEPENDANTS UNDER 11 YEARS				
	0	1	2	3	4
PROFESSIONAL	1.6(35)	2.8(14)	1.6(5)	2.5(6)	3.0(3)
INTERMEDIATE	1.2(32)	1.5(14)	1.5(8)	1.2(9)	2.0(10)
SKILLED MAN.	1.1(45)	1.1(20)	1.2(16)	1.1(11)	1.1(10)

1871	NUMBER OF PERSONS IN HOUSEHOLD	
	5	6
PROFESSIONAL	3.0(4)	0.0(0)
INTERMEDIATE	2.0(1)	0.0(0)
SKILLED MAN.	1.0(1)	1.5(3)

* SEE APPENDIX A, NOTE 7.

** SEE APPENDIX A, NOTE 12.

TABLE 73

BIRTHPLACES OF SERVANTS ACCORDING TO SOCIAL-ECONOMIC
GROUP OF EMPLOYER, 1851-1871

EMPLOYER'S SOCIAL-ECONOMIC GROUP*	% OF SERVANTS BORN IN:		
	ROCHDALE	REST OF LANCASHIRE	YORKSHIRE
1851			
PROFESSIONAL	26.5	11.8	26.5
INTERMEDIATE	37.7	11.7	15.6
SKILLED MAN.	47.3	20.5	8.6
	% OF SERVANTS BORN ELSEWHERE		CASES
1851			
PROFESSIONAL	35.2		102
INTERMEDIATE	35.0		77
SKILLED MAN.	23.6		93

TABLE 73 (CONT.)

BIRTHPLACES OF SERVANTS ACCORDING TO SOCIAL-ECONOMIC
GROUP OF EMPLOYER, 1851-1871

EMPLOYER'S SOCIAL-ECONOMIC GROUP*	% OF SERVANTS BORN IN:		
	ROCHDALE	REST OF LANCASHIRE	YORKSHIRE
1861			
PROFESSIONAL	16.4	12.3	26.2
INTERMEDIATE	19.3	15.7	25.3
SKILLED MAN.	35.8	22.2	17.3

	% OF SERVANTS BORN ELSEWHERE	CASES
1861		
PROFESSIONAL	45.1	122
INTERMEDIATE	39.7	83
SKILLED MAN.	24.7	81

TABLE 73 (CONT.)

BIRTHPLACES OF SERVANTS ACCORDING TO SOCIAL-ECONOMIC
GROUP OF EMPLOYER, 1851-1871

EMPLOYER'S SOCIAL-ECONOMIC GROUP*	% OF SERVANTS BORN IN:		
	ROCHDALE	REST OF LANCASHIRE	YORKSHIRE
1871			
PROFESSIONAL	12.1	12.8	15.7
INTERMEDIATE	18.3	16.3	9.6
SKILLED MAN.	31.9	15.6	11.2

	% OF SERVANTS BORN ELSEWHERE	CASES
1871		
PROFESSIONAL	59.4	140
INTERMEDIATE	55.8	104
SKILLED MAN.	41.3	116

* SEE APPENDIX A, NOTE 7.

TABLE 74

NUMBER OF INHABITANTS IN SETTLEMENTS WHERE SERVANTS BORN**
ACCORDING TO SOCIAL-ECONOMIC GROUP OF EMPLOYER, 1851-1871

EMPLOYER'S SOCIAL- ECONOMIC GROUP*	% OF SERVANTS BORN IN SETTLEMENTS CONTAINING FOLLOWING NUMBER OF PEOPLE:			
	UNKNOWN	OVER 5000	UNDER 5000	CASES
1851				
PROFESSIONAL	25.5	51.0	23.6	102
INTERMEDIATE	28.6	61.0	10.4	77
SKILLED MAN.	22.6	68.8	8.6	93
1861				
PROFESSIONAL	28.7	51.6	19.7	122
INTERMEDIATE	30.1	55.4	14.4	83
SKILLED MAN.	22.2	66.7	11.1	81
1871				
PROFESSIONAL	31.4	45.7	22.9	140
INTERMEDIATE	31.7	50.0	18.3	104
SKILLED MAN.	21.6	66.4	12.0	116

* SEE APPENDIX A, NOTE 7.
** SEE APPENDIX A, NOTE 18.

TABLE 75

OCCUPATIONS OF FATHERS AND SONS LIVING AT HOME IN BOLTON
1871

OCCUPATIONAL GROUP OF FATHER	TOTAL SONS	SONS IN SAME OCCUPATION AS FATHER	
		NUMBER	%
AGRICULTURE AND FISHERIES	10	3	30.0
MINING	21	12	57.1
BUILDING	58	20	34.5
METAL TRADES	119	47	39.5
TEXTILES	191	154	80.6
LABOURING	31	2	6.5
TRANSPORT	22	6	27.3
DEALING	53	16	30.2
PROFESSIONS	21	1	4.8
SERVICE	8	0	0.0

SOURCE: PRESTON (1977), 31.

TABLE 76

THE NUMBER OF SERVANTS EMPLOYED IN OLDHAM IN 1851 BY
EMPLOYERS WITH AN ESTATE OF MORE THAN £25,000

	'RURAL'	'TOWN'	TOTAL
LESS THAN 2 SERVANTS	21	9	30
MORE THAN 2 SERVANTS	6	22	28
TOTAL	27	31	58

SOURCE: FOSTER (1974), 177-79.

TABLE 77

PERCENTAGE OF OCCUPATIONAL GROUPS RESIDENT IN DIFFERING
SETTLEMENT TYPES, 1871

OCCUPATIONAL GROUPING	URBAN CENTRE	INNER PERIPH.	OUTER PERIPH.	INCORP. PERIPH.	NEW PERIPH.
AGRICULTURE	0.00	0.00	0.00	15.38	0.00
TEXTILES	0.75	4.85	10.07	6.34	20.15
METALS	0.00	9.09	22.73	9.09	31.82
COAL	0.00	0.00	0.00	0.0	0.00
BUILDING	0.00	10.53	26.32	21.05	0.00
WOODWORK	0.00	0.00	28.57	0.00	71.43
DRESS	0.00	7.14	21.43	0.00	7.14
TRANSPORT	0.00	0.00	0.00	0.00	20.00
LABOURERS	0.00	13.33	6.67	3.33	10.00
PROFESSIONS	0.00	0.00	99.99	0.00	0.00
COMMERCE	5.56	0.00	11.11	0.00	27.78
RETAILERS	10.00	15.00	5.00	7.50	25.00
SERVANTS	0.00	6.67	16.67	20.00	16.67
ALL HOUSEHOLDS	2.81	6.93	15.33	5.50	20.25

OCCUPATIONAL GROUPINGS INCLUDE WORKERS PROVIDING PRODUCTS
OR SERVICES IN THESE INDUSTRIES, OR RAW MATERIALS FOR THESE
INDUSTRIES.

FOR SETTLEMENT TYPES SEE APPENDIX A, NOTE 28.

TABLE 77 (CONT.)

PERCENTAGE OF OCCUPATIONAL GROUPS RESIDENT IN DIFFERING
SETTLEMENT TYPES, 1871

OCCUPATIONAL GROUPING	LARGE NUCL.	SMALL NUCL.	LARGE DISP.	SMALL DISP.	2-10 HOUSEH.S
AGRICULTURE	30.80	23.08	7.69	0.00	7.69
TEXTILES	35.07	10.82	0.00	1.12	4.48
METALS	18.18	9.09	0.00	0.00	0.00
COAL	41.67	16.67	0.00	0.00	16.67
BUILDING	21.05	15.79	0.00	0.00	0.00
WOODWORK	0.00	0.00	0.00	0.00	0.00
DRESS	46.43	3.57	0.00	0.00	3.57
TRANSPORT	20.00	40.00	0.00	0.00	0.00
LABOURERS	46.67	10.00	0.00	0.00	10.00
PROFESSIONS	0.00	0.00	0.00	0.00	0.00
COMMERCE	16.67	16.67	0.00	0.00	11.11
RETAILERS	32.50	5.00	0.00	0.00	0.00
SERVANTS	16.67	10.00	0.00	0.00	6.67
ALL HOUSEHOLDS	25.81	11.21	0.46	1.36	4.69

OCCUPATIONAL GROUPINGS INCLUDE WORKERS PROVIDING PRODUCTS
OR SERVICES IN THESE INDUSTRIES, OR RAW MATERIALS FOR THESE
INDUSTRIES.

FOR SETTLEMENT TYPES SEE APPENDIX A, NOTE 28.

TABLE 77 (CONT.)

PERCENTAGE OF OCCUPATIONAL GROUPS RESIDENT IN DIFFERING
SETTLEMENT TYPES, 1871

OCCUPATIONAL GROUPING	ISOL. DWELL.	URBAN BACUP	URBAN HEYWOOD	CASES
AGRICULTURE	15.38	0.00	0.00	13
TEXTILES	2.99	1.87	1.49	268
METALS	0.00	0.00	0.00	22
COAL	25.00	0.00	0.00	12
BUILDING	0.00	5.26	0.00	19
WOODWORK	0.00	0.00	0.00	14
DRESS	3.57	3.57	3.57	28
TRANSPORT	0.00	0.00	20.00	5
LABOURERS	0.00	0.00	0.00	30
PROFESSIONS	0.00	0.00	0.00	3
COMMERCE	0.00	0.00	11.11	18
RETAILERS	0.00	0.00	0.00	40
SERVANTS	0.00	6.67	0.00	30
ALL HOUSEHOLDS	0.81	3.78	1.09	22,604

OCCUPATIONAL GROUPINGS INCLUDE WORKERS PROVIDING PRODUCTS
OR SERVICES IN THESE INDUSTRIES, OR RAW MATERIALS FOR THESE
INDUSTRIES.

FOR SETTLEMENT TYPES SEE APPENDIX A, NOTE 28.

TABLE 78

PERCENT OF HOUSEHOLDS WITH MORE THAN ONE RESIDENT SERVANT
IN DIFFERING SETTLEMENT TYPES, 1851 AND 1871
EMPLOYERS IN SOCIAL-ECONOMIC GROUP 1**

SETTLEMENT TYPE*	% EMPLOYERS IN EACH SETTLEMENT TYPE WITH MORE THAN ONE SERVANT-CASES IN BRACKETS					
	PROFESSIONS		TEXTILE MANU.		PROPRIETORS	
	1851	1871	1851	1871	1851	1871
URBAN CENTRE OF ROCHDALE	100.0 (1)	100.0 (1)	100.0 (1)	----- (0)	----- (0)	----- (0)
INNER URBAN PERIPHERY	20.0 (5)	50.0 (2)	50.0 (2)	----- (0)	50.0 (2)	33.3 (3)
OUTER URBAN PERIPHERY	10.0 (10)	50.0 (2)	55.6 (9)	66.7 (3)	28.6 (7)	28.6 (7)
NEW PERIPHERY -INCORPORATED	----- (0)	----- (0)	----- (0)	100.0 (3)	----- (0)	0.0 (1)
NEW PERIPHERY -CONSTRUCTED	----- (0)	50.0 (4)	----- (0)	75.0 (4)	----- (0)	33.3 (3)
LARGE NUCL. SETTLEMENTS	100.0 (2)	33.3 (3)	25.0 (8)	40.0 (5)	0.0 (2)	50.0 (4)
SMALL NUCL. SETTLEMENTS	----- (0)	----- (0)	20.0 (5)	83.3 (6)	0.0 (1)	100.0 (2)
LARGE DISP. SETTLEMENTS	100.0 (1)	----- (0)	0.0 (2)	----- (0)	----- (0)	----- (0)

393

TABLE 78 (CONT.)

PERCENT OF HOUSEHOLDS WITH MORE THAN ONE RESIDENT SERVANT
IN DIFFERING SETTLEMENT TYPES, 1851 AND 1871
EMPLOYERS IN SOCIAL-ECONOMIC GROUP 1**

SETTLEMENT TYPE*	% EMPLOYERS IN EACH SETTLEMENT TYPE WITH MORE THAN ONE SERVANT-CASES IN BRACKETS					
	PROFESSIONS		TEXTILE MANU.		PROPRIETORS	
	1851	1871	1851	1871	1851	1871
SMALL DISP. SETTLEMENTS	----- (0)	----- (0)	100.0 (1)	----- (0)	----- (0)	----- (0)
2-10 HOUSEHOLDS	----- (0)	50.0 (2)	50.0 (2)	100.0 (2)	0.0 (2)	0.0 (1)
ISOL. DWELLINGS	----- (0)	100.0 (1)	100.0 (2)	----- (0)	----- (0)	0.0 (1)
URBAN BACUP	----- (0)	----- (0)	----- (0)	100.0 (1)	----- (0)	----- (0)
URBAN HEYWOOD	----- (0)	----- (0)	----- (0)	----- (0)	----- (0)	0.0 (1)
AVERAGE FOR GROUP	31.6 (19)	53.3 (15)	43.8 (32)	75.0 (24)	21.4 (14)	34.8 (23)

TABLE 78 (CONT.)

PERCENT OF HOUSEHOLDS WITH MORE THAN ONE RESIDENT SERVANT
IN DIFFERING SETTLEMENT TYPES, 1851 AND 1871
EMPLOYERS IN SOCIAL-ECONOMIC GROUP 1**

SETTLEMENT TYPE*	% EMPLOYERS IN EACH SETTLEMENT TYPE WITH MORE THAN ONE SERVANT-CASES IN BRACKETS			
	OTHER MANUFACTUERS		WHOLE SOCIAL GROUP	
	1851	1871	1851	1871
URBAN CENTRE OF ROCHDALE	----- (0)	----- (0)	100.0 (2)	100.0 (1)
INNER URBAN PERIPHERY	50.0 (2)	100.0 (1)	36.4 (11)	50.0 (6)
OUTER URBAN PERIPHERY	100.0 (1)	100.0 (1)	33.3 (27)	46.2 (13)
NEW PERIPHERY -INCORPORATED	----- (0)	100.0 (1)	----- (0)	80.0 (5)
NEW PERIPHERY -CONSTRUCTED	----- (0)	50.0 (2)	----- (0)	53.8 (13)
LARGE NUCL. SETTLEMENTS	----- (0)	----- (0)	33.3 (12)	41.7 (12)
SMALL NUCL. SETTLEMENTS	----- (0)	100.0 (1)	16.7 (6)	88.9 (9)
LARGE DISP. SETTLEMENTS	----- (0)	----- (0)	33.3 (3)	----- (0)

TABLE 78 (CONT.)

PERCENT OF HOUSEHOLDS WITH MORE THAN ONE RESIDENT SERVANT
IN DIFFERING SETTLEMENT TYPES, 1851 AND 1871
EMPLOYERS IN SOCIAL-ECONOMIC GROUP 1**

SETTLEMENT TYPE*	% EMPLOYERS IN EACH SETTLEMENT TYPE WITH MORE THAN ONE SERVANT-CASES IN BRACKETS			
	OTHER MANUFACTURERS		WHOLE SOCIAL GROUP	
	1851	1871	1851	1871
SMALL DISP. SETTLEMENTS	----- (0)	----- (0)	100.0 (1)	----- (0)
2-10 HOUSEHOLDS	----- (0)	100.0 (1)	25.0 (4)	66.7 (6)
ISOL. DWELLINGS	----- (0)	----- (0)	100.0 (2)	50.0 (2)
URBAN BACUP	0.0 (1)	----- (0)	0.0 (1)	100.0 (1)
URBAN HEYWOOD	----- (0)	----- (0)	----- (0)	0.0 (1)
AVERAGE FOR GROUP	50.0 (4)	85.7 (7)	36.2 (69)	58.0 (69)

* SEE APPENDIX A, NOTE 28.
** SEE TABLE 58 FOR OCCUPATIONAL GROUPINGS.

396

TABLE 79

PERCENT OF HOUSEHOLDS WITH MORE THAN ONE RESIDENT SERVANT
IN DIFFERING SETTLEMENT TYPES, 1851 AND 1871
EMPLOYERS IN SOCIAL-ECONOMIC GROUP 2**

SETTLEMENT TYPE*	% EMPLOYERS IN EACH SETTLEMENT TYPE WITH MORE THAN ONE SERVANT-CASES IN BRACKETS					
	FARMERS		SMALL MANU.		LARGE RETAIL	
	1851	1871	1851	1871	1851	1871
URBAN CENTRE OF ROCHDALE	----- (0)	----- (0)	----- (0)	----- (0)	0.0 (10)	0.0 (1)
INNER URBAN PERIPHERY	----- (0)	0.0 (1)	66.7 (3)	0.0 (1)	0.0 (7)	71.4 (7)
OUTER URBAN PERIPHERY	0.0 (1)	----- (0)	0.0 (1)	0.0 (1)	37.5 (8)	28.6 (7)
NEW PERIPHERY -INCORPORATED	----- (0)	----- (0)	----- (0)	----- (0)	----- (0)	100.0 (1)
NEW PERIPHERY -CONSTRUCTED	----- (0)	0.0 (1)	----- (0)	0.0 (4)	----- (0)	50.0 (10)
LARGE NUCL. SETTLEMENTS	0.0 (1)	0.0 (2)	0.0 (2)	0.0 (1)	0.0 (1)	0.0 (3)
SMALL NUCL. SETTLEMENTS	0.0 (3)	----- (0)	100.0 (1)	----- (0)	0.0 (2)	----- (0)
LARGE DISP. SETTLEMENTS	----- (0)	----- (0)	----- (0)	----- (0)	----- (0)	----- (0)

TABLE 79 (CONT.)

PERCENT OF HOUSEHOLDS WITH MORE THAN ONE RESIDENT SERVANT
IN DIFFERING SETTLEMENT TYPES, 1851 AND 1871
EMPLOYERS IN SOCIAL-ECONOMIC GROUP 2**

SETTLEMENT TYPE*	% EMPLOYERS IN EACH SETTLEMENT TYPE WITH MORE THAN ONE SERVANT-CASES IN BRACKETS					
	FARMERS		SMALL MANU.		LARGE RETAIL	
	1851	1871	1851	1871	1851	1871
SMALL DISP.	0.0	-----	-----	-----	100.0	-----
SETTLEMENTS	(1)	(0)	(0)	(0)	(1)	(0)
2-10	16.7	0.0	0.0	100.0	-----	100.0
HOUSEHOLDS	(6)	(1)	(2)	(1)	(0)	(1)
ISOL.	0.0	0.0	-----	50.0	-----	-----
DWELLINGS	(4)	(1)	(0)	(2)	(0)	(0)
URBAN	-----	-----	-----	-----	-----	-----
BACUP	(0)	(0)	(0)	(0)	(0)	(0)
URBAN	-----	0.0	-----	-----	-----	-----
HEYWOOD	(0)	(1)	(0)	(0)	(0)	(0)
AVERAGE FOR	6.3	0.0	33.3	20.0	13.8	46.7
GROUP	(16)	(7)	(9)	(10)	(29)	(30)

TABLE 79 (CONT.)

PERCENT OF HOUSEHOLDS WITH MORE THAN ONE RESIDENT SERVANT
IN DIFFERING SETTLEMENT TYPES, 1851 AND 1871
EMPLOYERS IN SOCIAL-ECONOMIC GROUP 2**

SETTLEMENT TYPE*	% EMPLOYERS IN EACH SETTLEMENT TYPE WITH MORE THAN ONE SERVANT-CASES IN BRACKETS			
	INDUST./COMERCIAL SERV.		WHOLE SOCIAL GROUP	
	1851	1871	1851	1871
URBAN CENTRE OF ROCHDALE	----- (0)	0.0 (1)	0.0 (10)	0.0 (2)
INNER URBAN PERIPHERY	100.0 (1)	50.0 (2)	27.3 (11)	54.5 (11)
OUTER URBAN PERIPHERY	40.0 (5)	16.7 (6)	33.3 (15)	21.4 (14)
NEW PERIPHERY -INCORPORATED	----- (0)	0.0 (3)	----- (0)	25.0 (4)
NEW PERIPHERY -CONSTRUCTED	----- (0)	33.3 (9)	----- (0)	33.3 (24)
LARGE NUCL. SETTLEMENTS	----- (0)	0.0 (4)	0.0 (4)	0.0 (10)
SMALL NUCL. SETTLEMENTS	----- (0)	0.0 (1)	16.7 (6)	0.0 (1)
LARGE DISP. SETTLEMENTS	----- (0)	----- (0)	----- (0)	----- (0)

TABLE 79 (CONT.)

PERCENT OF HOUSEHOLDS WITH MORE THAN ONE RESIDENT SERVANT
IN DIFFERING SETTLEMENT TYPES, 1851 AND 1871
EMPLOYERS IN SOCIAL-ECONOMIC GROUP 2**

SETTLEMENT TYPE*	% EMPLOYERS IN EACH SETTLEMENT TYPE WITH MORE THAN ONE SERVANT-CASES IN BRACKETS			
	INDUST./COMMERCIAL SERV.		WHOLE SOCIAL GROUP	
	1851	1871	1851	1871
SMALL DISP.	-----	-----	50.0	-----
SETTLEMENTS	(0)	(0)	(2)	(0)
2-10	-----	-----	12.5	66.7
HOUSEHOLDS	(0)	(0)	(8)	(3)
ISOL.	-----	-----	0.0	33.3
DWELLINGS	(0)	(0)	(4)	(3)
URBAN	-----	-----	-----	-----
BACUP	(0)	(0)	(0)	(0)
URBAN	-----	-----	-----	0.0
HEYWOOD	(0)	(0)	(0)	(1)
AVERAGE FOR	50.0	19.2	18.3	28.8
GROUP	(6)	(26)	(60)	(73)

* SEE APPENDIX A, NOTE 28.
** SEE TABLE 58 FOR OCCUPATIONAL GROUPINGS.

TABLE 80

PERCENT OF HOUSEHOLDS WITH MORE THAN ONE RESIDENT SERVANT
IN DIFFERING SETTLEMENT TYPES, 1851 AND 1871
EMPLOYERS IN SOCIAL-ECONOMIC GROUP 3**

SETTLEMENT TYPE*	% EMPLOYERS IN EACH SETTLEMENT TYPE WITH MORE THAN ONE SERVANT-CASES IN BRACKETS					
	SMALL RETAIL		ARTISAN/MANUAL		WHOLE SOCIAL GROUP	
	1851	1871	1851	1871	1851	1871
URBAN CENTRE OF ROCHDALE	0.0 (5)	0.0 (6)	----- (0)	----- (0)	0.0 (5)	0.0 (6)
INNER URBAN PERIPHERY	21.4 (14)	0.0 (15)	0.0 (6)	0.0 (5)	15.0 (20)	0.0 (20)
OUTER URBAN PERIPHERY	11.8 (17)	16.7 (12)	12.5 (8)	0.0 (5)	12.0 (25)	11.8 (17)
NEW PERIPHERY -INCORPORATED	----- (0)	0.0 (2)	----- (0)	0.0 (3)	----- (0)	0.0 (5)
NEW PERIPHERY -CONSTRUCTED	----- (0)	23.1 (13)	----- (0)	9.1 (11)	----- (0)	16.7 (24)
LARGE NUCL. SETTLEMENTS	20.0 (5)	11.1 (9)	0.0 (2)	16.7 (6)	28.6 (7)	13.3 (15)
SMALL NUCL. SETTLEMENTS	33.3 (3)	40.0 (5)	20.0 (5)	0.0 (4)	12.5 (8)	22.2 (9)
LARGE DISP. SETTLEMENTS	0.0 (2)	0.0 (1)	----- (0)	0.0 (1)	0.0 (2)	0.0 (2)

TABLE 80 (CONT.)

PERCENT OF HOUSEHOLDS WITH MORE THAN ONE RESIDENT SERVANT
IN DIFFERING SETTLEMENT TYPES, 1851 AND 1871
EMPLOYERS IN SOCIAL-ECONOMIC GROUP 3**

SETTLEMENT TYPE*	% EMPLOYERS IN EACH SETTLEMENT TYPE WITH MORE THAN ONE SERVANT-CASES IN BRACKETS					
	SMALL RETAIL		ARTISAN/MANUAL		WHOLE SOCIAL GROUP	
	1851	1871	1851	1871	1851	1871
SMALL DISP. SETTLEMENTS	0.0 (1)	----- (0)	----- (0)	----- (0)	0.0 (1)	----- (0)
2-10 HOUSEHOLDS	0.0 (2)	0.0 (2)	0.0 (3)	----- (0)	0.0 (5)	0.0 (2)
ISOL. DWELLINGS	0.0 (1)	----- (0)	0.0 (1)	0.0 (1)	0.0 (2)	0.0 (1)
URBAN BACUP	----- (0)	0.0 (2)	0.0 (1)	0.0 (2)	0.0 (1)	0.0 (4)
URBAN HEYWOOD	----- (0)	0.0 (1)	----- (0)	----- (0)	----- (0)	0.0 (1)
AVERAGE FOR GROUP	14.0 (50)	11.8 (68)	7.7 (26)	5.3 (38)	11.8 (76)	9.4 (106)

* SEE APPENDIX A, NOTE 28.
** SEE TABLE 58 FOR OCCUPATIONAL GROUPING.

TABLE 81

PERCENT OF TEXTILE MANUFACTURERS WITH MORE THAN ONE
RESIDENT SERVANT IN DIFFERING SETTLEMENT TYPES
RESULTS OF 1851 AND 1871 POOLED

SETTLEMENT TYPE*	% OF TEXTILE MANUFACTURERS IN EACH SETTLEMENT TYPE WITH MORE THAN ONE SERVANT	
	%	CASES
URBAN CENTRE OF ROCHDALE	100.0	1
INNER URBAN PERIPHERY	50.0	2
OUTER URBAN PERIPHERY	58.3	12
NEW PERIPHERY -INCORPORATED	100.0	3
NEW PERIPHERY -CONSTRUCTED	75.0	4
LARGE NUCL. SETTLEMENTS	30.8	13
SMALL NUCL. SETTLEMENTS	54.5	11
LARGE DISP. SETTLEMENTS	0.0	2

TABLE 81 (CONT.)

PERCENT OF TEXTILE MANUFACTURERS WITH MORE THAN ONE
RESIDENT SERVANT IN DIFFERING SETTLEMENT TYPES
RESULTS OF 1851 AND 1871 POOLED

SETTLEMENT TYPE*	% OF TEXTILE MANUFACTURERS IN EACH SETTLEMENT TYPE WITH MORE THAN ONE SERVANT	
	%	CASES
SMALL DISP. SETTLEMENTS	100.0	1
2-10 HOUSEHOLDS	75.0	4
ISOL. DWELLINGS	100.0	2
URBAN BACUP	100.0	1
URBAN HEYWOOD	-----	0
AVERAGE FOR GROUP	57.1	56

* SEE APPENDIX A, NOTE 28.

TABLE 82

NUMBER OF ADVERTISEMENTS FOR SERVANTS IN THE <u>ROCHDALE</u> <u>OBSERVER</u>, 1856-1871, AND THE NUMBER OF WORKHOUSE INMATES EMPLOYED AS SERVANTS, 1851-1871, IN EACH MONTH OF THE YEAR CUMULATIVE FIGURES FOR EACH MONTH

MONTH	ADVERTISEMENTS	WORKHOUSE
JANUARY	60	20
FEBRUARY	59	18
MARCH	52	19
APRIL	53	16
MAY	46	23
JUNE	41	23
JULY	64	16
AUGUST	51	8
SEPTEMBER	45	12
OCTOBER	43	15
NOVEMBER	39	12
DECEMBER	54	19

SOURCES: ROCHDALE PUBLIC LIBRARY.   NEWSPAPER COLLECTION.
LANCASHIRE RECORD OFFICE.   PUR 7.

TABLE 83

COINCIDENCE OF REGION OF BIRTH OF MASTER AND SERVANT
BIRTHPLACES OF SERVANTS IN HOUSEHOLDS HEADED BY EMPLOYERS
FROM DIFFERING REGIONS

REGION WHERE HEAD BORN	SERVANTS' REGION OF BIRTH (%)				
1851	ROCH-DALE	LANCS.*	YORKS.	ELSE-WHERE	NUMBER OF SERVANTS
ROCHDALE	50.0	14.8	10.4	24.8	162
LANCASHIRE*	29.4	29.4	20.6	20.6	34
YORKSHIRE	22.5	15.0	30.0	32.5	40
ELSEWHERE	20.0	11.1	28.9	40.0	45
ALL HEADS	38.2	15.2	16.6	30.0	283
1861	ROCH-DALE	LANCS.*	YORKS.	ELSE-WHERE	NUMBER OF SERVANTS
ROCHDALE	29.8	14.9	19.8	35.5	161
LANCASHIRE*	17.5	24.6	33.3	24.6	57
YORKSHIRE	20.0	16.0	20.0	44.0	25
ELSEWHERE	11.7	11.7	20.0	56.7	56
ALL HEADS	22.2	17.2	22.8	37.8	315

TABLE 83 (CONT.)

COINCIDENCE OF REGION OF BIRTH OF MASTER AND SERVANT
BIRTHPLACES OF SERVANTS IN HOUSEHOLDS HEADED BY EMPLOYERS
FROM DIFFERING REGIONS

REGION WHERE HEAD BORN	SERVANTS' REGION OF BIRTH (%)				
1871	ROCH-DALE	LANCS.*	YORKS.	ELSE-WHERE	NUMBER OF SERVANTS
ROCHDALE	22.5	11.2	12.9	53.4	240
LANCASHIRE*	22.6	32.3	6.5	38.7	62
YORKSHIRE	20.0	10.0	32.5	37.5	40
ELSEWHERE	9.4	7.6	0.0	83.0	53
ALL HEADS	20.9	14.4	11.9	52.8	402

* LANCASHIRE EXCLUDING THE ROCHDALE DISTRICT.

TABLE READS AS FOLLOWS: IN 1851, OF THE 162 SERVANTS WHO
WERE RESIDENT IN HOUSEHOLDS HEADED BY PERSONS BORN IN
ROCHDALE, 50% WERE BORN IN ROCHDALE, 14.8% WERE BORN IN THE
REST OF LANCASHIRE, AND SO ON.

TABLE 84

REGIONS WHERE SERVANT EMPLOYERS BORN, 1851-1871

REGION (%)	1851 SERV.* HEADS	1851 ROCH.** HEADS	1861 SERV. HEADS	1861 ROCH. HEADS	1871 SERV. HEADS	1871 ROCH. HEADS
ROCHDALE	57.0	64.7	49.8	61.0	60.3	59.0
REST OF LANCASHIRE	12.2	17.4	19.8	20.0	15.9	17.0
YORKSHIRE	12.7	9.5	9.8	8.5	10.0	9.5
S. ENGLAND	12.8	3.4	11.3	3.5	7.5	6.0
N. ENGLAND	1.7	2.5	1.3	0.5	0.8	0.5
WALES	0.9	0.0	0.8	1.0	0.0	1.0
SCOTLAND	1.8	0.0	3.0	0.5	2.9	1.0
IRELAND	0.9	2.0	4.2	5.0	1.8	6.0
ABROAD	0.4	0.5	0.0	0.0	0.8	0.0
CASES	228	201	233	197	282	200

* SERVANT EMPLOYING HEADS

** HEADS FROM THE ROCHDALE CONTROL SAMPLE.

SEE TABLE 41 FOR REGIONS.

TABLE 85

REGIONS WHERE SERVANT-EMPLOYING HEADS BORN BY
SOCIAL-ECONOMIC GROUP, 1851-1871

REGION OF BIRTH*	PROFESS.	INTERMED.	SKILLED/ MANUAL	ROCHDALE CONTROL
1851				
ROCHDALE	50.8	67.7	57.5	64.7
LANCS.	20.0	8.1	12.5	17.4
YORKS	6.2	13.0	16.2	9.5
S. ENG.	16.7	6.4	5.0	3.4
N. ENG.	3.1	0.0	5.0	2.5
WALES	0.0	0.0	1.3	0.0
SCOTLAND	3.1	3.2	1.3	0.0
IRELAND	0.0	0.0	1.3	2.0
ABROAD	0.0	1.6	0.0	0.5
CASES	65	62	80	201
1861				
ROCHDALE	52.2	44.8	56.6	61.0
LANCS.	20.2	16.4	19.7	20.0
YORKS	5.8	14.9	11.8	8.5
S. ENG.	10.1	7.5	6.5	3.5
N. ENG.	1.4	3.0	0.0	8.5
WALES	0.0	4.5	0.0	1.0
SCOTLAND	7.3	4.5	2.6	0.5
IRELAND	2.9	4.5	2.6	5.0
ABROAD	0.0	0.0	0.0	0.0
CASES	69	67	76	197

TABLE 85 (CONT.)

REGIONS WHERE SERVANT-EMPLOYING HEADS BORN BY
SOCIAL-ECONOMIC GROUP, 1851-1871

REGION OF BIRTH*	PROFESS.	INTERMED.	SKILLED/ MANUAL	ROCHDALE CONTROL
1871				
ROCHDALE	59.7	56.8	64.8	59.0
LANCS.	13.4	16.2	18.1	17.0
YORKS	14.9	8.1	8.6	9.5
S. ENG.	6.0	8.1	5.7	6.0
N. ENG.	0.0	2.7	0.0	0.5
WALES	0.0	0.0	0.0	1.0
SCOTLAND	6.0	6.8	0.0	1.0
IRELAND	0.0	0.0	1.9	6.0
ABROAD	0.0	1.4	1.0	0.0
CASES	67	74	105	200

* KEY:

LANCS. = LANCASHIRE EXCLUDING THE ROCHDALE DISTRICT

S. ENG. = ENGLISH COUNTIES TO THE SOUTH OF LANCASHIRE AND
YORKSHIRE

N. ENG. = ENGLISH COUNTIES TO THE NORTH OF LANCASHIRE AND
YORKSHIRE

SERVANTS BORN IN 'LANCASHIRE' EXCLUDED

TABLE 86

NUMBER OF GIRLS GOING OUT TO SERVICE FROM THE ROCHDALE
WORKHOUSES AND THE NUMBER OF THEIR EMPLOYERS, 1851-1870

DATE	NUMBER OF EMPLOYERS	NUMBER OF GIRLS
1851	20	13
1852	6	6
1853	9	8
1854	9	8
1855	11	9
1856	7	6
1857	7	7
1858	5	4
1859	13	12
1860	5	5
1861	9	8
1862	5	5
1863	9	9
1864	23	18
1865	18	15
1866	11	9
1867	5	5
1868	11	10
1869	15	13
1870	19	17
TOTAL*	216	140

* TOTAL NUMBER OF SEPERATE INDIVIDUALS CITED OVER PERIOD,
  1851-1870.
SOURCE: LANCASHIRE RECORD OFFICE. PUR 7.

TABLE 87

SOCIAL-ECONOMIC GROUPING OF EMPLOYERS OF SERVANTS FROM
THE ROCHDALE WORKHOUSE, 1851-1870

| | SOCIAL-ECONOMIC GROUP* | | | | | |
	1	2	3	4	5	CASES**
NUMBER	5	13	70	4	5	97
%	5.2	13.4	72.2	4.1	5.2	

* SEE APPENDIX A, NOTE 7.
** ONLY THOSE CASES WHERE OCCUPATIONS STATED.
SOURCE: LANCASHIRE RECORD OFFICE. PUR 7.

TABLE 88

NUMBER OF ADVERTISEMENTS FOR, OR BY, SERVANTS IN THE
ROCHDALE OBSERVER, 1856-1871

DATF	NUMBER OF SERVANTS SEEKING POSTS	NUMBER OF POSITIONS ADVERTISED BY EMPLOYERS
1856	2	8
1857	3	5
1858	1	4
1859	3	29
1860	2	31
1861	9	28
1862	3	28
1863	1	21
1864	4	20
1865	1	47
1866	2	31
1867	9	44
1868	12	76
1869	10	57
1870	8	66
1871	13	108

TABLE 88 (CONT.)

NUMBER OF ADVERTISEMENTS FOR, OR BY, SERVANTS IN THE
ROCHDALE OBSERVER, 1856-1871

DATE	AVERAGE NUMBER OF TIMES POSITIONS ADVERTISED*
1856	1.1
1857	1.0
1858	1.3
1859	1.5
1860	1.3
1861	1.2
1862	1.1
1863	1.6
1864	1.9
1865	1.3
1866	1.8
1867	1.6
1868	1.2
1869	1.2
1870	1.1
1871	1.0

* ANNUAL NUMBER OF INDIVIDUAL ADVERTISEMENTS PLACED DIVIDED
BY THE NUMBER OF POSITIONS TO WHICH THEY REFFERED.
SOURCE: ROCHDALE PUBLIC LIBRARY. NEWSPAPER COLLECTION.

TABLE 89

TYPES OF SERVANT SOUGHT BY EMPLOYERS, OR ADVERTISING FOR
PLACES, IN THE ROCHDALE OBSERVER, 1856-1871

SERVANT OCCUPATIONS (%)	POSITIONS OFFERED	POSITIONS SOUGHT	SERVANTS IN 1871 SAMPLE
GENERAL SERVANT	46.0	3.7	67.7
HOUSEMAID	7.6	6.2	8.2
HOUSEKEEPER	5.4	24.7	3.0
COOK	9.9	8.6	7.0
NURSE	18.1	16.1	8.5
KITCHEN MAID	0.7	1.2	0.5
BUTLER	0.0	3.7	0.0
MAN SERVANT	1.8	2.5	1.5
STABLE/GARDEN	10.7	33.3	0.2
CASES	609	81	402

SOURCES: ROCHDALE PUBLIC LIBRARY. NEWSPAPER COLLECTION.
1871 SAMPLE OF SERVANT-EMPLOYING HOUSEHOLDS IN
THE ROCHDALE REGISTRATION DISTRICT.

TABLE 90

NUMBER OF REGISTRIES ADVERTISING IN THE <u>ROCHDALE</u>
<u>OBSERVER</u>, AND THE NUMBER OF TIMES THEY ADVERTISED,
1856-1871

DATE	NUMBER REGISTRIES ADVERTISING	NUMBER OF SEPERATE ADVERTISEMENTS
1856	1	1
1857	1	1
1858	2	11
1859	2	4
1860	2	7
1861	2	2
1862	3	4
1863	2	2
1864	1	5
1865	0	0
1866	1	7
1867	2	2
1868	2	2
1869	7	43
1870	11	123
1871	9	72

TABLE 90 (CONT.)

NUMBER OF REGISTRIES ADVERTISING IN THE <u>ROCHDALE</u>
<u>OBSERVER</u>, AND THE NUMBER OF TIMES THEY ADVERTISED,
1856-1871

DATE	AVERAGE NUMBER OF ADVERT-ISEMENTS PER REGISTRY
1856	1.0
1857	1.0
1858	5.5
1859	2.0
1860	3.5
1861	1.0
1862	1.3
1863	1.0
1864	5.0
1865	0.0
1866	7.0
1867	1.0
1868	1.0
1869	6.1
1870	11.2
1871	8.0

TABLE 91

COMPARATIVE CHANGES IN WAGES IN DOMESTIC SERVICE AND
INDUSTRIAL WAGES FOR WOMEN (INDEX: 1900=100)

DATE	PRIVATE DOMESTIC SERVICE	FEMALE INDUSTRIAL OCCUPATIONS	DATE
1823-27	42	60	1824
28-32	46	58	1833
33-37	50	59	1840
38-42	54	61	1845
43-47	59	62	1850
48-52	59	65	1855
53-57	58	72	1860
58-62	60	73	1863
63-67	63	78	1866
68-72	69	84	1870
73-77	72	95	1874
78-82	84	98	1877
83-87	88	97	1880
88-92	92	98	1883
93-97	96	91	1886
1904	100	96	1891
07	103	98	1895
		100	1900

SOURCE: LAYTON (1908), 523.

418

TABLE 92

NUMBER OF SERVANTS IN ENGLAND AND WALES, 1851-1891

DATE	NUMBER* OF SERVANTS	SERVANTS AS % OF OCCUPIED POPULATION	OF ENTIRE POPULATION
1851	852,700	10.50	4.76
1861	1,072,800	11.68	5.35
1871	1,328,900	12.93	5.85
1881	1,434,600	12.82	5.52
1891	1,488,800	11.77	5.13

* INDOOR DOMESTIC SERVANTS, COACHMEN, GROOMS AND GARDENERS.
SOURCE: ARMSTRONG (1972), 255-81.

TABLE 93

OCCUPATIONAL GROUPING OF EMPLOYERS MENTIONED IN WORKS BY HORN AND BURNETT

OCCUPATIONAL GROUPING	HORN NO.	%	BURNETT NO.	%
TITLED	29	46.8	10	45.5
PROFESSIONS	14	22.6	4	18.2
INDUSTRIAL ENTREPRENEUR	1	1.6	0	0.0
PROPRIETOR/LAND	10	16.1	4	18.2
RETAILERS	3	4.8	1	4.6
ARTISAN/MANUAL	1	1.6	1	4.6
FARMERS	4	6.5	1	4.6
UNIDENTIFIED	0	0.0	1	4.6

SOURCES: HORN (1975), PASSIM; BURNETT (1974), PASSIM.

TABLE 94

INCREASES IN INCOMES, PRICES AND REAL INCOMES AMONGST
THE MIDDLE CLASSES, 1851-1911

PERIOD	INCREASE IN INCOMES OVER £150 (%)	INCREASE IN RETAIL PRICES (%)	INCREASE IN REAL INCOMES OVER £150 (%)
1851-1861	23.4	10.0	12.2
1861-1871	44.9	5.6	37.2
1871-1881	33.2	-10.0	48.0
1881-1891	16.4	-13.0	33.8
1891-1901	26.0	-1.5	27.9
1901-1911	24.0	11.6	11.1

SOURCE: BANKS (1954), 132.

TABLE 95

DECENNIAL INCREASE IN THE NUMBER OF COACHMEN, GROOMS AND
MOTOR CAR ATTENDANTS, COMPARED WITH THE INCREASE IN THE
NUMBER OF FEMALE SERVANTS AND THE SIZE OF THE POPULATION

| | DECENNIAL INCREASE (%): | | |
DATE	PRIVATE COACHMEN, GROOMS AND MOTOR CAR ATTENDANTS	FEMALE SERVANTS	TOTAL POPULATION
1851	-----	-----	-----
1861	40.0	28.1	11.9
1871	12.0	25.4	13.2
1881	NOT AVAILABLE	1.9	14.4
1891	NOT AVAILABLE	NOT COMPARABLE	11.7
1901	101.0 FOR 30 YEARS	8.2 FOR 20 YEARS	12.2
1911	20.0	1.3	10.9

SOURCE: FRANKLIN (1975), 221.

TABLE 96

TEN-YEAR DIFFERENCE IN PERCENT OF OCCUPIED WOMEN IN NINE
ECONOMIC SECTORS, 1851-1911

SECTOR	1851-1861	1861-1871	1871-1881
AGRICULTURE/ FISHING	-2.92	-1.46	-0.76
MINING	-0.09	0.00	-0.01
BUILDING	0.00	0.00	+0.04
MANUFACTURE	-0.23	-2.88	+0.22
TRANSPORT	-0.17	+0.08	-0.12
DEALING	+0.42	+0.75	+0.44
INDUST. SERVICE	-0.26	+0.14	-0.01
PUBLIC/PROFESS- IONAL SERVICE	+0.24	+0.29	+1.21
DOMESTIC SERVICE	+2.91	+3.08	-1.01

SECTOR	1881-1891	1891-1901	1901-1911
AGRICULTURE/ FISHING	-0.55	-0.43	-0.12
MINING	-0.06	-0.03	-0.03
BUILDING	-0.01	-0.05	-0.01
MANUFACTURE	+0.23	-1.52	-1.12
TRANSPORT	0.00	-0.03	+0.08
DEALING	+1.69	+0.94	+3.59
INDUST. SERVICE	+0.27	+0.85	+1.19
PUBLIC/PROFESS- IONAL SERVICE	+1.10	+1.09	+0.60
DOMESTIC SERVICE	-2.67	-0.82	-4.18

SOURCE: EBERY AND PRESTON (1976), 20.

TABLE 97

TEN-YEAR DIFFERENCES IN THE PERCENT OF THE OCCUPIED
POPULATION EMPLOYED IN AGRICULTURE

1801–1811 %	1811–1821 %	1821–1831 %	1831–1841 %	1841–1851 %	1851–1861 %	1861–1871 %
-2.9	-4.6	-3.8	-2.9	-0.5	-3.0	-3.6

1871–1881 %	1881–1891 %	1891–1901 %	1901–1911 %
-2.5	-2.1	-1.8	-0.4

SOURCE: DEANE AND COLE (1962), 142.